George Drake of Milwaukee, the only son of a widow, attired in the gray militia uniform of the First Wisconsin Volunteer Infantry. On July 2, 1861, near Falling Waters, Virginia, he became the first Wisconsin boy to be killed in combat in the Civil War. Courtesy Milwaukee County Historical Society.

WISCONSIN
in the CIVIL WAR

WISCONSIN
in the CIVIL WAR

The Home Front and the Battle Front, 1861–1865

Frank L. Klement

THE STATE HISTORICAL SOCIETY OF WISCONSIN
Madison : 2001

This publication was funded in part by
THE WISCONSIN HISTORY FOUNDATION
whose assistance the editors gratefully acknowledge.
Our special thanks as well to the
family and associates of Frank L. Klement.

LIBRARY OF CONGRESS CATALOGING-IN-PUBLICATION DATA

Klement, Frank L. (1908–1994).

Wisconsin in the Civil War:
The Home Front and the Battle Front, 1861–1865.

Includes bibliographical references and index.

1. Wisconsin—History—Civil War, 1861–1865.
I. Title.

E537.9.K54   1996   977.5'03—dc20   96-6259 CIP

ISBN 0-87020-286-3

⤙ *Preface* ⤚

THESE BRIEF INTRODUCTORY REMARKS might well be called "an explanation" rather than a Preface. As some readers may recall, *Wisconsin and the Civil War* was first published in 1962 as part of the *Wisconsin Blue Book*, that biennial compendium of political, historical, and bureaucratic data compiled by the Wisconsin Legislative Reference Library and published by the Department of Administration of the State of Wisconsin.

In the late spring of that year, Leslie H. Fishel, jr., director of the State Historical Society of Wisconsin and a member of the Wisconsin Civil War Centennial Commission, had proposed to the editor of the *Blue Book* that, as part of the nationwide commemoration of the Civil War Centennial, someone write a brief overview of Wisconsin's role in the war (1861–1865). At the next meeting of the commission, of which I happened also to be a member, Dr. Fishel moved that we find someone to write a piece for the *Blue Book*. The commission enthusiastically endorsed his proposal.

At that juncture, Professor William B. Hesseltine of the University of Wisconsin—another member of the commission—remarked in his characteristic basso profundo that he knew just the right person. Gesturing in my direction with his pipe, he said, "You've been chosen."

Now, Professor Hesseltine was a distinguished member of the University of Wisconsin's history department and a celebrated student of the Civil War. He had been my mentor at the University of Wisconsin, where I had earned my doctorate, and he was, at the time, also the president of the historical society. I greatly respected him, and I owed him a large professional and intellectual debt. I hated to say no, but I was teaching four courses at Marquette University at the time, and I was swamped with classwork. . . .

Before I could utter a word, Hesseltine growled, "The due date is around Thanksgiving." With that, I meekly submitted.

Ultimately, the deadline was extended to December 31, and my essay grew to more than a hundred pages. After its publication in the *Wisconsin Blue Book*, the State Historical Society of Wisconsin used the same plates to produce a booklet version of *Wisconsin and the Civil War*. Even though it had neither illustrations, bibliography, nor index, and though space constraints meant that I had to omit several important aspects of Wisconsin's role in the war, a gratifying number of readers seemed to consider my little booklet useful and instructive. Before long, it went out of print; but because a fire in the printing plant ruined the plates, no second printing was undertaken.

In 1993, on the rising swell of another wave of interest in the Civil War, the editors of the State Historical Society of Wisconsin approached me to ask whether I might be interested in revising and expanding my booklet, resetting the type, and upgrading it with illustrations, a bibliography, index, and other appurtenances. I was delighted at the prospect of giving *Wisconsin and the Civil War* this new lease on life. Like many another author, I was pleased to have the opportunity to rethink and revise what I had written thirty years earlier. What was more, I now had the opportunity to treat a number of topics I had, for one reason or another, given short shrift—for example, soldier voting-in-the-field, legal and constitutional aspects of the war, the military campaigns of 1864–1865, and the story of Wisconsin's black troops. I set to work at once.

About one-third of this book is entirely new material; the rest has been throughly revised and edited. Although it tells a fairly straightforward story, and still lacks footnotes, I am reluctant to concede that the text is not "scholarly," if only because it represents the distillation of a lifetime spent researching, writing, and thinking about the Civil War. I believe it is important for Americans to know something about the pivotal event in their history, because the outcome of the war, and its effects—indeed some of its underlying causes—are with us still.

I am grateful to the State Historical Society of Wisconsin for encouraging me and assisting in this endeavor. My special thanks go to Mrs. Jane L. Gray, assistant to the chair of the history department at Marquette University, who typed all of the new material; and to Ms. Judith A. Simonsen of the Milwaukee County Historical Society, who assisted with the bibliography and rounded up several of the illustrations.

I sincerely hope that the results will find a new audience, and that my book will justify William B. Hesseltine's assertion in 1962 that it was "a balanced, scholarly account of the total development of an American state involved in a great national crisis . . . [and] a story which deserves to be read, and deeply pondered, by every citizen of Wisconsin."

FRANK L. KLEMENT

Emeritus Professor of History
Marquette University
January, 1994

Publisher's Note About the Author

FRANK L. KLEMENT was born in northeastern Wisconsin in 1905—"a country boy who grew up on the banks of the Embarrass River," as he liked to say of himself. He did his undergraduate work at the Wisconsin State Teachers' College in Stevens Point and taught in Beloit and in rural schools before coming to the University of Wisconsin in Madison, where he earned a master's degree (1935) and a Ph.D. in American history (1946). After teaching briefly at Lake Forest College and at the Wisconsin State Teachers' College in Eau Claire, he joined the history faculty at Marquette University in 1948, where he spent the balance of his long and fruitful career as teacher and historian. He was the author of nine books and more than fifty articles, all of them about the Civil War era and most notably on the topic of northern dissenters. Among his best-known works are *Copperheads in the Middle West* (1960), *The Limits of Dissent: Clement L. Vallandigham and the Civil War* (1970), and *Dark Lanterns: Secret Political Societies, Conspiracies and Treason Trials in the Civil War* (1984). He retired from full-time teaching in 1975 but continued as an emeritus member of the Marquette University faculty until 1984.

Frank L. Klement died on July 29, 1994, shortly after putting the finishing touches on the manuscript for this, his final book.

⊰ *Contents* ⊱

Bismarck

Duluth

MINNESOTA

DAKOTA TERRITORY

Pierre

St. Paul

Minneapolis

WISCONSIN

Milwaukee

Madison

NEBRASKA TERRITORY

IOWA

Des Moines

Chicago

Mississippi River

Lincoln

ILLINOIS

Springfield

KANSAS

MISSOURI

Kansas City

Jefferson City

St. Louis

Island No. 10

Pittsburg Landing

ARKANSAS

Memphis

Shiloh

Corinth

INDIAN TERRITORY

Little Rock

Helena

Holly Springs

Red River

MISSISSIPPI

TEXAS

LOUISIANA

Vicksburg

Jackson

Natchez

Alexandria

Austin

Baton Rouge

New Orleans

0   75   150 miles

The Western Theater

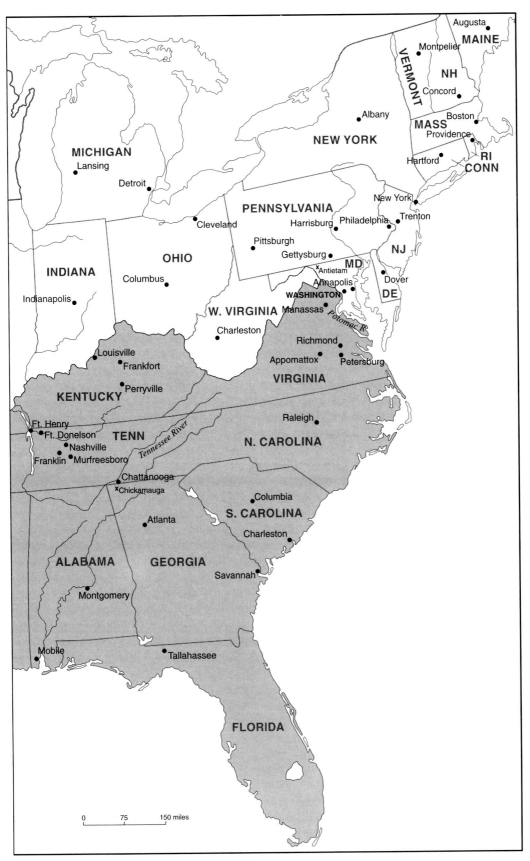

The Eastern Theater

WISCONSIN
in the CIVIL WAR

Wisconsin in 1860

1

Wisconsin in 1860

THE CITIZENS OF WISCONSIN celebrated their twelfth year of statehood in 1860. In the preceding decade, Wisconsin had taken gigantic steps forward, and the state's newspaper editors and boosters proudly pointed to an unbroken record of growth and achievement. The population had climbed to 775,881—a gain of 470,490 or 154 per cent over that of 1850. Two million more acres of farmland had felt the plow's reversing power. Thanks in part to the McCormick reaper, portions of southern Wisconsin had become part of the wheat belt; indeed, Wisconsin ranked second in the nation in wheat production, and 1860 came to be known as "the golden year." In the southwestern corner of the state, strong-backed miners dug deeper into the veins of galena, the bluish-gray lead ore. Lumbermen and their logging crews cut and milled the state's vast timber resources. They guided huge rafts of lumber down the Mississippi and its tributaries or towed them to Chicago to help build that city, and cities to the west. Milwaukee had mushroomed in size and importance, claiming a population of 45,000 in 1860. Some Milwaukeeans optimistically believed that "the Cream City" would one day surpass Chicago in size and importance. The two cities were spirited rivals, each claiming to be the foremost port on Lake Michigan. Madison, meanwhile, had gradually been transformed from a country village into a growing and bustling capital city. Several railroads spanned the state from east to west. Canal promoters planned a huge project which would allow steamers to go from Lake Michigan to central Wisconsin, where the old trading outpost of Portage stood on the Wisconsin River. The state's motto, "Forward," seemed to be an appropriate one.

Yet, in 1860, Wisconsin retained many of the attributes of a frontier state. Surplus capital was scarce; debt was commonplace; barter was widely practiced. Spurious banknotes circulated freely. Manufactured goods contributed but little to the state's annual income. Indigent school districts paid their schoolma'ams a mere fifty cents a day.

The number of oxen about equaled the number of horses; swine outnumbered sheep; sheep outnumbered milch cows. No cheese factory had yet been established, and Wisconsin butter was disparaged in the East as "Western grease." Approximately five-sixths of the state's inhabitants tilled the soil for a living. Men outnumbered women by 40,000. And King Forest still ruled the northern half of the state.

Most of the state's inhabitants lived along the Lake Michigan area or in the southern tiers of counties, the soil of which was among the nation's richest. That population was truly a varied one. Transplanted Yankees were numerous in some of the southern and eastern counties. Rufus King, editor of the Milwaukee *Sentinel*, bore the name of his grandfather, a signer of the United States Constitution. Beloit College had its roots in "the Yankee exodus." Few lead miners, on the other hand, listed Massachusetts or New York as their native states. They usually told the census taker that they were born in Illinois or Missouri. Although a few slaves had previously been used in the lead-mining industry, less than 1 per cent of Wisconsin's population had been born in the slave states of the South.

More than a third of the state's population was of foreign birth. Of these, nearly half had come from various German states. Wisconsin, of course, catered to the German immigrants of the 1850's. In New York, state agents met ships loaded with German immigrants and painted rosy pictures of opportunities in the Badger State. Milwaukee, Ozaukee, and Kewaunee counties, especially, held heavy concentrations of German-Americans. Twenty German-language newspapers were published in Wisconsin in 1860—proof of the high literacy of the German immigrants. Those thrifty and hard-working newcomers had no difficulty establishing themselves and sharing in the state's growth and prosperity.

There were other notable nationality groups besides the German-Americans. About 60,000 proudly called themselves Irishmen. Most of them lived in the cities, although many dug canals and built railroads in the hinterlands. In the cities, the Irish-Americans worked on construction projects, served as millhands, and walked the policeman's beat. (Haughty sons of New England contemptuously termed them "the beasts of burden of America.") Norwegian-Americans numbered about 20,000. Trempealeau, La Crosse, Dane, and Racine counties, among others, had considerable numbers of these Scandinavians. Racine County was heavily Danish. There were Belgians in the Door peninsula and in Ozaukee County. Bangor, in La Crosse County, and New Glarus, in Green County, had sizable Swiss settlements. Holland, in Sheboygan County, was a noted Dutch community. There were a few Bohemian (Czech) colonies along Lake Michigan. Welshmen and Cornishmen from southeastern England were numerous in the lead-mining fields. Other and lesser-known foreign groups were scattered here and there. Free Negroes numbered 1,171. There were also approximately 10,000 Indians, of whom some 1,017 were enumerated by the census taker as "civilized."

This diverse population reacted in different ways to the reform movements of the 1850's. Sherman M. Booth, a transplanted Yankee, became the state's best-known abolitionist. The antislavery movement found many ex-Yankees in its ranks. The so-called "Forty-eighters"—liberals and reformers who had fled Germany after the collapse of the revolutionary movements of 1848 —ardently supported Booth and the abolition movement. Carl Schurz, the state's best-known Forty-eighter, ardently championed the cause of the slave. Most German-American workers, however, feared emancipation, which they believed would release "a flood of cheap labor" upon the North, cutting living standards even lower. The Irish workmen also viewed emancipation with alarm, fearing economic competition from the slaves who would be freed. The Irish and Germans therefore had no use for Sherman Booth and the abolitionists. Some called him "a polecat" and applauded the court decisions which went against the radical reformer.

The temperance or prohibition movement also stirred the Wisconsin populace in the 1850's. Its chief strength lay in those Wisconsin communities settled by Yankees and New Yorkers. Temperance advocates honored a prominent eastern pro-

hibitionist when naming Walworth County. In 1846 and 1851 Maine had passed state prohibition laws, and many of the ex-New Englanders living in the Badger State thought it wise were Wisconsin to emulate Maine's example. The Irish-Americans and German-Americans, on the other hand, viewed prohibition as unwise and unwarranted. They called the advocates of the Maine law "Mainiacs." The prohibition movement became enmeshed in partisan politics. Democratic leaders, supported by German-American voters, prevented a prohibition law from being enacted. Dismayed but not disheartened, the prohibitionists continued to agitate for their cause, hoping that their "moral crusade" might yet triumph.

While the reformers argued passionately against slavery and in favor of temperance, most citizens of Wisconsin wrestled with their own problems. Debt-laden farmers cleared their fields of rocks and stumps and hoped for bounteous crops so they could remove the liens on their farms and earn a new lease on life. Bankers tried to flush out and rid the state of the "wildcat" notes that destabilized the economy. Manufacturers prodded their workers to produce more and better goods for wider markets. Brewers smacked their lips as they tasted their product and toasted the future. Brawny puddlers sweated and toiled in the state's three iron smelters. Miners complained that the veins of galena were growing less productive, and some stopped working their water-filled shafts. Sturdy woodsmen sharpened their axes and saws for a grand assault on the virgin pineries. But while the state's agents and editors preached the gospel of optimism, Wisconsin bonds and butter continued to enjoy "an evil repute" in the eastern markets.

⇥ 2 ⇤

The Election of 1860

THE POLITICAL PICTURE of the 1850's in Wisconsin was both a complex and a changing one. The Democratic party dominated in the early 1850's. Frauds of various kinds—what one historian termed "scandalous irregularities"— characterized the administration of Democratic

Governor William A. Barstow and helped to make the fledgling Republican party respectable. On the national scene, the Southern wing of the Democratic party held the reigns of government, and Wisconsin members of that party fussed and fretted. President James Buchanan, himself a Democrat, contributed to the Democratic disaffection by trying to force a pro-slavery constitution upon Kansas. Senator Stephen A. Douglas of Illinois split with President Buchanan on the question of Kansas; and Wisconsin Democrats who held federal posts through the patronage of President Buchanan felt obliged to oppose Douglas. But most Wisconsin Democrats sympathized with Douglas and looked to him as a leader. They liked his advocacy of western interests, his promotion of railroads, his faith in a dynamic and expansive America. They also liked his moderate stand on the emotional issues of the day, his boldness of speech, and his flair for dramatics. In 1860, most Democratic editors avowed that Douglas was their favorite presidential candidate. They wanted Wisconsin delegates to their party's national convention to put the name of the "Little Giant" at the head of the ticket.

But not all Democrats agreed. The editor of the Tomah *Chief*, for example, argued that Horatio Seymour of New York had many things in his favor. The editors of the Madison *Argus* and the Milwaukee *Enquirer* also opposed Douglas and offered a variety of suggestions. This apparent split of the Democratic party on the national scene cast an aura of gloom over the state's party leaders. "Family quarrels," noted one, "are distasteful and spell disaster."

Wisconsin Republicans, on the other hand, had every reason to be eager and optimistic. From its beginnings in 1854 in a little white schoolhouse in Ripon, the Republican flame had spread across Wisconsin like a prairie fire. The billowing smoke in northern skies from Minnesota to Maine proved that Republican fires were burning brightly.

Governor Alexander Randall, reelected in 1859 to another two-year term, wore the Republican label. Republicans far outnumbered Democrats in the state legislature, and Randall's partisans hoped to consolidate their position in the 1860 elections. Wisconsin Republicans looked back upon the election of 1856 with some satisfaction. John C. Fremont, their presidential candidate in

Alexander W. Randall (1819–1872), governor of Wisconsin during the critical years 1858–1862. (H32)341.

1856, had run well and carried the state with 55 per cent of the vote. Republicans believed that they were even better off in 1860. They viewed the Democratic position on homesteads, internal improvements, and slavery as very vulnerable. They awaited the political contest of 1860 confidently, chafing at the bit.

Wisconsin Republicans proposed several different men to head their national presidential ticket. A Racine Republican thought Fremont was the best bet again. "In our opinion," wrote the Racine scribe, "justice, honor, expediency, and the desire of success, should compel the party to give Fremont a chance for victory, as he had before the honor of a defeat." Other Republican prophets proposed Salmon P. Chase of Ohio, Edward Bates of Missouri, and Simon Cameron of Pennsylvania. As a boom for William H. Seward of New York spread, the name of Seward captured the imagination of Wisconsin Republicans. Rufus King of the Milwaukee *Sentinel* and Carl Schurz waved the Seward banner energetically and predicted that Seward would be the choice of both Wisconsin Republicans and the nation.

Abraham Lincoln's name was never seriously mentioned, even though he had visited the state in 1859, when he had spoken in Milwaukee, Beloit, and Janesville. At their state convention in February, Wisconsin Republicans named ten delegates to attend their party's national conclave. No one expressed surprise when the ten were instructed to vote for William Seward.

In the months that followed, however, the political stew thickened. The state's Democratic delegates who went to Charleston to attend their party's national convention and nominate Stephen Douglas found their party hopelessly split. A rump session which met later in Baltimore put the names of Douglas and Herschel V. Johnson at the head of its ticket. The southern wing of the Democracy countered by holding its own nominating convention, naming John C. Breckinridge and Joseph Lane. Hopelessly divided over candidates and strategy, the Democrats suddenly faced disaster.

Wisconsin's Republican delegates who went to Chicago to nominate Seward likewise failed in their mission. The delegates and campaign managers who favored Lincoln effectively checked the Seward boom. On the third ballot, Lincoln received the necessary majority; and Carl Schurz, in an effort to heal the factional wounds, then seconded the motion to make Lincoln's nomination unanimous. Wisconsin delegates even divided over selecting Hannibal Hamlin of Maine as Lincoln's running mate. Yet they accepted the ticket and returned home hoping that the homestead plank and the no-slavery-in-the-territories provisions of their platform would appeal to Wisconsin voters.

While Lincoln conducted a stay-at-home campaign, receiving delegations and visitors, Douglas and the Democrats waged a vigorous fight. His itinerary took him into Wisconsin, where he gave formal speeches in Milwaukee and Fond du Lac. The incivility tendered Douglas by a jostling, jeering mob in Kenosha, where he attempted to give an impromptu speech, should have been a hint to Wisconsin Democrats that all was not well.

Wisconsin Republican leaders, meanwhile, began active work for Lincoln. They actually generated some enthusiasm for their candidate. They organized "Wide-Awake" clubs to march in torchlight parades, applaud at rallies, and cheer party orators. They built wigwams, imitating on a small scale the Chicago building where Lincoln had been nominated. They pointed out that Lincoln was a westerner, a common man, and a practical politician. They talked up "Honest Abe" and praised the homely virtues of railsplitting. Rufus King brought William Seward into Wisconsin to enliven the campaign. Republicans never tired of emphasizing that their homestead plank should appeal to Wisconsin residents; it proposed that a head of family could obtain a free 160-acre farm through "actual settlement and cultivation." Professional politicians recognized that pro-Lincoln sentiment grew stronger with each passing day. The Republicans had a good candidate and good issues. The Democrats had Stephen A. Douglas— and little more. So the Democrats tried negative tactics. They tried to scare the Irish and Germans into voting Democratic by tying Know-Nothing (anti-foreigner) straps around the Republican elephant. They claimed that Lincoln's election would precipitate a national crisis. (Which it did.) But partisan Democrats knew that the tide had turned and that the Republicans would sweep Wisconsin. It was not a question of who would win, but by how much the Republican candidate would carry the state.

The election returns of November 4, 1860, elated Wisconsin Republicans, who carried the state by more than 20,000 votes. The final count read: Lincoln, 86,110; Douglas, 65,021; Breckinridge, 889; and John Bell of Tennessee, a scant 151. Forty-six of the state's fifty-seven counties recorded Republican majorities. Consequently, Wisconsin Republicans added to the hold they had on the state legislature. Furthermore, Republicans had swept most of the other northern states and put Lincoln in the White House. Governor Alexander Randall was pleased. So was Carl Schurz. Incorrectly and egotistically, Schurz credited himself with delivering the German vote to Lincoln; he boasted that his speaking tours had produced 200,000 votes for Lincoln and believed he deserved much credit for making Lincoln president.

While Republicans celebrated, the Democrats wore long faces. Flavius J. Mills of the Sheboygan *Journal* spoke the mind of the Democrats: "Every shout of victory makes us feel sad and gloomy." The less disconsolate Democrats screened a few cheerful facts out of the ashes of defeat. Milwaukee remained a Democratic stronghold, and a few other lakeport cities also returned Democratic majorities. Furthermore, the vast majority of Wisconsin's German-Americans had voted for Douglas and the Democratic ticket. And Democrats knew that Schurz had talked through his hat. The counties most heavily populated by Germans returned Democratic majorities; Schurz's home town, Watertown, gave Douglas 452 votes to Lincoln's 271. (Douglas even carried Schurz's own ward, 100 to 33.) The Democratic schism, the Lincoln image, and the homestead plank—not Schurz's officious oratory—had put Lincoln into the White House.

When the excitement of the election of 1860 died down, the campaigners returned to their jobs. They wondered what the future held. They wondered how the South in general—and South Carolina in particular—would react to Lincoln's election. They hoped that the dire threats made by Southern "ultras" before and during the campaign would be forgotten. But they knew that an uneasy peace existed in the land, and that civil war was a real possibility.

⊰ 3 ⊱

The Secession Crisis

THOSE DEMOCRATIC EDITORS who had earlier warned their readers that Lincoln's election would produce a crisis leaned back in their chairs and assumed an I-told-you-so attitude when several Southern states scheduled "special conventions." The South Carolina legislature issued a call for a "secession convention" as soon as Lincoln's election was assured. The call specified that delegates would be elected on December 6, 1860, and would meet on December 17. Both Alabama and Mississippi set elections for a secession convention scheduled for January 7. Other states of the lower South also set convention machinery in motion.

Wisconsin's worried residents disagreed upon the action which should be taken by the federal government. Some, who thought slavery a curse or blot upon the nation, were glad to see the slave states depart the Union. These few "radicals" repeated Horace Greeley's dictum: "Let the wayward sisters go in peace." Others wished that An-

drew Jackson were back in the White House to take stern corrective action against the defiant Southern states. They wanted the federal government to coerce South Carolina and hang some rebels. These coercionists heaped abuse upon President Buchanan, accusing him of timidity and inaction. Even some Douglas Democrats, who had learned to hate Buchanan, laid the lash upon the president. Marcus Mills ("Brick") Pomeroy of the La Crosse *Democrat* blasted Buchanan as "a weak and imbecile old fool." Pomeroy, who was destined to become Lincoln's most bitter critic in the war years, said Buchanan lacked a backbone and called him "a traitor to his Country."

Most Wisconsin Democrats, however, took their cue from Stephen A. Douglas, who supported compromise. They hoped that the national crisis could be resolved without bloodshed and claimed that compromise had become the standard and proper policy. "Our Country," wrote a moderate, "was conceived in compromise and maintained by compromise. Truly, compromise is the American Way."

While some timid souls wondered what views they should adopt, Governor Alexander Randall took steps to shape public opinion. As the acknowledged leader of the Republican party in Wisconsin, his opinions would carry considerable weight. Bewigged, slight in build, and genteel in appearance, Randall even looked like a prophet. He had worked his way up the political ladder and he knew he was a good judge of men and issues. He possessed an abundance of energy and was an excellent organizer. As a longtime worker in the political vineyards, he knew who the faithful were. He had a good mind and considerable administrative ability. He was an excellent speaker who had a knack for coining catchy phrases as well as solemn sentences. There was no question where Governor Randall stood on the vexing questions of secession or coercion. In his first inaugural address (January, 1859), Randall had said that Wisconsin would "never consent to a disunion of the States." Later, he labeled Southern threats of disunion as "unpatriotic, undignified, and disgraceful."

When the Wisconsin legislature convened on January 10, 1861, Governor Randall had his message ready. He addressed a joint session, advising an eager audience of his views on both state and national issues. He forcibly restated his opposition to both slavery and secession. He argued that Abraham Lincoln's election was legal and that he must be installed as president "over all the States," north and south. "A state," contended the governor, "cannot come in the Union as it pleases and go out when it pleases." Once in, it must stay in. He warned Southern secessionists that Wisconsin would help to sustain the government and enforce its laws. He stated his creed tersely: "Secession is revolution; revolution is war; war against the government of the United States is treason."

Two dismal efforts to resolve the crisis occurred in the national capital. In Congress, a Kentuckian named John J. Crittenden took the lead in proposing compromise. Each house of Congress, in time, established a committee to consider the Crittenden proposals. Wisconsin had a member on each of the two congressional committees. Congressman John F. Potter served on the Committee of Thirty-three established by the House of Representatives. Senator James R. Doolittle

James R. Doolittle (1815–1897), Republican and United States Senator, 1856–1869. (D484)8204.

served on the Committee of Thirteen established by the Senate. Stalwart Republican congressmen—Potter among them—joined hands with Southern extremists to nullify congressional efforts at compromise.

The second compromise effort took place outside the halls of Congress. The border state of Virginia took the lead in proposing a national peace convention, to convene in Washington on February 4. The Virginia legislature, in a resolution and an invitation, asked each state to send commissioners. Virginia hoped that such a convention might develop a climate in which the olive branch of peace and compromise might flourish. Virginia's invitation reached Governor Randall's desk, and on January 27 he forwarded the resolution to the Wisconsin legislature. Most of the Democratic legislators wanted commissioners sent, although they feared that Governor Randall might sabotage the convention by sending "stiff-backed" anti-compromise representatives. Most Republican legislators opposed sending any delegates. Wyman Spooner, leader of the radical Republicans in the assembly, denounced the Virginia invitation as a summons "to compromise the honor and dignity of Wisconsin." Carl Schurz wanted a set of anti-compromise commissioners appointed. (Characteristically, he hoped to be one of the commissioners.)

But inaction and indecision followed a protracted and heated debate. Consequently, Wisconsin failed to send any commissioners to the national peace convention. The assemblage in Virginia, after considerable debate, ratified some compromise proposals and recommended those proposals to Congress. But Congress chose to ignore the proposals and they met death by default.

As Wisconsin Democrats dreamt of peace and compromise, the sky grew darker and more ominous. The states of the lower South had seceded from the Union and organized themselves as the Confederate States of America. The angry jurisdictional dispute over Fort Sumter in South Carolina and Fort Pickens in Florida might bring a hail of bullets at any moment. Governor Randall, a realist and a Republican, appraised the situation correctly: he anticipated that coercion would become official federal policy after Lincoln was installed in the White House. As a party strategist and prophet, he knew his state must prepare for the worst. The storm clouds were real; they could not be dissipated by wishful thinking. So he urged the Wisconsin legislature to strengthen the militia laws and ready the state for the war which loomed on the horizon. He wanted to transform the state militia into a well-organized and well-armed institution.

Tradition and practice dictated that every "able-bodied free male white" between the ages of eighteen and forty-five belong to the state militia. Whether a lumberjack living in the woods near Superior, a fisherman tending his nets off Sturgeon Bay, a raftsman residing at Prairie du Chien, or a construction worker in Milwaukee, each was technically a member of the state militia if he met the requirements of age, health, and residency. In his message of January 10, 1861, Governor Randall pointed out that the number of persons subject to military duty in the state exceeded 130,000.

The state militia, however, could not be an effective force unless the militiamen were organized into companies, the companies into regiments, and the regiments into brigades. In 1860, Wisconsin's adjutant general (titular head of the state militia) reported that forty-two uniformed volunteer companies, in various stages of efficiency, were "organized and armed." Twelve others had applied for "organization and equipment." The militia, of course, was far from being ready for war. On the state level, its principal purpose and occupation seemed to have been to manufacture military titles for aspiring politicians. On the local level, the militia company usually functioned more as a social club than a military unit and was dressed for a parade rather than for war. Although the state supposedly furnished the arms (muskets for the infantry and cannon for the artillery), each company designed and secured its own uniforms. Some companies were dressed in blue, others in green or red. Uniform styles varied as much as the caps, hats, and shakos—sometimes plumed and cumbersome—which served as headgear. The more imaginative or affluent militia companies patterned their uniforms after those worn by the French Zouaves or those devised by the Italian revolutionary Garibaldi for his "red-shirts." After the initial organization, the typical militia company seldom met for drill; no one expected an invasion from Canada nor an Indian uprising.

Small wonder, then, that Governor Randall

urged the legislature to strengthen the state's militia laws. In addition, he urged the adjutant general to bring the uniformed militia up to a standard of efficiency and to have plans in readiness if the federal government called upon the states to furnish troops. Largely owing to Governor Randall's foresight and energy, Wisconsin was in better condition than any other midwestern state to answer Lincoln's call for troops when it came.

4

Wisconsin's Reaction to the Fort Sumter Affair

A LARGE DELEGATION from Wisconsin watched Abraham Lincoln, a prominent citizen of Illinois, become Abraham Lincoln, sixteenth President of the United States, on March 4, 1861. Both Governor Randall and Carl Schurz were anxious to give the new president advice on how to distribute the basketful of political plums. There was fear in some Republican circles that Lincoln would not be firm and forthright enough. Early in April, Randall visited President Lincoln to pledge his personal support of a policy of coercion.

Most of the state's citizens pursued a policy of watchful waiting. While Radical Republicans (meaning those who actively opposed slavery) denounced disunion as treason, most Democratic spokesmen wishfully talked of compromise. They hoped for a compromise which would negate the chief plank of the Republican party platform. The editor of the Milwaukee *Free Press* denied that the federal government had the right to coerce a state into remaining in the Union. He hoped that time would cool the national passions and make peaceful reunion possible. "Brick" Pomeroy of the La Crosse *Democrat* wrote in a like vein, declaring that coercion was "a pretty thing to talk about," but impractical, impossible, and dangerous.

The telegraphic dispatches from the East shocked Wisconsin. First came the news that on April 12 troops from South Carolina had attacked Fort Sumter—hurled shot and shell at U.S. troops and the American flag. Not long afterward came the news that Fort Sumter had surrendered. Next

Pre-war lithograph depicting officers of the Milwaukee Light Guard, a militia unit commanded by Capt. (later Col.) John C. Starkweather. (X32)5868.

came word that President Lincoln had called for 75,000 troops to serve for three months to quell "the insurrection."

Word of the surrender of Fort Sumter reached Milwaukee and Madison on April 14. Prominent citizens of both cities sponsored war or indignation meetings. The newspapers whipped up public emotion. The agitated editor of the Milwaukee

Sentinel asked for revenge: "Animated by the infernal spirit which produced this rebellion, the South has needlessly inaugurated this war. Let the Government now draw the sword and throw away the scabbard. Let us hear no more of *Peace*, till it comes in appeal from the trembling lips of conquered traitors." The Madison and Milwaukee war meetings were successful affairs. They featured patriotic speeches, martial music, cheers for the Union, and resolutions which expressed the indignation of the people. The editor of the Milwaukee *Sentinel* expressed his indignation in poetry:

Fort Sumter! Fort Sumter is taken!
The flag of our fathers hauled down!
Bold hearts of the Union awaken,
And prove you are sons of renown.
All ties of your party now sever,
And flock round your standard so true;
Compromise now? Oh never! No! Never!
The sword and the red, white, and blue.

Other Wisconsin cities also sponsored indignation meetings. The mayor of Oshkosh, a one-time Democratic delegate to his party's national convention at Charleston, headed the call for the "Union meeting" in the city. The editor of the Oshkosh *Northwestern* also preached the gospel of revenge and retaliation: "The Southern rebels have BEGUN the conflict! With them rests all of the responsibility and the CRIME of flinging the firebrand of CIVIL WAR. . . . The RIGHT *must* prevail, and the Nation's honor will be *vindicated!*" War meetings in La Crosse and Green Bay drew huge crowds. In the Democratic stronghold of Fond du Lac, an enthusiastic crowd raised $3,500 to fit out volunteers and support their families. Flags flew on every hand until "the whole Northern heavens seemed a perfect aurora borealis of stars and stripes." Members of militia companies hurriedly put their affairs in order and polished their muskets. The state was truly aroused!

Leaders of Wisconsin's two political parties seemed to be trying to outdo each other in preaching patriotism and pledging loyalty to country. Stephen D. Carpenter of the Madison *Patriot* had long been an ardent advocate of compromise. But after the fall of Fort Sumter, "Pump" Carpenter wanted vengeance and no quarter. "Let blood flow," he wrote with stony heart, "until the past is atoned, and a long future secured to peace, prosperity, happiness, and honor." "Brick" Pomeroy hurriedly discarded his views on coercion and compromise, offering instead to organize a volunteer company to serve with the army. Senator Timothy O. Howe, a Republican, complimented the Democrats for rallying to Lincoln's call, for shelving partyism, and for denouncing

Handbill issued in Waupun warning "rebel sympathizers" against tampering with military recruitment. (X3)17933.

South Carolina and "the rebels." He noted that "party lines burned, dissolved by the excitement." "The Democrats generally," wrote a member of President Lincoln's cabinet, "are offering themselves to the country."

When Governor Randall heard of Lincoln's call for 75,000 troops, he took immediate action. He asked all "patriotic citizens" to organize themselves into companies and report their readiness to the governor. He called the legislature into session to amend the militia act, to arm and equip the soldiery, and to vote bonds to finance the state's war effort. He reported that the state's quota for Lincoln's first call was a single regiment of ten companies of seventy-eight men each, plus officers.

Commanding officers of the organized militia companies telegraphed to Madison, offering their men to the governor. Many were anxious to be the first accepted for federal service. Some of the commanding officers hurried to Madison to use their personal influence or make a special plea. The Madison Guard, one of the militia companies headquartered in the state capital, gained the distinct honor of being the first company accepted by the governor. Within a week, thirty-six companies had offered their services. The governor either had to turn down twenty-six offers, convince the Secretary of War in Washington that more troops were needed, or organize some reserve regiments.

This response to the call for troops was heart-

Raw recruits, 1861, from a drawing in Battles and Leaders of the Civil War.

ening indeed. But it was also embarrassing. Limiting Wisconsin's quota to one regiment of ten companies would result in many disappointed patriots. As so often happens when war breaks out, many of these patriots feared that the war would be a short one and they would lose out on the glory. Men and officers not accepted into the First Wisconsin Volunteer Regiment moaned about their misfortune: "We'll spoil for want of a fight."

Flooded with offers of the volunteers, Governor Randall sent a telegram to Simon Cameron, Lincoln's Secretary of War. Randall urged Cameron to accept two additional Wisconsin regiments, even suggesting that the president call for 100,000 more men. He advised that the call be for three-year rather than three-month troops. (Randall did not seem to realize that Lincoln's call for three-month troops was based upon the limitations specified in a federal act of February 18, 1795.) Other governors besides Randall wanted the Secretary of War to accept more than the assigned quotas. Cameron, of course, had to reject the offers of the generous and patriotic governors; he replied courteously that "one regiment for the present would suffice." Governor Randall, reluctant to take "no" for an answer, sent other telegrams to the Secretary of War. Finally—and foolishly, as it turned out—Cameron asked Randall to cease recruiting altogether, even suggesting that he cancel all other enlistments except for the one regiment.

Governor Randall wisely ignored this advice from Washington. He believed that more troops would be needed, and he asked his adjutant general to continue raising and organizing the volunteers. On April 22—just eight days after Lincoln's first call—the governor proudly reported that the First Wisconsin was organized and ready, that a second regiment was in camp, and that five more were being formed. Events were to prove that Randall was far-sighted as well as patriotic and energetic.

In addition to raising men, there was the problem and responsibility of arming and equipping them. The state arsenal contained a few rusty and outdated items: six old brass cannons, 135 outdated flintlock muskets, 796 percussion muskets, 811 rifles, 101 rusty pistols, 158 sabers, forty-four swords, and fifty-six tents. Governor Randall tried hard to secure sufficient muskets to equip his regiments. His soldiers wanted them for drill and practice. Randall obtained some promises and for a while thought he had first chance on some muskets stored in the Rock Island Arsenal in Illinois. When those promises failed to materialize, both Randall and the soldiers were disappointed. Consequently, when Wisconsin's first regiments left the state, they were still without their arms, and they received them only after they arrived in Washington. Such dilatory practices undermined morale. Wisconsin recruits talked facetiously of using slingshots or pitchforks as weapons. But the truth was, many soldiers were destined to go into combat without ever having fired a military musket.

The situation as to clothing, tents, and equipage was somewhat better. Here Governor Randall took the initiative. Assured that the federal government would reimburse the states for expenses incurred in raising and equipping their troops, Randall consulted with Wisconsin's quartermaster general, William T. Tredway. Aware that ordering uniforms from New England factories would entail delay, Randall and Tredway decided to purchase the material from eastern merchants and then have the uniforms made in Wisconsin. Despite rivalry and arguments over "contracts" and "favoritism," this arrangement worked fairly well. However, since the state had purchased gray material, the first eight Wisconsin regiments wore uniforms the same color adopted by Confederate troops. (This was to prove embarrassing and decidedly unhealthy in combat.) Governor Randall also called upon the women of the state to supply quilts and blankets. Patriotic women organized quilting bees and responded nobly to the call.

Disorganization in Washington, especially in the offices of the War Department, plagued the governors who tried to raise troops for Lincoln's call. The exchange of letters between Randall and the Secretary of War showed mutual distrust and disagreement. Other midwestern governors also expressed disgust at the federal government's "conduct of the war." They felt there was a lack of cooperation and coordination—as well as timidity—on the part of the government. A governors' conference, which Randall attended, met in Cleveland, Ohio, on May 3, 1861. Randall's outspoken criticism of the federal government made him a prominent spokesman among his peers, and after the governors formulated their "demands" they delegated Randall to convey their instructions to President Lincoln.

Randall also gained the spotlight by means of his oratory. The citizens of Cleveland serenaded the governors and each of the executives had an opportunity to repay the applause with a few appropriate remarks. Randall's fiery rhetoric stole the show. He wanted the Union army to "blaze a broad track through the whole South, from Montgomery to Charleston." Continuing in the same vein, he said, "Rebellion and treason are abroad in our land. . . . We know where this commenced and we know where it must end. . . . Charleston should be razed till not one stone is left upon another, till there is no place for the owl to hoot nor the bittern to mourn. Had I the power of the thunderbolts of Jove, I would wipe out not only traitors but the seeds of traitors."

On May 6, Governor Randall conveyed the "views and suggestions" of his fellow governors to President Lincoln. The governors, said Randall,

Camp Randall, Madison, where thousands of Wisconsin troops prepared for war, from a wartime lithograph. (X3)18122.

wanted the federal government to act more efficiently, show more enthusiasm, and develop a dynamic plan of action. He urged Lincoln to call 300,000 more men into the service. (There was irony in this. Early in the war, the governors dictated to Lincoln—they told him what to do. Later on, as the power of the executive branch grew, Lincoln would dictate to the governors—they were his loyal and obedient servants.)

⊰ 5 ⊱

Baptism of Fire

AFTER ADJUTANT GENERAL Augustus Gaylord selected the ten militia companies which would make up the First Wisconsin Volunteer Infantry Regiment, he ordered them to rendezvous at Camp Scott in Milwaukee, named after Gen. Winfield Scott, then general-in-chief of the United States Army. Wisconsin residents remembered Gen. Scott as a hero of the Mexican War as well as the Whig candidate for the presidency in 1852. In 1861, however, Scott was no more fit to serve as general-in-chief than Camp Scott was fit to receive recruits. The seventy-five-year-old general was irritable, vain, and gout-afflicted; the newly established camp had no barracks, an inadequate water supply, and no fence surrounding the encampment.

Still, when the troops arrived, they found the carpenters hard at work, building barracks, mess halls, and supply quarters. Visitors flooded the camp, so it was soon necessary to put up picket lines to keep the guests out and the recruits in. One mother, carrying two warm mince pies when she came to visit her soldier-son, was stopped by a picket who informed her that visitors were forbidden at that hour. An agreement resolved the problem. The sentry ended up with one of the pies and the mother had a chance to visit her son.

Col. John C. Starkweather, the Milwaukeean who commanded the First Wisconsin, chafed because the camp was incomplete and because no arms were forthcoming. For a time, the four Milwaukee companies which were part of the First Regiment stayed at home during the night and reported to the camp each morning. Col. Stark-

John C. Starkweather (1839–1909), colonel of the First Wisconsin Volunteers. (X3)50389.

weather was more concerned about the absence of muskets. He knew that a firearm was more important to a soldier than a hammer or saw to a carpenter. He complained to the governor and to the state adjutant general; but he drilled his men, nonetheless. They spent long hours learning the complicated maneuvers of close-order drill which would serve them well amid the confusion and terror of the battlefield. Most citizen-soldiers quickly accepted the regimentation of army life and expressed a wish to fight the rebels.

While the First Wisconsin was still encamped in Milwaukee, Col. Starkweather sadly reported the death of one of the recruits. John H. Monroe, a private in Company C, had accompanied some companions down to the Milwaukee River for a swim. He slipped into a deep hole and drowned—Wisconsin's first casualty of the Civil War.

Col. Starkweather recognized that his regiment lacked a regimental banner. (Civil War regiments generally carried such a flag, in addition to the national colors, as a guide or rallying-point as well as a record of battles.) The colonel's wife and some other women set to work to fill the need.

They secured some brightly colored silk and sewed a banner which was later carried on two-score battlefields. On May 8, Mrs. George H. Walker, wife of one of the early founders of Milwaukee, formally presented the flag to the regiment and its colonel in impressive ceremonies at Camp Scott before a crowd of 5,000.

A month later, the First Wisconsin, consisting of 794 officers and men, entrained for Madison. The soldiers, tired of drill, were anxious for action. A large crowd gathered to take part in "the great farewell." Church bells rang, bands played, and cheers mingled with tears as the train pulled out of the station and the soldiers set out on the first leg of a trip that would take them to war.

The trip from Madison to Washington, D.C., seemed like a triumphal tour. Crowds lined the tracks and cheered the Wisconsin troops in every city through which the train passed. Usually the regiment disembarked from the train when it arrived on the western edge of the city. They then paraded down the main street and boarded another train at the other end of town. A correspondent of the New York *Tribune* who watched the First Wisconsin parade in Harrisburg, Pennsylvania, was either duly impressed or unduly optimistic. He predicted that the "martial looking" colonel and his "well-trained" recruits would "ring the knell of traitors who get within rifle dis-

tance." Unfortunately the regiment had not yet received its weapons.

From Washington, the First Wisconsin was shipped by train to Harpers Ferry and the Shenandoah Valley in northern Virginia. There it joined the command of Gen. Robert Patterson. The Harpers Ferry area had earlier been visited by a Confederate force commanded by Col. Thomas J. Jackson (who had not yet earned the nickname "Stonewall"). Jackson's marauders cut the Baltimore & Ohio Railroad, captured some rolling stock, and withdrew up the Shenandoah Valley on June 15. Another Confederate, Gen. Joseph E. Johnston, superseded Jackson and withdrew his forces to Winchester, a more tenable position. Gen. Patterson had reoccupied Harpers Ferry just before the First Wisconsin joined his command.

Patterson ordered his army to move up the Valley toward Martinsburg. As his apprehensive regiments edged forward, they encountered some Confederate pickets and outposts. A slight skirmish occurred on July 2 at a place called Falling Waters. Company B of the First Wisconsin was engaged, and there a bullet struck Pvt. George Drake near the heart. A companion who bent over him to examine the wound heard Drake utter but one dying word: "Mother!" Another member of Company B, Sgt. Warren M. Graham, also received a mortal wound at Falling Waters and died several days later. Thus, the First Wisconsin was

Union troops departing for the front, from Battles and Leaders of the Civil War.

baptized by blood, and George Drake became the first Wisconsin soldier to be killed in action.

When President Lincoln and Gen. Scott ordered Gen. Irvin McDowell and the Union army to advance on Richmond, the Confederate capital, in early July of 1861, Gen. Patterson also received orders to advance and "engage the enemy." But Patterson and his army of 18,000 men (including the First Wisconsin) stood idly by while Patterson's opponent reinforced the Confederates at First Bull Run, the first major battle of the war. However, another Wisconsin regiment, the Second, received its baptism of fire at First Bull Run.

The story of the Second Wisconsin dated back to April, 1861. Governor Randall did not follow the suggestion of Secretary of War Cameron that all volunteers not incorporated into the First Wisconsin be sent home. Instead, Randall assembled twenty more companies at the fairgrounds of the state agricultural society on the western edge of Madison. The first ten companies accepted into service formed the Second Wisconsin, and Governor Randall named S. Park Coon colonel of the regiment. Col. Coon, a well-known Milwaukee Democrat, repaid the honor by naming the army camp at the fairgounds on the western edge of Madison "Camp Randall."

These soldiers, who had volunteered originally for three months, had a chance to change their term of volunteering to three years. This was in line with President Lincoln's proclamation of May 3, 1861. Almost all the recruits accepted the three-year condition; a few went home, but their places were soon filled by other eager volunteers. The men of the Second Wisconsin received drill instructions and exercises under the direction of Lt.-Col. Henry W. Peck, who had spent two years at West Point. Even Col. Peck praised the ability of the soldiers of the Second Wisconsin to do "by the left flank" or "left front into line." Bedecked in their new gray uniforms, the regiment prepared to leave for Washington on June 20. Elaborate ceremonies preceded the departure of this second regiment of Wisconsin troops. Governor Randall witnessed the parade and gave the farewell speech. "By the shedding of blood," said Randall like a prophet of old, "atonement has always been made for great sins. This rebellion must be put down in flood, and treason punished by blood." After giving the governor three cheers, the recruits (totaling 1,048 officers and men) filed aboard the

railroad coaches and headed for the nation's capital. The regimental band of thirty-four pieces performed creditably, adding to the occasion.

Col. Coon and the Second Wisconsin arrived in Washington on June 25. After receiving their weapons—clumsy, outmoded Belgian muskets—the regiment joined the army of Gen. Irvin McDowell, commanding the Department of Northeastern Virginia. After a few days in camp on the outskirts of Washington, the Second Wisconsin marched into Virginia to Fort Corcoran, one of a series of forts guarding the approaches to the national capital. There the Second Wisconsin was joined with three New York regiments and a battery of artillery from the regular army to become Sherman's Brigade. Col. William Tecumseh Sherman, a West Pointer who evolved into one of the great Union commanders, reviewed his troops and wondered how these raw recruits would perform in battle.

He did not have to wait long to find the answer. Sherman soon recognized that Col. Coon was a political appointee who (as he put it) "knew no more of the military art than a child." Sherman solved the problem by naming Col. Coon to his staff and elevating Col. Henry W. Peck to command of the Second Wisconsin.

Preparatory to advancing upon Richmond, Gen. McDowell assigned Sherman's Brigade to Gen. Daniel Tyler's Division (the First Division). Then, at Gen. Scott's order, McDowell's "mass of men" moved south and west toward Centreville and Manassas Junction in northern Virginia. Confederate Gen. P.G.T. Beauregard, ordered by President Jefferson Davis to defend Manassas Junction, gathered a motley army just north of the railroad and behind a creek called Bull Run. Beauregard's lines extended from Union Mills to the Stone Bridge crossing on the Warrenton Turnpike.

After the Union troops reached Centreville, Gen. McDowell ordered a halt until provisions arrived and until his reconnaissance units located the main bodies of Confederate troops. Gen. Tyler, commanding the First Division and with the Second Wisconsin taking part, conducted a "reconnaissance in force," probing for the enemy in the vicinity of Blackburn's Ford and eventually permitting a skirmish to become a "serious engagement." The Union force paid a high price to find out that the Confederates were entrenched in

William T. Sherman (1820–1891), from a photo made late in the war. (X3)50386.

strength across Blackburn's Ford. Tyler, recognizing that he had exceeded his instructions when he became seriously engaged at Blackburn's Ford, took his dispirited troops back to Centreville and meekly relayed his findings to Gen. McDowell.

Gen. McDowell decided to outflank the Confederate left, opening the Stone Bridge as a gateway for some of his troops. He began the flanking movement on July 21. While two divisions took part in the flanking movement, Gen. Tyler's Division feigned an attack upon the Stone Bridge. This diversion was poorly executed and the Confederate forces guarding the bridge soon learned of McDowell's flanking movement. The Confederates moved to their left to engage the Union brigades which had crossed at a ford several miles upstream from the Stone Bridge. By noontime, the outmanned Confederates had retreated across the Warrenton Turnpike to the plateau-like brow of Henry House hill, contesting every foot of ground. But the morning's battle had heavily favored the Union army.

Meanwhile, most of Gen. Tyler's troops had also crossed Bull Run, some at the Stone Bridge and some a quarter-mile upstream. Sherman's Brigade, with the Second Wisconsin leading the way, crossed upstream and took part in the pursuit.

Atop the plateau, the Confederates regrouped. They rushed in reinforcements, reformed their lines, and pushed back the attacking Federals. (It was here that Jackson stood "like a stone wall.") After a brief lull in the fighting, the Federals attacked in force, trying to push the Confederates off the hilltop and into the woods. Sherman's Brigade was part of this earnest effort to dislodge the enemy. Col. Sherman sent two of his regiments forward, holding the other two in reserve. The Second Wisconsin and the Thirteenth New York fought their way up Henry House hill under heavy fire. Confederate musketry thinned the ranks of the two attacking regiments. Close-range artillery fire took a toll. The Union line, with the Wisconsin boys in the center, wavered and began to break. Soon both the Second Wisconsin and the Thirteenth New York were retreating in considerable disorder.

Col. Sherman observed their repulse, scowled, and puffed on his cigar. He then ordered the Wisconsin and New York boys to reform their lines and renew the assault. Once again the Second Wisconsin fought its way back to the brow of the hill—and a second time it was "repulsed in disorder." The regiment was in no condition to try another attack. Instead, Sherman sent his other two regiments forward. They too reached the hilltop, only to be driven back to the woods where they had sheltered while awaiting their turn to get into the fight.

Repulsed from the hilltop, Gen. McDowell knew it was futile to try to rally his men and make another attack. Consequently, he gave orders to withdraw across Bull Run and toward Centreville. Sherman's Brigade, with the Second Wisconsin leading the way, withdrew in good order across Bull Run, retracing its steps. Confederate cavalry caught up with him, but Sherman coolly ordered his four regiments to form a hollow square, fix bayonets, and keep the enemy at bay. His tired soldiers repulsed the cavalry attack and then continued to retire in orderly fashion toward Centreville. There they encamped, worn out and exhausted.

Much of the the rest of the Union army fell back from the battlefield in considerable disorder,

New York troops in zouave uniforms under Sherman's command in action at Henry House hill, from Battles and Leaders of the Civil War.

causing Gen. McDowell to abandon the notion of making a stand at Centreville. Sherman, then, aroused his brigade and led it into Washington, where he took stock and wrote his report on the role played by his brigade in the first major battle of the Civil War.

Truly, the Second Wisconsin had earned its spurs. The regiment reported heavy losses: twenty-three men killed, sixty-five wounded, and sixty-three missing (mostly prisoners). Only four regiments in McDowell's entire army recorded heavier casualties at First Bull Run. Considering the fact that these were green troops, they had fought amazingly well. In days to come, the Second Wisconsin would become a part of the most famous brigade in the entire Union army.

One other Wisconsin regiment saw action in the first year of the Civil War: the Third Wisconsin. It also was formed of ten companies and mustered in for three years. So many northern and northeastern Wisconsin counties were represented in the Third that some mistakenly referred to the recruits as "the wild woodsmen of the North." This regiment rendezvoused at a camp near Fond du Lac where they drilled and learned the myster-

ies of camp life. The Third Wisconsin left for the East on July 11, 1861. At a camp in Hagerstown, Maryland, the troops received modern Springfield rifle-muskets. Then the regiment crossed the Potomac into northern Virginia. It missed the First Battle of Bull Run, but it was ready to defend Washington if the Confederates should try to take the capital.

While waiting for blue uniforms to replace their gray ones, the Third Wisconsin received a rather bizarre assignment. Pro-Southern members of the Maryland legislature planned to meet secretly at Frederick on September 17, 1861. Those secessionists hoped to take Maryland out of the Union, giving a boost to Confederate morale, dividing the state, and endangering Washington. Federal authorities, however, learned of the secession scheme. Guided and accompanied by federal agents, the Third Wisconsin stole into Frederick, where they surrounded the building in which the would-be rebels were meeting. With loaded muskets and fixed bayonets, the Wisconsin soldiers rounded up the secession-minded legislators and marched them off to Fort McHenry, where they were interned. President Lincoln's orders, executed efficiently and secretly by the Third Wisconsin, helped to keep Maryland in the Union.

In addition to arresting the Maryland legislators, the Third Wisconsin was linked to a minor engagement at Harpers Ferry. Three companies of the regiment journeyed to Harpers Ferry to prevent a shipment of wheat from being captured by the enemy. Rebel troops appeared, planting some howitzers atop a hill overlooking the supply route. The commander of the Union detail ordered his troops, including the three Wisconsin companies, to drive the Confederates from the hilltop. Once attacked, the Confederates fired a few volleys and then retreated post haste. It was a minor skirmish. But for the six Wisconsin boys who died there, this brief hillside encounter was as deadly as any battle.

≈ 6 ≈

Banks and Bonds, Business and Politics

WHILE GOVERNOR RANDALL preached patriotism and organized regiments for war, an economic depression afflicted the state's economy. The depression was a hydra-headed monster. It threatened to destroy the state's banking system. It pushed some manufacturing plants to the brink of bankruptcy. It caused many commercial firms to close their doors. Lawyers and professional men complained of the hard times. The unemployed paraded the streets of Milwaukee; a few shouted angrily that they wanted bread. Farmers complained of "ruinous prices" as farm surpluses piled up in their granaries. Newspaper publishers moaned too; subscribers did not pay for their papers and advertisers cut costs and corners.

The closing of the Southern market by the Union blockade of the Mississippi River pinched Wisconsin less than her sister states to the south. By 1860, the Wisconsin economy depended upon an eastern and British market reached through the Great Lakes waterway or by east-west railroad lines. But Wisconsin lumbermen who had rafted logs or lumber down the Mississippi in the spring of 1861 were now forced to sell their products at punishingly low prices.

The state banking system likewise received a terrible jolt when Southern states seceded and the war began. Many Wisconsin bankers had invested their capital in Southern bonds which they had turned over to the state bank comptroller, who issued them an equal amount of paper money. Prior to the secession crisis, Missouri and North Carolina "sixes," and Louisiana "sevens," could be bought at considerably less than face value and exchanged with the state comptroller at face value, making them a seductive investment. In 1860 the comptroller had reported that he had $5 million in bonds on hand to validate the $5 million in authorized bank notes. However, three-fifths of those bonds were of the five most heavily indebted Southern states, meaning that bankers had bought them at considerable discount.

The secession of the Southern states drove the value of the bonds even lower—to the point of worthlessness. The state bank comptroller now instituted "depreciation levies," which some banks could not meet. Thirty-eight Wisconsin banks closed their doors in rapid succession and two-score more tottered on the brink. Some Milwaukee bankers, among them the powerful Alexander Mitchell, saw an opportunity to elimi-

Alexander Mitchell (1817–1887), Milwaukee banker and railroad magnate. (X3)50395.

nate some of their banking competitors by chal-
lenging their depressed currency. On Friday, June
21, 1861, Mitchell and some fellow bankers secretly listed the bank notes of ten more banks as
"unacceptable." The bankers then cleansed their
vaults of the questionable currency, passing it on
to manufacturing firms when they picked up their
weekly payroll packages. The next day—and after
the close of banking hours—some of Milwaukee's
manufacturers ended the work week by paying
their unwitting workers in the virtually worthless
currency.

On Monday, June 24, Mitchell and his fellow
bankers publicly listed the currency of the ten
specified banks as "discredited and unacceptable." Workers who had received their week's pay
in the discredited currency complained bitterly,
claiming they had been defrauded. A mob gathered and some men muttered threats; a riot ensued in which they broke into Alexander
Mitchell's bank. Some smashed windows. Others
lugged the furniture and papers outside where
they lit a bonfire—some called it "a bondfire."
The mob then marched on two other banks, dam-
aging property and talking of lynching the
bankers.

City authorities called upon the army officers
at Camp Scott to furnish soldiers to quell the rioters. Firemen, using fire hoses, and soldiers, bran-
dishing bayoneted rifles, dispersed the mob and
put an end to "the bank riot of 1861." The
bankers appraised the damage to their property as
bordering on $40,000.

Alexander Mitchell recognized that quite a
number of other state banks were in precarious
straits. Blacklisting their banknotes might produce
another riot, and more bank failures would surely
lead the populace to distrust banks even more. So
Mitchell and other bankers proposed a scheme
which would help the "depressed" banks. Those
banks could substitute Wisconsin war bonds for
the questionable Southern bonds. That scheme
could benefit the state treasury as well as the trou-
bled banks. A Wisconsin agent had tried to dispose of the state's war bonds on the eastern
money markets, but Wall Street gave him the cold
shoulder; New York money men had no faith in
Wisconsin's pledges and promissory notes. But
the bankers' scheme—a legislative committee later
called it "financial hocus-pocus"—helped save
some of Wisconsin's tottering banks and enabled

embarrassed state officials to dispose of most of
the $1,250,000 in war bonds.

The fall months of 1861 were also trying times
for Wisconsin farmers. Wheat and corn prices slid
downhill, lower and lower. In some areas corn
sold for as little as 10 cents a bushel, and some
farmers burned their crop for fuel rather than dispose of it for a pittance. Potatoes also begged for
buyers; butter was a drug on the market. Farmers
felt their flat pocketbooks when mortgages and
interest payments fell due. As hard times spread
gloom over the entire state of Wisconsin, many
transmuted their economic grievances into political action. They denounced the party in power
and blamed Republicans for bringing on both the
bad times and the war.

Immense purchases of foodstuffs for the European market failed to benefit the midwestern
farmers. East-west railroads and the Great Lakes
freighters raised their rates regularly, higher and
higher. The carriers charged all that the traffic
would bear, depriving the farmer of his just due.
"The railroads have put up their tariff on freights
to almost an embargo price," complained one
newspaperman. "They are literally skinning the
West alive, by advantage of the Mississippi blockade." The editor of the *Wisconsin Farmer* joined
in the rising chorus of criticism. "The farmers
work like heroes to produce their great crops of
wheat," he editorialized, "and then practically
give to shipowners and transportation companies
. . . all the product of their toil."

Democrats tried to make political capital out of
the high freight rates and prevailing hard times.
They pointed out that New England and New
York capitalists owned the railroads of the West,
and they claimed that the same crowd "owned"
the Republican party as well. They also emphasized that the Morrill Tariff of February 10, 1861,
and the supplementary act of August 5, 1861,
aided New England and injured the West. "The
West has been sold to the Eastern manufacturers
by the politicians," wrote a carping critic; "the
tariff is not a war measure, but a New England
protective measure by which she expects to lay the
great agricultural West tributary at the feet of her
cotton and woolen mills." Frederick W. Horn, a
prominent Cedarburg Democrat, resigned his captaincy in the militia rather than fight in a war
which would, as he said, "plunder" the Middle
West "for the benefit of Pennsylvania iron mon-

Frederick W. Horn (1815–1893), Democrat of Cedarburg.
(X3)50397.

gers and New England manufacturers." The observant editor of the Sheboygan *Journal* noted that coffee prices rose sharply even as domestic farm prices spiraled downward. Sarcastically, he suggested that the Republicans aid the war effort by "buying lots of coffee at thirty or thirty-five cents a pound."

Emboldened Democrats became critical of both President Lincoln and Governor Randall. They wrote and spoke of "the coming oppressive taxation" and of "general ruin" as silent partners in the gubernatorial election of 1861. Some Democrats, ignoring the facts of history, blamed the "Black Republicans" more than the Southern "Fire-Eaters" for the nation's dilemma and the civil conflict.

After the debacle of First Bull Run, the Wisconsin Republicans recognized that defeat on the military front and economic troubles on the home front would aid the opposition party. They tried to counteract the Democratic trend in two ways: by overtly generating patriotism and by organizing the so-called Union party, which they asserted would unite all "loyal Americans" under the same banner. Of course, this was really a cloak for their own political aspirations; they hoped to persuade ambivalent Democrats into supporting a war to preserve the Union. War meetings and patriotic speeches stoked the fires of patriotism. Republican editors reminded their readers that South Carolinians had fired upon the American flag at Fort Sumter and that "the rebels" had defeated the Union army at Bull Run. Republicans contended that all who criticized either Lincoln or Randall were undermining the war effort. They labeled all Democratic critics "rebels," "secessionists," and "traitors." Republicans wrote of the need for "unity," asking the Democrats to wave the flag of patriotism and to cease aiding the enemy.

Republican party strategists also used the Union party idea effectively. Instead of issuing a call for a Republican state convention, the Republican state committee issued a call for a "Union party" convention. Such a convention would indicate an absence of partisanship in the naming of a slate of state officials. The Republicans caught some prominent Democrats in their Union party web. Even such straitlaced Democrats as "Pump" Carpenter of the Madison *Patriot* and "Brick" Pomeroy of the La Crosse *Democrat* got entangled in the Union party movement early in the war years.

Governor Randall would have liked a third term, but he correctly gauged the direction of the political wind. He was also tired of politics. The depression of 1861 deepened the political unrest that was already so widespread over Wisconsin. Randall had alienated a number of prominent and wealthy Republicans. He was criticized because some military uniforms were made of "shoddy" (meaning they practically dissolved in the first rain) and because Wisconsin bonds were scorned by bond buyers in the East. Furthermore, the railroad interests had turned against him. Wisely, the governor let President Lincoln know that he would be available for a federal position—and soon thereafter he was promised the post of minister to Rome.

When Randall removed himself from the gubernatorial race, a backstage struggle for party leadership ensued. Republicans preached the unity theme to Democrats—but argued among themselves over candidates and policy. The "Madison Regency," headed by "Boss" Elisha W. Keyes of Madison, tried to reassert its hold upon the party. Milwaukee Republicans also jockeyed for position.

*Elisha W. Keyes of Madison (1828–1910), boss of the state's
Republican party.* (X3)1766.

The Union party convention met in Madison on September 24. Republicans, hiding backstage, pulled the strings. The delegates, almost all of the Republican persuasion, named Louis P. Harvey of Southport (Kenosha) as their gubernatorial candidate. The delegates gave three of the nine places on the ticket to "War Democrats" but saved the choice spots for members of their own party. The astute editor of the Prairie du Chien *Leader* saw the hand of Republicanism behind the Union party scheme and labeled it "an invitation to all Democrats to join the Republican Party."

Democrats, of course, hoped that the "Republican situation" would redound to the advantage of the Democratic party. They went to work with a will, believing that economic conditions would favor the party out of power. Their state convention met in Madison on October 8, 1861. The delegates publicly stated that the Union convention

was but a Republican scheme; they drafted resolutions criticizing both the Randall and Lincoln administrations. They named a full slate of Democrats for the nine state offices, with farmer-Democrat Benjamin Ferguson of Dodge County as their gubernatorial candidate.

Although both Ferguson and Harvey campaigned energetically, interest inevitably centered upon soldiering and the Civil War. Both candidates lacked color, and so did the campaign. The Union ticket carried the day. Harvey won the governorship with 53,777 votes to Ferguson's 45,575. The Union party stratagem helped enable the Republicans to win the election and control the statehouse, if not the legislature.

Republicans celebrated Louis P. Harvey's inauguration on January 6, 1862, and then turned to the task of winning the war. Democrats studied the election returns more carefully. They had increased their seats in the state senate. They had a chance to control the state assembly, believing that "fusion," an unkind term for the Union party movement, had cheated them of a greater number of seats in the legislature. They therefore began to speak of the "folly of fusion" and also resolved not to be caught in any more "Republican traps" where "the Republican cat was well concealed under the Union meal."

7

The Ninety-Four-Day Governor

THE ELECTION OF 1861 had put an unusual man into the governor's chair in Madison. Louis P. Harvey had served as secretary of state during Governor Randall's second term. He was more conservative than Randall, and he was not in the good graces of the Radical Republican junta headed by "Boss" Keyes of Madison. Harvey was a good speaker and an experienced politician. He could look back upon a checkered and active career. Born in New England in 1820, he was part of that great "Yankee exodus" which flooded portions of the Upper Mississippi Valley. First he settled in Southport, where he taught school, edited the Southport *American*, and espoused Whig doctrines. He gained the postmastership of Southport, attended the state constitutional conventions, and served as a state senator. In 1847 he moved to Rock County, where ex-Yankees were especially numerous. There he met and married Cordelia A. Perrine. While operating a general store, he was active in church groups and political affairs. He, more than any other man, was responsible for building a new Congregational church in Waterloo (later renamed Shopiere). He became the idol of temperance preachers because he bought a distillery in order to demolish it and erected a gristmill on the site.

The collapse of the Whig party after 1852 seemed to check Harvey's political ambitions. With many another transplanted Yankee, he moved into the newly established Republican party, and he helped to build a strong party organization in Rock County. His services to the cause of Republicanism paid dividends. In 1856 he was one of Wisconsin's delegates to the Republican national convention which nominated John C. Fremont. In 1859 he was rewarded with his party's nomination for secretary of state. After the election, Harvey took up residence in Madison and worked hard in his new office. The next year he campaigned for Lincoln, giving political speeches in various Republican strongholds. By helping Lincoln to win the presidency, Harvey enhanced his own reputation and his own political fortunes. As secretary of state, he kept his name before the public. When Randall decided not to seek a third term, Harvey seemed like the logical successor. He had many friends and few enemies; he had a reputation for honesty and integrity.

In his first message to the legislature on January 10, 1862, Governor Harvey proved that he intended to be "the soldiers' friend." He insisted that the legislature amend the Soldier Volunteer Aid Act so that more funds would be available to more soldiers. The reluctant legislators gave Governor Harvey only half a loaf. The state had earlier agreed to pay $5 a month to the family of every enlisted man, but the state coffers were empty and many families had failed to receive their allotments. Consequently, patriotism sometimes gave way to despair and genuine hardship. Governor Harvey urged that soldiers and their families receive preferential treatment—that the promised aid be forthcoming.

About mid-February, the state treasurer, in charge of relief funds, reported again that the re-lief barrel was empty and urged the governor to obtain additional funds. Harvey immediately dispatched a special message to the legislature, requesting immediate action. He reminded the legislature that thirteen Wisconsin volunteer regiments were in the field, that 3,100 claimants had filed for dependents' pay, and that the "soldiers' fund" cupboard was bare. "In many instances," he continued, "the $5 per month pledged by the state is the sole dependence of a helpless family against cold and hunger." He pointed out that the state's failure to fulfill its promises to the volunteers embarrassed the state officials as well as the soldiers' families. However, the legislative wheels turned but slowly. Not until April 5 did the legislature provide for the transfer of $50,000 from the general fund to the relief fund. It was easier to make promises than to keep them.

In 1861, Congress and the president had tried to establish a system by which some of the volunteer soldier's monthly pay might get home to help his family. A federal law authorized each state to be represented by three commissioners whose chief job was to collect the allotments from the soldiers in the camps and distribute them to the

Louis P. Harvey (1820–1862), ill-starred governor for only ninety-four days. (X3)2293.

dependents. The states were expected to pay the salaries of the appointees even though they received their commissions at Lincoln's hand. These commissioners—always good Republicans—were in a position to help their party, unless they helped themselves too much.

Governor Randall had initiated the practice of sending a state agent or "good Samaritan" into the field with each regiment. Democrats believed that the "Samaritan system" aided the political party in power, and they cynically referred to these state agents as "political commissars" and "keepers of the political conscience of the regiments." There was a measure of truth in this charge. When Harvey replaced Randall in the governor's chair, he revised the system so he could name his own state agents. Harvey's political friends and "deserving party workers" gained the state agent posts, blending military with political activities.

While Governor Harvey worked hard at being "the soldiers' friend," the telegraph brought some good news. Brig. Gen. Ulysses S. Grant had led a land-and-water expedition against a pair of Confederate forts in northwestern Tennessee. Grant's name made the headlines when Fort Henry surrendered on February 6, 1862. He then turned his attention towards Fort Donelson, some ten miles to the east, where it guarded a bend of the Cumberland River. Grant's demand for an "unconditional surrender" and the resultant capture of 15,000 Confederates at Donelson made him the hero of the hour. Although no Wisconsin regiments took part in the Henry-Donelson campaign, state residents were well aware that Grant was a westerner and that the victory had been won by western troops.

The telegraph also brought some good tidings from the East. There, in early March, the Federal ironclad *Monitor*, the so-called "cheese-box on a raft," had dueled for several hours on even terms with the famous Confederate ironclad *Merrimac* off Hampton Roads, Virginia. Both ships gave and took punishment; the North claimed a victory when the *Merrimac* retired. This dramatic contest also thrilled Wisconsin citizens, who exaggerated the importance of the brief contest between the two ironclads.

Early in April, word reached Wisconsin that Grant's forces in Tennessee were on the move again. There was the anticipation of battle and the hope of victory. Four Wisconsin regiments of in-fantry had joined Grant's command: the First, the Fourteenth, the Sixteenth, and the Eighteenth. The First had been reorganized; most of the three-month volunteers had reenlisted for three-year terms. Instead of being sent back to the East, they were sent down to Louisville and then to join Grant. The Fourteenth had been organized in November of 1861. Commanded by Col. David E. Wood, it was sent to Savannah, Tennessee. The Sixteenth and Eighteenth were green regiments, part of the division commanded by Gen. Benjamin Prentiss. The Eighteenth had left Milwaukee for the front just a week before.

Gen. Prentiss' division formed the left wing of Grant's army. It would be the first to encounter the enemy if the Confederates moved straight north from their encampment twenty miles away near Corinth, Mississippi; but neither Prentiss nor Grant expected a Confederate attack. The Confederate commander, Gen. Albert Sidney Johnston, decided to attack Grant's army before it was reinforced by some 20,000 men under Gen. Don Carlos Buell's command. Johnston knew that Buell had orders to join Grant, so he was anxious to join battle with Grant before the reinforcements arrived.

Gen. Johnston and his Confederate troops devised one of the most successful surprise attacks of the war, and they caught Grant napping. Early Sunday morning, April 6, 1862, a portion of Johnston's army stormed out of the woods, drove in Gen. Prentiss' pickets, and fell upon his surprised and disordered soldiers, who were still encamped near Pittsburg Landing on the Tennessee River. Soon Prentiss' entire division, including the two regiments of green Wisconsin troops, felt the brunt of Johnston's attack. The division wavered and fell back, threatening disaster to the entire army, but Grant managed to rally his crumbling lines. Prentiss' division reorganized and held fast. Soldiers of the Sixteenth and Eighteenth Wisconsin fought and died in a clearing that became known as the Hornet's Nest and near a shallow watering place later designated Bloody Pond. In one sector, Wisconsin troops had a hand in repulsing thirteen successive Confederate charges.

By noon, the battle lines extended over several miles in wooded terrain adjacent to the river, and death was everywhere. Gen. Johnston, anxious to turn the scales, personally led the afternoon assault in a determined effort to crush Grant's left, where Prentiss' division stubbornly held on against odds.

Troops of Prentiss' division fighting in the Hornet's Nest at Shiloh, from Battles and Leaders of the Civil War.

Johnston fell, mortally wounded, but the Confederate attack continued. It was more than Prentiss and his troops could take. Some retreated, leaving Prentiss in an exposed position. He decided that the cause was hopeless. Late in the afternoon, surrounded and outnumbered by the enemy, Prentiss surrendered the remains of his division—some 2,200 men, his Wisconsin troops among them.

Grant's main force held off the enemy until nightfall. Then some of Gen. Buell's reinforcements showed up—including the Fourteenth Wisconsin, which arrived about midnight from Savannah, Tennessee, anxious to redeem the honor lost by Prentiss' troops. Reinforced, Grant and Sherman feverishly bolstered their lines to stave off a renewed Confederate assault.

Bitter fighting continued into the following day. But Grant's lines held, and the battle became a series of localized attacks and counterattacks. During the afternoon of April 7, the Fourteenth Wisconsin received orders to capture a troublesome Confederate battery, some distance away. The regiment captured the battery—on its fourth effort. Later, Gen. Grant singled out the regiment for special praise and recognition.

By evening the Confederates decided they had

had enough. During the night, they withdrew from the field. Each side, of course, claimed a victory. Grant's army had been surprised and badly mauled, but it held the field when the Confederates withdrew. Grant lost 13,000 killed, wounded, and captured. The Fourteenth Wisconsin reported fourteen killed and seventy-nine wounded or missing. The Eighteenth lost twenty-four killed, eighty-two wounded, and 174 missing (the latter being part of the 2,200 men who surrendered with Gen. Prentiss). The Sixteenth had the longest casualty list; it lost more than a fourth of its men in this first great battle in the western theater of war—known as Shiloh in the North and Pittsburg Landing in the South.

Grant's losses were considerably higher than those suffered by the Confederates (about 11,000), but the South had lost Gen. Johnston, one of its best generals, and Shiloh could justly be called a narrow Union victory.

When reports of Shiloh and the heavy Wisconsin losses arrived via telegraph, Governor Harvey publicly expressed concern. He called upon the citizens of the state to contribute medical supplies and offered to deliver the supplies personally to the camps and hospitals in Tennessee. Wisconsin

Union steamboats at Pittsburg Landing on the Tennessee River, where Gov. Harvey drowned.
From Battles and Leaders of the Civil War.

citizens answered the governor's call for contributions with more than ninety crates of supplies. The governor then recruited some volunteer surgeons to accompany him on his "mission of mercy" to the battlefields.

Governor Harvey visited a number of hospitals near the Shiloh battlefield, seeking out Wisconsin soldiers and distributing the medical supplies. He also visited some of the regiments in camp. On the evening of April 17, he wrote a letter to his secretary in Madison, saying he was glad he had undertaken his mission to the front. "Thank God for the impulse which brought me here," he wrote with feeling. "I am doing a good work and shall stay as long as I am profitably employed."

The governor's errand of mercy ended tragically. On April 19, 1862, while transferring from one steamboat to another at Pittsburg Landing, he lost his balance and fell into the Tennessee River. It was dark, and the current was swift and treacherous. Harvey's body was recovered ten days later, nearly sixty miles downstream.

When news of the disaster reached Madison, sadness reigned and the governor's many friends

mourned unashamedly. After his body was shipped home for burial, his grieving wife Cordelia watched them lower it into the grave. Louis P. Harvey had been governor for only ninety-four days. Wisconsin had lost a good executive. The soldiers had lost a friend.

The Military Draft of 1862

THE SUDDEN AND SHOCKING DEATH of Governor Harvey elevated Edward Salomon to the statehouse. In some ways he was an unknown quantity. He was but thirty-three years old. He was a German-American and a newly naturalized American citizen. He was less the political partisan than Harvey had been; in fact, he was an eleventh-hour convert to Republicanism who had been a self-proclaimed Democrat early in his Wisconsin career. His antislavery sentiments, however, made him uneasy in a party dominated nationally by Southern Democrats. In 1860 he announced his support of Abraham Lincoln, and he adopted the Republican label. When Republicans looked around for a German-American whom they could put on the slate of candidates for state office, someone suggested his name; he was a well-known lawyer and he might attract the votes of some German-Americans. Thus it was purely a matter of political expediency that Edward Salomon had a place on the Republican ticket and in November, 1861, became the lieutenant-governor of Wisconsin. Then destiny and the death of Harvey put him in the governor's chair.

Yet Governor Salomon proved that he was deserving of the confidence that had been placed in him. He was a decent governor. He never sacrificed his personal convictions for partisan favors. He possessed a good deal of administrative ability, considerable common sense, and devotion to duty. When defending the interests of his state against the demands of the War Department in Washington, he proved himself prudent and persistent.

In Washington, Simon Cameron had resigned

Governor Edward Salomon (1828–1909). (X3)15371.

under fire as Secretary of War and a crusty Ohioan named Edwin M. Stanton took his place. The new Secretary of War erred in disbanding the federal recruiting service early in 1862. Someone had convinced Stanton that enough troops were already in arms. But news of Grant's heavy losses at Shiloh and Gen. George B. McClellan's failure in the Peninsular Campaign against Richmond caused the Secretary of War to reverse his decision to stop recruiting. Somewhat embarrassed, Stanton had to ask the governors to furnish more troops. On July 2, 1862, President Lincoln called for 300,000 volunteers to serve for three years. A month later, he asked for 300,000 more nine-month men. The federal government set Wisconsin's quota for the various calls at 42,557 men.

Congress recognized that some states might not be able to raise their quotas through volunteering. (As the realities of actual combat dawned on the public, there was diminished enthusiasm for military service.) So, in mid-July of 1862, Congress provided for a draft into the state militia by the state authorities—if quotas were not filled by volunteering. The Congressional act outlined procedures in cases where states had no draft systems.

Governor Salomon wrestled with the problem of breaking the state quota of 42,557 into county quotas. There was the problem of giving credits to those counties which had furnished volunteers generously in the first year of the war. Furthermore, an enrollment of all eligible males had to be made before a fair draft could be executed and credits be given. It was evident to Salomon that the federal government wanted the men, but not the responsibility for recruiting or drafting them into the military. While busy with men and mathematics, Salomon received another request from the Secretary of War, who informed him that Wisconsin was required to furnish 5,904 additional men to raise depleted regiments to full strength. If these men were not furnished by the first of September, Stanton warned, a special draft should be held to fill the depleted ranks of the existing regiments.

Governor Salomon's arithmetic showed him that Wisconsin had already furnished five regiments more than previous quotas had required. He therefore wanted these "excessive soldiers" credited to the state and deducted from the new levies. In any case, the governor was reluctant to resort to conscription. He pretended that it was possible to meet the new quotas by volunteering and a generous bounty system, by which men were encouraged to enlist by the offer of cash bounties to be paid by the state.

Salomon knew that a state-executed draft was political dynamite. The odium of the draft would center upon the governor's office, for the draft would have to be executed under the governor's orders. Republican political leaders were especially concerned, for 1862 was an election year in which six Congressmen and half the state legislators were up for election. A draft would lessen Republican chances of sweeping the election. Then, too, Salomon rationalized, the draft would impede the fall harvest. So he sent his excuses to Washington, hoping that a controversy over correct quotas might delay the draft until after the November elections. But Secretary of War Stanton imperiously brushed aside such excuses and objections. On August 15, 1862, he ordered Governor Salomon to execute the draft and meet the quotas assigned to Wisconsin.

Secretary of War Edwin M. Stanton (1814–1869).
(X3)50387.

The governor reluctantly set the machinery of the draft in motion. He named Levi B. Vilas of Madison, a respected and well-known banker and "War Democrat," to serve as state draft commissioner. With the aid and advice of Vilas, Salomon named a draft commissioner and an examining physician for each county. The enrollment of all men between the ages of eighteen and forty-five proceeded rapidly. Then, in September, Governor Salomon called the legislature into session so that laws could be passed which would make conscription more equitable and efficient. But the politically minded legislators did not want their names linked to any draft laws. They made excuses and adjourned without passing any, leaving the responsibility solely on the governor's doorstep.

Although enrollment proceeded rapidly, there was widespread disaffection. An old state law exempted both firemen and militia officers from conscription. When the draft was announced, there was a rush by many to sign up as firemen. Since the number of firemen in companies was not set by any law or regulation, some fire companies soon were bloated with ten times as many members as they needed. The governor finally felt compelled to limit exemptions to those on the fire company rolls prior to the announcement of conscription.

Enrolling officers were also embarrassed by the large numbers of Wisconsin men who claimed physical disability. Many who had previously been hale and hearty became unbearably lame and chronically ill. New diseases swept over the state like epidemics. So many visited the examining surgeon's office in Fond du Lac that state officials shook their heads in disbelief; someone placed a sign reading "Cowards' Headquarters" over the surgeon's door. The surgeon charged with examining Manitowoc County enrollees granted so many exemption certificates that Governor Salomon had to take action, declaring all Manitowoc County exemption certificates invalid and appointing a new examining surgeon. Surgeon Gen. Erastus B. Wolcott, who supervised the system, tried to enforce the law honestly and fairly—and no one questioned his integrity or efficiency. Gradually the number of exemptions and complainants decreased.

Governor Salomon, himself a foreign-born citizen of Wisconsin, was personally embarrassed by the large number of German-Americans who filed exemptions as "aliens." State laws gave the vote

Erastus B. Wolcott (1804–1880), Wisconsin's surgeon general. (X3)14850.

to foreign-born residents who declared their intent to become citizens. Thus many men had voted who had not completed the naturalization process. Both Governor Salomon and Secretary of War Stanton therefore ruled that all who had filed their "declaration of intent" should be subject to the draft. Many German-Americans angrily disagreed with that interpretation. They claimed they were still aliens, and some even renounced their declarations to become citizens. Many filed appeals and claimed they should not be enrolled or drafted. Some "skedaddled" to Canada or left for the Far West. "Draft malaria" seemed to be a popular disease, and there were claims that the Canadian climate brought back good health. In the nineteenth century, it was relatively easy for people to disappear from a community and become drifters or start new lives elsewhere. They were difficult to trace, and there was no mechanism for keeping track of men who left to visit friends or relatives and never returned. Federal and state officials tried their best to prevent the flight of potential draftees, but when the gateway to Canada was closed, the runaways went elsewhere. Wisconsin contributed substantially to a

sudden increase in the population of the north woods and the western territories.

Opposition to the draft was centered in those counties which held a large percentage of German-born residents, many of whom had emigrated to escape conscription in their homelands. (In the nineteenth century, prior to the unification of Germany in 1871, the term "German" applied to immigrants from Prussia, Hannover, Mecklenburg, and scores of other German principalities as well as to Austrians, Belgians, Luxembourgers, and Swiss.) When German immigrants arrived in New York City, many had been greeted by Wisconsin agents who painted a glowing picture of the freedom and opportunities Wisconsin offered. The state draft seemed to be a violation of those promises. Who would pay the mortgage when it fell due if the breadwinner was away in the army?

Furthermore, the German-Americans did not understand the long-time controversy between North and South. Their spokesmen in the Democratic party blamed the "Black Republicans" more than the South for the war. Such Democratic newspapers as the Milwaukee *See-Bote* and the Port Washington *Ozaukee County Advertiser* dealt harshly with President Lincoln and Governor Salomon. Spokesmen Peter V. Deuster and Frederick W. Horn railed against both abolitionists and Republicans, condemning them in the same breath. There was no question but that there would be widespread opposition to the draft in Wisconsin's Germanic communities.

Governor Salomon, on the advice of political friends, postponed the draft until after the elections of 1862. He used the excuse that the delay would enable the counties to show good faith by raising their quotas through volunteering. And in fact the campaign to raise Wisconsin's quota by volunteering was quite successful. Most counties raised their allotments and toasted their success. But Washington, Ozaukee, Sheboygan, Brown, Fond du Lac, and Milwaukee counties lagged behind—and each contained a large element of Germans. Reluctantly, Governor Salomon ordered a draft to take place in the counties which had not furnished their quotas.

In the autumn of 1862, Milwaukeeans carrying "No Draft" signs marched up and down the streets of Milwaukee. There was fear in some quarters that the disorganized protest against the draft might turn into disorder. In Sheboygan, mal-

Recruiting poster for the Twenty-fifth Wisconsin Volunteer Infantry, July, 1862. (X3)50509.

contents talked of trouble when the draft began in their county, and a defiant crowd threatened to become a mob. The courageous draft commissioner, however, drew his revolver and defied the crowd. His boldness chilled riot fever, and he then proceeded with the draft without further incident. There was also threat of mob action in West Bend, Washington County, when a crowd gathered to watch and protest against the draft proceedings. Some members of the crowd threw stones and eggs, but the authorities overawed the crowd. In Port Washington, however, the dam of discontent burst: a full-scale riot ensued.

Port Washington Democrats placed some of the blame on the undercurrent of discontent at Governor Salomon's door. An almost all-Catholic regiment had earlier been recruited in Washington and Ozaukee counties. The rank and file thought they were entitled to have a Catholic chaplain, but

Governor Salomon ignored the wishes of the majority of the regiment in naming the chaplain. Friends and relatives of the soldiers grumbled openly. The governor also chose to ignore the wishes of prominent Democrats in the naming of the draft commissioner and the examining surgeon, who was authorized to exempt men from the draft for physical shortcomings of one kind or another. Dissatisfied Democrats complained that too many exemption certificates were granted by the examining surgeon to prominent Republicans, generally men of social position and wealth. Small wonder that a groundswell of disaffection existed and that it spelled t-r-o-u-b-l-e.

William A. Pors, the draft commissioner for Ozaukee County, set November 10, 1862, as the day for the draft lottery. Early that morning a crowd of Germans and Luxembourgers gathered before the steps of the county courthouse. Some shouted "No draft." Others declared their opposition to a war to free the slaves. Grumbling and complaining, they gave courage to one another. When Pors began the lottery, some of the bolder men pushed forward, shouting angrily. The rest joined in noisy protest. In moments, the crowd became a mob. A couple of burly fellows seized the draft commissioner and pushed him down the steps of the courthouse, where others pummeled and kicked him.

The mob then turned its attention to the machinery of the draft, destroying the box containing the names of those who could be drafted. Some rioters seized other enrollment records and started a fire in the street. While the mob was venting its rage on the draft machinery, commissioner Pors got up and ran for his life, pursued by some women and children. He escaped into the basement of the building which housed the post office. There he locked himself in the cellar and listened anxiously to the noise outside.

The mob, meanwhile, sought additional outlets for its anger. Some of the rioters led a portion of the rabble to the "handsome, well-furnished dwelling" that commissioner Pors called home. They invaded and ransacked his house, tore clothing to ribbons, threw jam and jelly over the rugs and carpets, and wrecked the furniture. The vengeful mob visited seven more homes, all owned by prominent Republicans who had endorsed the draft, and destroyed what they could. Sometimes they made bonfires out of furniture and furnishings dragged from the homes. Someone decided that they needed a large "No Draft" banner which could be prominently displayed. A group visited a local storekeeper and forced him to paint the banner, which they carried up and down the main street, chanting "No draft! No draft!" Some dragged a small cannon down the street and set it up on a pier—as if defying the authorities to send a troop of soldiers by water. That evening many of the tired mobsters visited the saloons, seeking to bolster their courage or to forget their folly.

When the word of the rioting reached Governor Salomon's desk, he shook his head in disbelief. It was his duty to enforce the law, and here was open opposition to his authority. Salomon ordered six companies of the Twenty-eighth Wisconsin Regiment, quartered in Milwaukee, to suppress the Port Washington insurrection, arrest the rioters, and help enforce the draft. The troops soon put the draft commissioner back in business. They arrested approximately 150 persons for their part in the draft riot and overawed the citizenry. The draft commissioner, with troops and gleaming bayonets at his side, finished the draft without further incident.

Gauging the temper of the anti-draft sentiment in Milwaukee, the draft commissioner of Milwaukee County wisely delayed the draft for another week. He wanted troops at his side when the machinery of the draft would be set in motion. Troops helped to supervise the lottery when the draft was finally begun. No trouble occurred; those whose names were called caused no incidents. Sullenly or willingly, the new conscripts began the transition from citizens to soldiers of the Union armies.

Flavius J. Mills of the Sheboygan *Journal*, like many other Democrats (and plenty of Republicans as well), expressed sympathy for the conscripts and antipathy to the draft. "In Heaven's name," he wrote, "let us have no more of this conscription—a system which the most prescriptive monarchial government would scarce resort to." It was true that the state draft of 1862 could hardly be called a success. Indeed, the state's principal military officer termed it "a miserable failure." As Adjutant General Augustus Gaylord wrote: "The total number drafted in the State under the call of August 4, 1862, was 4,537; of which 2,875 reported at camps of rendezvous. Of these, 988 were discharged; 19 deserted from

camp; 129 were furloughed until further orders, by the Governor, to await the decision of the War Department in their cases, equivalent to a discharge; and the balance, 1,662, failed to report."

9

The Indian Scare

WHILE GOVERNOR SALOMON wrestled with the complex problems of enrollment and conscription, disturbing news of an Indian uprising came to his desk. The same news spread throughout the state and precipitated the famous "Indian scare" or "people's panic" of 1862.

The episode stemmed out of long-standing grievances among the Sioux of southern Minnesota, who were unhappy when new white settlements appeared in territory upon which they still had claims. The Indians had been deprived of their hunting grounds by treaties concluded in the 1850's. Now they were hungry, and increasingly they grumbled about the fraud practiced on them by government traders and the governmental red tape which delayed tribal annuity payments. The young braves, especially, were weary of the white man's chicanery and persecution. A setting existed which could produce an incident—and an incident could lead to war.

Gen. Augustus Gaylord (left) scanning draft rolls, c. 1862.
(X3)17938.

The incident occurred at Acton, Minnesota, on August 17, 1862. Four young braves, while drunk, stopped at a white settler's cabin to demand food and whiskey. An argument ensued and the Indians killed the occupants. Sobered by the experience, the four miscreants called upon Chief Little Crow to protect them. Little Crow expected that the army would punish the entire tribe, so he determined to strike the first blow. Little Crow and a portion of the tribe took to the warpath. Suddenly, southern Minnesota was aflame with an Indian war. The Sioux began a series of forays and massacres in the vicinity of New Ulm, which they besieged. Within seven days, Sioux raiders had killed over 400 men, women, and children.

Settlers in western Wisconsin feared that the outbreak would extend to their settlements. There were also rumors that various Wisconsin Indians would join the Minnesota Sioux on the warpath. Some settlers let their fears cloud their judgment. An "Indian scare" engulfed the western and northwestern portions of the state and gradually spread eastward. Panic-stricken settlers dreamed of scalping parties and tomahawk-swinging assailants. They mistook mystified peaceful Indians for mortal enemies and imagined that the woods were filled with bloodthirsty redmen. "Every bush," wrote a witness later, "had an Indian behind it, every moan of the wind was an Indian signal, [and] the hoot of an owl was the infuriated whoop of an army of savages."

A paroxysm of irrational fear swept Wisconsin. Hundreds and then thousands of residents of the rural areas fled to the larger settlements. The people of Beldenville migrated en masse to River Falls, "stampeding like cattle while not an Indian was within fifty miles." In Dunn County "the whole population of the county was in commotion and on the move." For four days (August 29–September 1), a constant stream of settlers streamed into Menomonie, fully convinced that the Indians were close behind them, murdering every white person they could overtake and destroying the settlements as they progressed.

In most cases, the fugitives left everything behind in their mad race to keep ahead of their imaginary pursuers. Some loaded their belongings into wagons, arriving in nearby cities with their bedding and provisions. A few of the more frightened frontiersmen burned or destroyed some of their property or provisions so the Indians would not seize them. One panic-stricken settler reportedly dumped a quantity of flour into an adjacent river and then embarked in a boat down the Cedar River, heading back for "Pennsylvany."

Entire settlements were sometimes deserted. The Indian scare struck the settlement of Massee in Dunn County on the morning of Sunday, August 21. Church services had just ended when some breathless alarmists reported that the Indians were on their way. The alarm spread like wildfire. Massee settlers made a mad dash for Downsville. "When we arrived there," a participant related, "it seemed as though everybody in that vicinity was there; some had their household goods, but each had some sort of a weapon of defense, all the guns, axes, pitchforks, and scythes were there."

Far northern Superior, swept by fear, put itself in the hands of an emergency "committee of public safety." It was the responsibility of that vigilant band to care for the hundreds of nearby settlers who sought safety in Superior. The committee issued an order requiring all residents to stay and sleep within prescribed boundaries. It also drafted all men between the ages of eighteen and sixty for guard and sentinel duty. People believed that the Sioux would sweep in from the west and the Chippewa from the south.

Even eastern and southern Wisconsin succumbed to the Indian panic of 1862, which reached its peak in this area on September 3–4. Word reached Chilton that Centerville in Manitowoc County—on the Lake Michigan shore!—had been burned. It was rumored that most of the residents of Holland in Brown County had been murdered and that a belligerent band of savages was advancing on New Holstein. Some people heard that Manitowoc had been destroyed, that Sheboygan had been plundered and Plymouth sacked. Appleton and Fond du Lac promptly succumbed to the hysteria which was sweeping the countryside and bringing a flood of fugitives into those cities. Fond du Lac authorities sent out an expedition to ascertain the truth of the rumors that most of the villages west of the city had been "wrecked and ruined." A local editor who accompanied the expedition wrote: "On every road we could see dozens of wagons, all loaded down with women and children fleeing towards the city—no men were along—all had been left at home to fight. Everywhere on the road we saw empty houses, flying families, and numerous picket-guards . . . armed with old shotguns and awaiting the first attack. . . . Every family met was asked if they had seen the Indians—and sure enough in that whole trip of fourteen miles not a person could be found that had seen an Indian, though all were satisfied that the said Indians were but a short distance behind them. And so the various parties sent out returned without finding the trace of an Indian, and seeing nothing but deserted country."

Appleton residents were as excited as those of Fond du Lac. A report reached Appleton on September 3 that the Indians were burning and massacring in the town of Morristown and "marching on in their butchery." Some residents of Appleton hustled off to Oshkosh; others gathered at the city hall to plan a defense. The editor of the Appleton *Crescent* advised calmness, remarking sardonically that the hysteria was so widespread that half a dozen Indians could have easily taken possession of the city.

Even the Milwaukee area took part in the scare. As fleeing settlers from the countryside streamed into Port Washington and Milwaukee, fugitives outdid each other in starting new rumors and magnifying old ones. It was reported, for example, that Waukesha had been attacked, that West Bend was ablaze, that Pewaukee had been destroyed. All Ozaukee County was gripped by the panic. It was rumored that Cedarburg had been burned and that scalping parties were active throughout both Washington and Ozaukee counties. Governor Salomon, who was visiting Milwaukee at the time, ordered a company of militia to seek out the Indians in the area north and west of the city. Capt. Charles Lehman and his militiamen spent several days in fruitless search. Some of his soldiers, weary of marching after the elusive Indians, visited grog shops to regain enthusiasm for their chore.

A Milwaukee *Sentinel* reporter wrote an article which heaped ridicule upon the "Indian hunters" and their wild-goose chase. The article blended sarcasm, satire, and criticism in equal portions. When Capt. Lehman and his militiamen returned to Milwaukee, dusty and bone-tired, a friend showed the distraught officer the *Sentinel* article. Boiling with indignation, Lehman marched his company downtown and to the *Sentinel* building, where he lined up his troops, went inside, and cor-

nered the offending reporter. First he drew his sword and laid it aside; then he unbuckled his scabbard and with it gave the reporter a sound beating. When he felt that the insult had been avenged, Capt. Lehman rejoined his company outside. Sensible Milwaukeeans were ashamed of the incident.

But this was a season for folly in Wisconsin. Even Governor Salomon, who was ordinarily a realist, fell victim to the panic. On September 3 he excitedly telegraphed Secretary of War Edwin M. Stanton, asking for 150,000 rounds of ammunition: "Appeals are daily made to me for arms and ammunition. Families are leaving their homes for fear of the wandering bands. I am well satisfied that these Indians have been tampered with by rebel agents. The people must be protected. Prevention is better than cure. I have furnished to different localities all the state arms, some eight hundred that we have, and must send more. More arms must be furnished immediately. . . ."

The Secretary of War was not impressed. He refused to take Governor Salomon's request seriously and demanded evidence that there really was an Indian invasion of Wisconsin. He did not believe that "reasonable necessity" existed. Salomon responded tartly, claiming he was better qualified than bureaucrats in far-off Washington to judge an emergency and a "reasonable necessity."

The governor's anxiety during the Indian scare was revealed in still another way. He sent an emergency call for Capt. Maurice M. Samuel to hurry back to Wisconsin from the war front, and he named him a "special agent" to visit the Chippewa and find out their intentions. Samuel, a fur trader of twenty years' standing with the Chippewa, visited his friend, Chief A-que-en-zse. The chief assured him that the Chippewa wanted only peace, but were fearful lest the panic-stricken whites attack without cause. Two other agents, James Clark and James McCloud, visited other Indian tribes to reconnoiter and investigate. All the Indians asserted that their intentions were "only the best."

When his special agents reported their findings, Governor Salomon was somewhat embarrassed. He had crawled out on a limb, and his agents had sawed it off. But not until the war was over and Wisconsin had entered the postwar era did Salomon realize how silly and ill-founded the Indian scare of 1862 had been.

Governor Salomon's mistrust of Wisconsin's Indians did them an injustice. In fact, the Indians proved not only peaceable but also loyal to the Union. They furnished between 500 and 600 soldiers to Wisconsin regiments—out of an Indian population approximating 9,000. The Menominee, with a total population of 1,879, sent forth 125 soldiers, one-third of whom died in the service of the Union. The Oneida, who numbered less than 1,100, furnished 111 soldiers. The Munsee and Stockbridge, with a total population of 338, supplied forty-three.

While Wisconsin panicked in 1862, the War Department took steps to quash the Sioux uprising in Minnesota. The Secretary of War quickly created the Department of the Northwest, with headquarters in Milwaukee. The War Department then dispatched Gen. John Pope, whose wings had been clipped at the second Battle of Bull Run, to head the new department. Under the supervision of Gen. Pope, Col. Henry Hastings Sibley led a force of army regulars and Minnesota militia against the Sioux. Sibley defeated the Indians in a series of battles and captured more than a thou-

Indian recruits being sworn into military service. (X3)10058.

sand prisoners, of whom thirty-eight were subsequently hanged—the largest execution in American history.

The defeat of the Minnesota Sioux and the arrival of annuity payments for the Wisconsin Indians helped to convince any restless would-be warriors that peace was the best policy. Soon thereafter, common sense began to return, and gradually affairs in upstate Wisconsin returned to normal. But the memory of the Indian scare remained. "The human family is at times ridiculous or frightened or desperate or foolish or cowardly," noted a latter-day historian, "but never until the Indian scare of 1862 were the dwellers of . . . Wisconsin possessed of all five of these attributes at once."

⊰ 10 ⊱

Politics and the Elections of 1862

WHILE UNION AND CONFEDERATE armies fought along a far-flung military front, the political pot boiled vigorously on the home front. In 1862, events seemed to favor the Democrats, the party of opposition. The controversy over the state draft bore political overtones. The depression of 1861 left marks that were not yet erased. When prices climbed upward, wages lagged far behind. There was labor unrest; some claimed that labor paid too heavy a price. Furthermore, Democrats openly declared Lincoln's military policy a failure. They took the position that Grant's victory at Fort Donelson and Commander David Farragut's capture of New Orleans were offset by the casualties at Shiloh and the lost battles in Virginia. Although Grant claimed the edge at Shiloh, his heavy losses had shocked the North, and there were even some demands for his dismissal.

In Virginia, things were even worse. There, Gen. Robert E. Lee had administered a series of stern lessons in tactics and strategy to Union generals George B. McClellan and John Pope. Lee forced Gen. McClellan to admit failure in the Peninsular campaign (as the grand effort to capture Richmond was called), and he gave Gen. Pope a sound thrashing at Second Bull Run in late August of 1862. When Democrats spoke of "military incapacity" and "Republican bungling," they had no trouble convincing those who would listen.

Democratic legislators also tried to dig up arguments and issues which could be used in the fall political campaign. Democrats exposed the hocus-pocus by which state bonds had been substituted for Southern bonds in order to "save" the banking system. Democrats also condemned the "political commissar" arrangement by which Republican a governor appointed Republican agents to accompany each regiment to the field—what Democrats sneeringly called "the wet nurse system." They charged that Wisconsin had spent twice as much per soldier as any other loyal state in the North. In addition, a Democratic committee of legislators offered proof that soldiers in the field had received free Republican newspapers—what they termed "unvarnished Republican propaganda"—while Democratic newspapers mysteriously failed to reach their soldier-subscribers.

The spring elections of April, 1862, also gave heart to Wisconsin Democrats. The trend everywhere seemed to be back toward the Democratic party; Republicanism seemed to be in retreat. So Democrats anxiously looked toward the fall elections of 1862. They were eager to gain control of the state legislature and county offices, and of Wisconsin's congressional delegation.

The Democrats warmed up for their state convention with a series of local meetings which featured speakers who criticized the Republican party and ended with the selection of delegates to the state convention. A Milwaukee rally of August 6 received favorable mention in the Democratic press. Eloquent speakers chided the Lincoln administration for its "sins" and warned Republicans that the November election was "judgment day." The Milwaukee rally named Edward G. Ryan, among others, as one of its delegates to the Democratic state convention: he would prove to be the man of the hour.

The Irish-born Ryan was both able and irascible. After living awhile in Racine he moved to Milwaukee, seeking a bigger pond for his croaking. He gained a reputation as a first-rate lawyer and a silver-tongued orator. A well-read and articulate disciple of Thomas Jefferson, he frankly labeled himself a Jeffersonian Democrat. He was a lone wolf who cared nothing for what others thought of him. Few loved him, but he was feared and respected by many.

Edward G. Ryan (1810–1880), brilliant lawyer and the voice of Democratic party opposition to the war. (X31)10902.

The executive committee of the state Democratic party asked Ryan to serve as chairman of the resolutions committee. He set to work preparing a party platform (meaning a major speech) which he would present at the state convention. He wrote and rewrote his address, sharpening the criticism of the Lincoln administration and polishing the literary style of what he entitled "An Address to the People by the Democracy of Wisconsin."

The state convention met in Milwaukee on September 3, 1862. After a few preliminaries and some partisan oratory, Ryan presented the report of his committee. He then read his long and scholarly address. It was adopted by the membership, although some conservative delegates felt it was too partisan and far too critical of the Lincoln administration. All, however, admitted that it was a learned political treatise, steeped in the doctrines of Jeffersonian Democracy. In time, it ceased to be called "An Address to the People by the Democracy of Wisconsin" and came to be known simply as the "Ryan Address." (Ryan's enemies would call it "the Copperhead Bible.")

Aware that Republicans would accuse Democrats of being "disloyal," Ryan incorporated an explanation of a citizen's loyalty and duty into his address: "The Administration may err, but the Constitution does not change. And when the Administration violates the Constitution, loyalty to the Administration may become disloyalty to the Union. . . . In days of civil discord and convulsion, there is danger of patriotism being blindfolded, mistaking the object of its faith and transferring to the servant of the altar the devotion due only to the altar itself."

With his speech, Ryan declared open warfare upon the Lincoln administration. He viewed President Lincoln's suspension of the writ of habeas corpus as unconstitutional in nature and dictatorial in design. He believed the President's suspension of Democratic newspapers was a threat to basic rights. He criticized the wave of arbitrary arrests (especially in Illinois, Ohio, and Iowa) as a threat to the civil processes. He viewed Lincoln's war upon the Confederacy as the product of fanaticism—of Northern abolitionists on the one hand and Southern radicals on the other. He defined slavery as "a great social evil" but insisted upon its legality and its practicality. He also argued that only the Democratic party had the ability to end the war and reunite the country. "We are for the Constitution as it is," Ryan stated in his final sentence, "and the Union as it was."

Most Democratic newspapers in Wisconsin printed the "Ryan Address" in its entirety. Several Democratic editors, however, recognized that the document was too learned and too philosophical to capture the public imagination. A few believed that the document was also immoderate and overly partisan; they termed unfair Ryan's criticism of a government that was struggling to crush disunion and reunite the nation.

Instead of trying to answer the contentions which Ryan incorporated into his address, Wisconsin's Republicans appealed to the spirit of patriotism. They declared the speech treasonable and branded its author a traitor. They claimed that those who criticized the Lincoln administration were aiding the Confederate enemy. Charges and countercharges enlivened the political campaign.

When President Lincoln issued his preliminary proclamation of emancipation on September 22, 1862, effectively ending slavery in the rebellious states, he gave Democrats an issue upon which they could capitalize. Democrats could now claim that the Republicans had perverted a war to save the Union into a war to free the slaves. Democratic editors and orators blasted the emancipation policy and made it one of the chief issues of the 1862 political campaign. "We are willing to fight till death for the common good of a common people," wrote "Brick" Pomeroy of the La Crosse *Democrat*, "but will not be forced into a fight to free the slaves." The editor of the Green Bay *Advocate* denounced Lincoln's proclamation of September 22 as "a political measure" and a "rash act"—"one of a series of imbecile and disastrous steps." He did not believe that military need dictated that policy. Flavius J. Mills of the Sheboygan *Journal* termed Lincoln's proclamation "a youthful indiscretion" and denounced it as an "unconstitutional act." The editor of the Oshkosh *Courier* incorporated the same anti-emancipation arguments into his editorial columns, saying he feared that Lincoln's "political medicine" would kill both the patient and the doctor. Others pointed out that this was but another unnecessary and unconstitutional act—and that necessity was ever the excuse of tyrants.

Republican party strategists feared that the political winds were blowing in the Democratic direction. They needed some practical devices which would produce Republican votes. In 1861, they had used the "Union party" stratagem successfully. This time they pulled a different rabbit from their magical hat: a proposal to give the vote to soldiers in the field and to use the soldiers' vote to hold back the resurgent Democrats.

11

Soldiers Voting-in-the-Field, 1862–1864

WISCONSIN REPUBLICANS had grown concerned about the fall elections of 1862 long before they were scheduled to take place. Although Abraham Lincoln had carried the state by

20,000 votes over three opponents in November of 1860, Louis P. Harvey, the Republican gubernatorial candidate in November of 1861, had received only 5,000 more votes than his Democratic opponent. After Governor Harvey's death in the spring of 1862, Edward Salomon took over the governor's chair; but he proved to be a rather listless leader at a time when the Republican party needed a dynamic one. Furthermore, the economic depression of 1861–1862 that visited the Upper Midwest took a heavy toll in Wisconsin. More than three dozen banks closed their doors during the first year of the war, and farm prices hit bottom. Democrats blamed the party in power in Washington and Madison for the hard times—and pocketbook issues always affect election returns. Then there were the military failures. Gen. U.S. Grant's success in the western theater of war did not balance Union defeats in the eastern theater.

Democrats had made gains in both the fall elections of 1861 (when the state officers were elected) and the spring elections of 1862 (mainly for local officials). Therefore they looked forward to the 1862 fall elections when seats in the state legislature and six congressional seats were at stake.

But Republicans still controlled the state legislature in the summer of 1862, and they had cooked up a brilliant scheme to improve their chances at the polls: they would solicit votes from Wisconsin soldiers on duty elsewhere! This idea of counting the votes of soldiers scattered in camps and distant battlefields was not new; in fact, it had first been put into effect by quite a number of Confederate states as a means of ensuring control of their state legislatures. Then Missouri Unionists and Republicans had borrowed the idea because they needed the soldiers' votes to keep their state loyal to the Union. Governor Samuel J. Kirkwood of Iowa recognized a good political stratagem when he saw one; he called the Iowa legislature into session on September 3, 1862, and two weeks later signed a soldier-voting law. His action impressed Horace Rublee, chairman of the Republican central committee and editor of the *Wisconsin State Journal* in Madison, who thereupon convinced Governor Salomon that "the army voting scheme" would help the party in Wisconsin too.

On September 10, 1862, Governor Salomon called the state legislature into special session in Madison. The governor's message emphasized the need and desirability of giving soldiers the vote. As he put it, serving in the army should not lead to "the loss of one of the most important rights of citizenship."

Both houses of the legislature set to work drafting a soldier-voting law. The gist of it was that Wisconsin's soldiers, whether in camp or on the march, could vote in the spring and fall elections. Three ranking regimental officers were to act as election inspectors and count the votes, whereupon they would "make a statement of the results in writing." Since most Wisconsin colonels were Republicans, Democrats fully expected to get the short end of the stick. In both the assembly and the senate, Democrats argued against a soldier-voting bill. "The soldiers are not asking or demanding such privileges or right," one Democrat in the lower house wrote in a minority report,

Governor James T. Lewis (1819–1904), "the soldier's friend." (X3)15549.

"and in our opinions it is simply a scheme . . . to gain some advantage to their party in the future." The Democratic editor of the Madison *Wisconsin Patriot* was more blunt, terming the proposal "a cheat—a humbug—a fraud."

The soldier-voting bill passed both houses of the legislature, 19 to 7 in the state senate and 52 to 40 in the assembly. On September 25, acting governor James T. Lewis signed the bill into law.

In its first test, the bill proved its worth to the Republicans. It prevented Democrats from gaining control of the state assembly, and soldier votes reversed the results in many county elections. The soldier vote did not affect the results in the fall congressional elections, in which Democrats captured three of the state's six seats in the House of Representatives and overall polled nearly 20,000 more votes than they had in the gubernatorial election of 1861. They increased their membership in both houses of the state legislature and regained many posts in county government. The editor of the Sheboygan *Journal* chirped: "Fall fashions—Democratic victories." The returns cheered the Democrats and jolted the Republicans. Nevertheless, the Republicans maintained control of the Wisconsin legislature, though by reduced margins: 18 to 15 in the state senate and 54 to 46 in the assembly.

Democrats felt that the soldier-voting law deprived their party of "justice." Democratic newspapers, receiving word from friends at the front, alleged instances of fraud. It was said that Republican colonels destroyed Democratic ballots, denied the ballot to companies from Democratic districts, and gave "patriotic speeches" to their regiments the night before the election. It was alleged that colonels who turned in one-sided army votes were rewarded with promotions. Someone reported that the Second Wisconsin Regiment returned more Republican votes than there were men in the regiment. One soldier wrote to his newspaper: "Our Col. made a speech to the regiment on the eve of election, in favor of Amasa Cobb [the Republican candidate]." A soldier "is under too much influence to cast a free and independent vote," he added, calling the soldiers' voting scheme "a perfect humbug." The Democratic editor of the *Wisconsin Patriot* said much the same thing: "The scheme is like a jug handle—on one side." No Democrat was more bitter and disillusioned than George B. Smith, the Madison

George B. Smith (1823–1879), Democratic lawyer and politician. (X3)50388.

lawyer and state legislator who had once served as attorney-general of Wisconsin. He knew the game of politics and he feared for the future of the country. He was especially critical of the many arrests of Democrats made by U.S. marshals in nearby states. Smith also believed Lincoln's emancipation policy was unconstitutional and unnecessary. He stated his opposition to Lincoln's policies in the legislature and on the stump. He also expressed his disapproval of presidential policy in his diary. His last entry of 1862 read: "The President of the United States is responsible for the miserable state of things, and for this and many special and arbitrary acts which he has committed and authorized to be committed, I solemnly believe that [he] ought to be impeached and legally and constitutionally deposed from the high office of President of the United States."

Democrats arranged to challenge the soldier-voting act in the state supreme court. The case was known as *Ex rel. Chandler v. Main*, and it stemmed out of a county election where the soldier vote gave Main the office which Chandler had won on the home vote.

The state supreme court was headed by Chief

Justice Luther S. Dixon. Democrats hoped for a favorable verdict because Judge Dixon had written the court's decision for *In re Kemp*, reprimanding President Lincoln for suspending the writ of habeas corpus. While the court's decision was pending, the Republican-controlled legislature made a bid for a favorable decision by amending the soldier-voting bill to have it apply to the election of judges as well. (Dixon was up for reelection the following April.) Furthermore, while the decision was pending, Republicans named Dixon their judicial candidate for chief justice of the Wisconsin supreme court.

Ever the realist, Chief Justice Dixon sided with the other two judges to give the Republican party a victory. Subsequently, in the spring elections of 1863, the soldier vote saved Dixon's seat on the court. M. M. Cothren, the Democratic candidate, received 56,840 home votes to Dixon's 51,498. But the soldier vote totaled 9,440 for Dixon and only 1,747 for Cothren; this swung the election to Dixon. Republican political strategy in the form of soldier voting-in-the-field paid handsome dividends.

Democrats complained, some saying that soldier voting was "the rotten scheme of corrupt

Luther S. Dixon (1825–1891), chief justice of the Wisconsin Supreme Court. (X3)46869.

politicians." They pointed to some of the results: the Seventh Wisconsin regiment cast 309 votes for Dixon, none for Cothren; the Fifteenth Wisconsin cast all of its 239 votes for Dixon; the Third Wisconsin gave Dixon 347 votes and only one for Cothren. "The Republican State and military offices," wrote the Democratic editor of the Sheboygan *Journal*, "are very smart in manufacturing votes from the army."

Wisconsin Republicans saw the political tide turn their way in the last half of 1863 and they looked toward the fall elections with renewed hope. That summer, Union victories at Gettysburg and Vicksburg had conferred respectability upon the Lincoln administration and its war policies. The economic depression of 1861–1862 that had plagued the Upper Midwest also gave way to war prosperity. Furthermore, the soldier-voting scheme would be even more useful to Republicans as the army increased in size.

The Republicans held their state convention in Madison on August 10, 1863, calling it a "Union convention" to attract sympathetic Democrats and undecided voters. "Boss" Keyes of Madison played a major role in sidetracking Governor Salomon's bid to get renominated. Instead the gubernatorial nomination went to James T. Lewis. The convention named Col. Lucius Fairchild, who had lost an arm at Gettysburg, as the Republican candidate for secretary of state. Then and later, Fairchild's empty sleeve helped to attract votes to the Republican slate. The Democratic party, badly divided into peace and war factions, chose a straitlaced Milwaukee assemblyman, Henry L. Palmer, as its gubernatorial nominee.

In the November election, the Republicans won handily, electing their entire slate of state officers. They would have won even without the soldier vote, but votes from the field did help the party retain control of both houses of the legislature. And with each successive election, the soldier vote was better "controlled." (Of every fifteen soldier votes cast in the 1863 election, the Republicans received fourteen!)

In the final year of the war, as war-induced prosperity and increasing numbers of Union military victories influenced voters, the soldier vote in Wisconsin lost its importance. On the national level, the presidential election of November, 1864, pitted Lincoln against the popular Gen. George B. McClellan. On the state level, the contest was for seats in the state legislature and the election of six members of Congress.

In the national election, Lincoln received 68,887 home votes and 8,895 soldier votes, a grand total of 77,782. McClellan received 61,586 home votes and 1,844 soldier votes, or 64,430 in all. So Abraham Lincoln once again carried Wisconsin, even though his 20,000-vote margin of 1860 had narrowed somewhat to around 13,000 votes.

In the 1864 election in the First Congressional District, Republican incumbent Halbert E. Paine of Milwaukee had his seat saved by the soldier vote. (He was an ex-colonel of Wisconsin infantry who had lost a leg in combat before returning home to run for Congress.) Paine received 12,043 home votes to 12,791 for his Democratic opponent, John W. Carey. But the soldier vote wiped out Carey's narrow margin and dashed his hopes. Paine received 1,673 soldier votes, giving him a total of 13,716; Carey received only 439 soldier votes for a total of 13,230. Several state legislators likewise owed their election to votes cast by

Halbert E. Paine (1826–1905), colonel of the Fourth Wisconsin Infantry. (X3)17239.

soldiers in the field, and soldiers' ballots gave some county officials their victories as well.

The end of the war relegated the soldier-voting ploy to the background. But it had helped to keep the Republican party in firm control of Wisconsin's machinery of government during the war. Republicans rightly regarded the soldier vote as a clever and effective stratagem. Democrats—probably with good cause—regarded it as devious and highly partisan in conception and corrupt in execution. It was not until 1871 that the voting-in-the-field act was repealed by the state legislature.

⊰ 12 ⊱

Copperhead High Tide, 1863

THE FIRST SIX MONTHS of 1863 were trying and troublous for the Lincoln administration. Negative reaction to the Emancipation Proclamation, the threat of federal conscription, and a dearth of military victories cast a cloud of gloom over the North. War weariness and a spirit of defeatism added weight and momentum to a peace movement which found many adherents in Wisconsin.

During these months, the term "Copperhead" came into popular usage. It was a smear term coined by Republicans and used against their political enemies, the Democrats who refused to accept emancipation of the slaves as a legitimate object of the war. It was also applied to Democrats who argued that peace and reunion could be achieved by means other than war. Republicans claimed that such Democratic dissenters resembled that venomous snake with the copper-colored head. They claimed that, just as the snakes were poisonous, the dissenting Democrats were pro-Southern in their views, literally "rebels in the rear."

Democrats tried to give their own meaning to the term "Copperhead." Some of them cut the head of the goddess of liberty out of the old copper cent and contended that the terms "Copperhead" and "Liberty" were synonymous. One Democratic editor defined a Copperhead as "a man who designs to maintain our system of free government as our fathers founded it, as their successors administered it, and as we and posterity are bound by every motive of interest, patriotism, and honor to continue it." But over time, the Republican rather than the Democratic meaning of the term was written into history.

Wisconsin Democrats who had criticized Lincoln's preliminary proclamation of emancipation vented their rage against the president when he issued the final proclamation on January 1, 1863. Peter V. Deuster, editor of the Milwaukee *See-Bote*, wrote harsh editorials. He warned his readers that their jobs would be washed away by the flood of cheap labor. White workingmen, he wrote, would now lose their jobs to black freedmen. He entitled an editorial "Abolition the Worst Enemy of the Free White Laborer," and he advised his fellow German-Americans: "Workmen! Be careful! Organize yourself against this element which threatens your impoverishment and annihilation."

Flavius J. Mills of the Sheboygan *Journal* also criticized Lincoln for bowing to abolitionist pressure. He felt that Lincoln had deceived Democrats about his war aims and he expressed his bitterness in the issue of May 7, 1863: "All the support the war has ever received from Democrats was originally obtained by a base cheat, an infamous swindle, a damnable deception. The Democratic party trusted and was betrayed. 'The War for the Union' was cordially supported by Democrats all over the North. It turned out to be a war of abolition, of violation of the Constitution, a war by the Eastern oligarchy."

It was in the early months of 1863 that "Brick" Pomeroy of the La Crosse *Democrat* abandoned moderation for madness. His aversion to the abolition of slavery chilled his patriotism, and he lambasted the Emancipation Proclamation with both barrels. But it was a trip to Helena, Arkansas, which transformed him into a vicious critic of Lincoln and the government. Carrying a special pass from Governor Salomon, Pomeroy visited friends who were assigned to the Army of the Southwest—meaning Missouri and Arkansas, a backwater of the war after 1862. Pomeroy accompanied Union troops as they chased guerrillas, foraged for food, and raided plantations to confiscate cotton and free the slaves. Illicit trafficking in confiscated cotton seemed to be the chief occupation of many army officers; speculation and corruption were rife. Watching the army in action

caused Pomeroy to lose all respect for Lincoln and his generals. "If the enemy is to be conquered," he queried, "why in God's great name do we not march troops to battle instead of cotton fields?" He became even angrier when he saw army contractors and cotton agents descend like vultures upon the army.

When he was not sloshing through the Arkansas mud or playing poker and listening to camp gossip, Pomeroy wrote letters from camp and exposés for several newspapers. His disclosures and his increasingly intemperate letters were published in such newspapers as the Chicago *Times*, the Milwaukee *Evening News*, and of course his own La Crosse *Democrat*. His racy reports cursed the "devilish vandalism" of the soldiery, for he was critical of the army policy of scouring the countryside for provisions. "When God has forgotten us, and men rule but to plunder," he wrote, "the people may well begin to pause and tremble." With the ardency of the reformer he put his despair and disdain into words: "The war is not being carried on to preserve the Union. Such talk is all bosh. Once in the country simplicity of our heart, we thought so; but the truth has dawned upon our vision full and clear. Were there no presidents to make—did there not exist parties in the North and South which appeal to the passions and prejudices rather than reason—were there no cotton in the South—no chance to *steal* in one day more than a man can *earn* in a lifetime—were there no rich speculators and moneyed men, as selfish and unprincipled as the devil himself, now controlling this crusade, there would be peace today over the land."

This trip to Arkansas opened Pomeroy's eyes to the more squalid aspects of the war. He wrote of a hospital ship as "a boat load of pain and misery" and of amputated arms and legs as the "true trophies of war." He described the war as "a waste of men, blood, and treasure." "The more I see of this war," he grumbled, "the more I feel like swearing at the fanatical fire-eaters and abolitionists who brought it on." The more Pomeroy wrote and editorialized, the more he convinced himself that the South could not be whipped, that dishonesty dominated the army, and that the Lincoln administration was corrupt and incompetent. Pomeroy deluded himself into believing that the war had degenerated into what he termed "a murderous crusade for cotton and niggers." He rained malediction on Gen. Benjamin Prentiss, who commanded the Arkansas sector where Pomeroy was visiting. He referred to Helena as "a second Golgotha." He asserted that generals were changed frequently in the Arkansas cotton country so that many generals would have a chance to line their pockets. Each week's revelations and reports were longer, more pungent, and more insulting to the general whose hospitality he enjoyed.

When Gen. Prentiss eventually saw Pomeroy's scandalous reports in a copy of the Chicago Times, he turned purple with rage. He ordered the editor arrested and brought into his presence, where he gave him a vicious tongue-lashing. Then he ordered Pomeroy to get out of his sight and out of the Arkansas sector, warning him that if he ever came back within his jurisdiction, he would have him arrested as a spy.

Embittered but impudent, "Brick" Pomeroy returned to La Crosse and the editorial offices of the Democrat. There he dipped his quill in more poisonous ink and began writing ever-more-scurrilous editorials. He denounced Abraham Lincoln and "the imbecility of the Administration." The President was "a fool," "a flat-boat tyrant," and a "blockhead." He called the president "hell's vice-agent on earth," "a usurper," "a deceiver," "a fanatic." Pomeroy's self-indulgent exercises in abuse and slander earned him national notoriety, and he got some of the attention he craved. Other editors, both Democratic and Republican, reprinted some of Pomeroy's editorials. Democratic editors republished the comments to prove that Lincoln was unworthy and that the critics were bold. Republicans republished them to show that Pomeroy was insane and deserving of being called a traitor. "Brick" Pomeroy made name-calling an art, but his reputation suffered, and eventually he lost much credibility, even among those who opposed Lincoln's prosecution of the war.

But Pomeroy was not the only Wisconsin Democrat to hunt headlines in 1863. Edward G. Ryan of Milwaukee, a towering figure among Wisconsin's lawyers and jurists, also gained a reputation as an avowed enemy of the Lincoln administration.

When the Ozaukee County draft rioters were arrested in November of 1862, they were turned over to federal authorities. They were to be tried by an army court martial in accordance with a presidential order which subjected persons who

Marcus "Brick" Pomeroy (1833–1896), vitriolic editor of the La Crosse Democrat. (X3)17968.

resisted the draft to military law. It also suspended the writ of habeas corpus in such cases. Edward G. Ryan was incensed at the presidential order, which he believed robbed citizens of their basic civil rights. So he volunteered his services on behalf of the defendants—meaning the draft rioters—and he argued their case on behalf of a writ of habeas corpus before the Wisconsin Supreme Court. He won the case and thereby added to his reputation.

Flushed with victory, Ryan argued a second anti-administration case before the Wisconsin Supreme Court in February, 1863. This time he sought a writ of habeas corpus for some draft evaders who were being held by military authorities. He argued that draft law of 1862, which authorized states to draft men into the state militia in order to meet state quotas, was unconstitutional. Ryan's chief argument was that Congress had illegally and unconstitutionally delegated legislative power to the president. This time the justices of the Wisconsin Supreme Court brushed aside Ryan's arguments, and their decision (*In re Griner*) endorsed administration policy.

Edward G. Ryan was an extraordinary orator as well as an accomplished lawyer. He criticized President Lincoln from the speaker's platform as well as in the courtroom. In a notable speech in Milwaukee in May of 1863, Ryan told 15,000 partisan Democrats that Lincoln was anxious to establish "a military despotism." He denounced Lincoln's advisors as "fools" and "knaves" and called the President "a mere doll, worked by strings . . . a weak, vain, amiable man" who was "totally unfit" for the high position which he held.

Ryan was especially critical of the summary treatment accorded Clement L. Vallandigham, an ex-congressman, prominent Ohio Copperhead, and outspoken critic of Lincoln and the federal government. Vallandigham had been arrested by military authorities and tried by a military commission instead of a civil court. To Ryan and other Democrats, the Vallandigham case was proof that Lincoln was anxious to destroy popular government and establish a dictatorship.

Events and the passage of time would prove that the Copperhead critics, like Ryan and Pomeroy, had misjudged Lincoln and had fallen victim to their own fears. But the many military defeats suffered by Union armies and the wave of arbitrary arrests of 1862 turned some Democrats into defeatists. There existed a growing war-weariness—fertile ground for a peace movement. Quite a few prominent Wisconsin Democrats took up the cause of "peace and compromise," claiming that any peace which restored "the Union as it was" would be an honorable peace. In fact, they were quite unrealistic; they had no definite peace proposals to offer; they were simply waving the olive branch. "Brick" Pomeroy of the La Crosse *Democrat* put some of this widespread peace sentiment into words: "The people do not want this war. Tax payers do not wish it. Widows, orphans, and over-taxed working men do not ask or need this waste of men, blood, and treasure. There is no glory to be won in a civil war, no more than in a family quarrel. If politicians would let this matter come before the people, there would be an honorable peace within sixty days. But so long as blind leaders govern and

fanaticism rules the day, so long will there be wars, tears, and desolation."

Pomeroy was not the only prophet of gloom and doom in Wisconsin. There were others who could see no silver lining, who saw only the dark clouds and who misunderstood the man in the White House. These conservatives did not understand that the winds of change were blowing. Their wartime slogan ("The Constitution as it is, the Union as it was") proved that they looked toward the past. As conservatives, they feared the changes which the war was bringing to America.

Flavius J. Mills of the Sheboygan *Journal* was another Democrat who feared for the future and spoke out for peace. He did not trust Lincoln, nor did he believe that the Lincoln administration could restore the Union. "When will the hideous Moloch who holds the press and sword of this nation," he asked dejectedly, "call off his dogs of war, and suffer peace once more to bless our bleeding country?" Even some Republicans lost hope and plumped for peace. The Fox Lake *Gazette*, edited by a Republican, suggested that a national convention be substituted for further warfare as a means to peace and reunion.

Thus the first six months of 1863 were days of despair in many circles. The low point probably occurred in early May of that year, when Robert E. Lee's Confederate army dealt yet another stinging defeat to the Army of the Potomac at the Battle of Chancellorsville in northern Virginia. Not surprisingly, this period marked the high tide of Wisconsin Copperheadism. But Northern victories in the field would soon induce change in the political climate and enhance Abraham Lincoln's standing as president and savior of the Union.

⊰ 13 ⊱

The Iron Brigade

NO BRIGADE IN THE ENTIRE Union army gained more renown or suffered heavier battlefield losses than the Iron Brigade, a unit of the Army of the Potomac which contained three of Wisconsin's finest regiments. It was toasted in the North and respected even in the South. "Here comes those damned black-hat fellers again," dis-

mayed Confederates said more than once, in rue-
ful tribute to the fighting men of the Iron Brigade.

The Iron Brigade came into existence on October 1, 1861, less than three months after federal
troops were routed at First Bull Run. On that day
Gen. George B. McClellan assigned the Seventh
Wisconsin, newly arrived in Washington, to a
brigade containing the Second Wisconsin, the
Sixth Wisconsin, and the Nineteenth Indiana. Mc-
Clellan placed the four regiments under the command of Brig. Gen. Rufus King of Milwaukee.
Later on, the Wisconsin and Indiana regiments
were joined by the Twenty-fourth Michigan, increasing the size of the brigade to approximately
5,000 officers and men at full strength. It was the
only "all-western" brigade in the Army of the Potomac (the principal Union army in the eastern
theater); its men wore distinctive broad-brimmed
black hats; and it compiled a record of gallantry
and sacrifice unequalled by any other brigade in
all of Mr. Lincoln's armies.

Only one of the four regiments assigned to
Gen. King could boast of battlefield action at the
time the brigade was created: the Second Wisconsin, which had suffered severely at First Bull Run
in 1861. Its men viewed themselves as battle-
tested veterans, and some of them expressed con-
tempt for "the greenhorns" who were brigaded
with them. A harsh winter in camp during 1861–
1862, however, broke down the barrier between
the old and the new soldiers; the old as well as the
new suffered from flu and dysentery, and all fretted about inadequate supplies and the bitter cold.
During that winter, Capt. John Gibbon's Battery
B of the Fourth U.S. Artillery was attached to
King's brigade. Because Gibbon was short of artillerymen, he hand-picked a number of infantrymen from the ranks of King's four regiments.
Good relations soon developed between the artillery company and King's infantrymen. The soldiers from Wisconsin genuinely respected Gibbon's army regulars, and Gibbon in turn called
the infantry volunteers "the finest material for soldiers I ever saw."

Initially, King's brigade and two New York
brigades made up the division commanded by
Gen. Irwin McDowell, the unsuccessful commander at First Bull Run. But the growing size of the
army called for institution of the corps system,
and the commander of the Army of the Potomac,
Gen. McClellan, therefore grouped several divi-

Rufus King (1814–1876), commander of the Iron Brigade.
(X3)11287.

sions together to create an army corps. Gen. Mc-
Dowell stepped up to command this new First
Corps and Gen. King was promoted to command
of a division. Col. Lysander Cutler of the Sixth
Wisconsin took temporary command of King's
old brigade.

On March 17, 1862, Gen. McClellan trans-
ported most of his army by water to Fortress
Monroe at the tip of the James River peninsula to
launch his assault against the Confederate capital,
Richmond—what became known as the Peninsu-
lar campaign. At President Lincoln's command,
the First Corps (30,000 men) was detached to
guard the national capital. Gen. McDowell ordered Col. Cutler to take his brigade across the
Potomac and occupy Fredericksburg, Virginia.
There the brigade waited several months while
McClellan fought a series of battles as he slowly
advanced up the peninsula toward Richmond.
While at Fredericksburg, however, the "Western
Brigade" acquired yet another new commander:
Brig. Gen. John Gibbon, the West Pointer who
had earlier joined the brigade as captain of Com-
pany B of the Fourth U.S. Artillery.

Gibbon was a professional soldier—hard-nosed
and efficient, forthright and capable. He had faith

in himself and in his men. It was he who transformed first-rate raw material into first-rate soldiers, and he who ordered black-plumed hats for his "Western Brigade." It was under his leadership that the unit won its famous nickname and became the best-known brigade in the Union army.

It was not until the end of August, 1862, however, that Gibbon's westerners finally saw hard action. By that time Gibbon's brigade was a part of King's division of McDowell's corps, under the overall command of Gen. John Pope. While Pope's main force moved toward Manassas Junction and the old Bull Run battlefield, King's division of 10,000 men moved along the Warrenton Turnpike. On August 28, toward sunset, King's brigades were strung out along the road. After the lead brigade had passed out of sight over the hills east of a farmstead of a man named Brawner, Gibbon put his brigade in motion. Suddenly a portion of Stonewall Jackson's command emerged from a nearby railroad embankment and lined up for battle. Gibbon's brigade was caught by surprise. Soon Jackson's entire division and part of Gen. Richard Ewell's division—5,200 of Lee's best veterans—engaged Gibbon's 2,100 raw troops. (Eventually reinforcements raised the odds to 6,400 to 2,900 in favor of the Confederates. Furthermore, twenty-two Confederate field pieces op-

posed the six guns of Battery B.) An English observer attached to Jackson's staff guessed that the outnumbered Union soldiers would be swept from the field.

Thus began the Battle of Brawner Farm. It was a brutal, head-on battle—a stand-up, give-and-take affair. The opposing forces faced each other at a maximum range of seventy-five yards, exchanging volley for volley at this deadly range. There was no lying down, no cover or entrenchment, no maneuvering. Neither side advanced, but neither would retreat. They fought for two hours.

When darkness set in, the firing ceased by mutual consent and the fighting ended on the same spot where it had begun. The dead lay in neat rows where they had fallen. Both sides were badly battered. The Confederates had suffered 2,200 casualties out of 6,400 engaged. Gibbon reported 133 dead, 539 wounded, and seventy-nine missing—a total of 751 casualties, or 33 per cent of the brigade. In addition, Gibbon lost seven of twelve field-grade officers. The Second Wisconsin suffered the heaviest casualties among the four regiments. Of its 500 effectives, 298 were killed or wounded on Mr. Brawner's farm—almost 60 per cent casualties! Gen. Gibbon later said it was "the most terrific musketry fires" he had "ever listed to." The English observer who

Company I, Seventh Wisconsin Volunteer Infantry, Virginia, 1862.
Note the distinctive black hats. (X3)26132.

saw the battle from start to finish wrote: "The men who faced each other that August evening fought with a gallantry that has seldom been surpassed." Ten days before the Battle of Brawner Farm, Gibbon had referred to his men as "green troops." After this battle of August 28 he always referred to them as "the brigade I have the honor to command."

From Brawner's farm the "Black Hats" continued their march to Manassas. As reserves, they played little part in the Second Battle of Bull Run. But when Gen. Pope, defeated and despairing, withdrew toward Washington, Gibbon's brigade helped cover his retreat. In Washington they again marched down Pennsylvania Avenue and past the White House. While the head of the column cleared the street ahead, Gibbon's brigade rested and waited on the fringe of the White House lawn. President Lincoln came out with a pail of water in one hand and a dipper in the other. He moved among the men, offering water to the tired and thirsty. Some Wisconsin soldiers drank from the common dipper and thanked the president for his kindness.

Several weeks later, on September 14, Gibbon's brigade passed its second test under fire. Gen. McClellan, once again in command of the Army of the Potomac after the defeat of Pope at Second Bull Run, moved his troops westward. He had learned that Lee's forces were launching an invasion of Maryland. At Turner's Gap on South Mountain, the advancing Federals found 1,100 Confederate defenders blocking their way: five regiments of Gen. D. H. Hill's division. The commanding officers assigned Gibbon's brigade the task of opening the gap. Gibbon personally led the brigade toward the enemy and up the slope. Generals McClellan, Joseph Hooker, and Ambrose Burnside were all nearby, watching the "Black Hats" deploy and attack. Confederate artillery fire was heavy and the rattle of musketry added to the din. Gibbon's men moved forward relentlessly through the smoke, undaunted, and drove the enemy from their positions.

McClellan nodded his head in satisfaction. Turning to Gen. Hooker, he remarked, "They must be made of iron." So, on the rocky slope of South Mountain, Gibbon's "Western brigade" acquired a name. Henceforth they were known as the Iron Brigade. In clearing Turner's Gap, the brigade added to its reputation—and its combat

Capt. Wilson Colwell, Second Wisconsin Infantry, killed at South Mountain on September 14, 1862. (X3)40390.

casualties: thirty-seven killed, 251 wounded, thirty missing.

Three days later, at Antietam in northern Maryland, the Iron Brigade once more clashed with Stonewall Jackson's crack troops. In the opening attack of the day, the Iron Brigade struck against the Confederate left wing, driving Jackson's men out of a field of ripening corn—known forever after as the Corn Field—only to be counterattacked and driven back by Gen. John B. Hood's Texas brigade. From start to finish, it was a desperate fight. "The men are loading and firing with demoniacal fury and shouting and laughing hysterically," wrote Major Rufus Dawes of the Sixth Wisconsin afterward. "We push over the open fields half way to [the white brick Dunker church]. The powder is bad, and the guns have become very dirty. It takes hard pounding to get the bullets down, and our firing is becoming slow. A long and steady line of rebel gray, unbroken by the fugitives who fly before us, comes sweeping down through the woods around the church. They raise the yell and fire. It is like a scythe running through our line. . . . This was the most dreadful slaughter to which our regiment was subjected in the war."

The carnage of Antietam was simply appalling, and it continued from dawn to dark. September 17, 1862, was—and remains—the bloodiest single day in all of America's wars. One of Gibbon's aides described the scene as "a great tumbling together of all Heaven and earth." Of the 800 officers and men of the Iron Brigade who had marched into battle that morning, 343 were wounded or killed. It was the third bloodbath in which Gibbon's brigade had been involved.

Gen. Lee's army of invasion, battered all along the line, retreated from Antietam and returned to Virginia. Gen. McClellan did not pursue Lee closely, as Lincoln so fervently wanted him to do; to this day, some insist McClellan could have swept the retreating Confederates into the Potomac and perhaps ended the war at Antietam. But McClellan's casualties had been very heavy and—always the cautious general—he counted his losses rather than his opportunities. He failed to deliver a knockout blow.

McClellan did commend his troops for their valor, reserving special praise for the Iron Brigade. To the governor of Wisconsin he wrote: "I add . . . the expression of my great admiration of the three Wisconsin regiments in Gen. Gibbon's brigade. I have seen them under fire, acting in a manner that reflects the greatest possible credit and honor upon themselves and their state. They are equal to the best troops in any army in the world."

The three severe encounters in which Gibbon's men had fought so creditably had reduced the brigade's strength from 4,000 men to less than a thousand. Gen. Gibbon therefore requested that another regiment of Westerners be added to his command. The corps commander subsequently assigned the Twenty-fourth Michigan to Gibbon's brigade. The brigade commander inspected his new regiment on October 9, 1862. The newcomers felt that Gibbon received them "with considerable reluctance" and that the battle-scarred veterans of the Iron Brigade extended "a pretty cool reception." Evidently the proud and battle-tested veterans were not yet sure that the "boys from Michigan" deserved to wear the black hats.

Late in October the reorganized and refitted Army of the Potomac again crossed into Virginia.

Union troops attacking through the Corn Field, Antietam, from Battles and Leaders of the Civil War.

The corps commander asked Gibbon to report to his headquarters and brusquely offered Gibbon command of a division. Gibbon accepted the promotion, although he was reluctant to leave the Iron Brigade. "My first feeling," recorded the hard-shelled soldier, "was one of regret at the idea of being separated from my gallant brigade." They had gained fame together, and he never forgot the brigade for which he had genuine respect. In the postwar years, when invited to a soldiers' reunion in Wisconsin, Gibbon paid the Iron Brigade the supreme compliment: "I was not a Wisconsin soldier, and have not been honorably discharged, but at judgment day I want to be with the Wisconsin soldiers."

Solomon Meredith, who had started out as the colonel of the Nineteenth Indiana and had later been promoted to brigadier general, took charge of the Iron Brigade after Gibbon left to command a division. The next test of the Iron Brigade occurred on the battlefield of Fredericksburg. On that battlefield the Iron Brigade fought as part of the Union left, at the other end of the line that Gen. Ambrose Burnside's army repeatedly attacked an impregnable Confederate position. As a

Col. Solomon Meredith, commander of the Iron Brigade at Gettysburg. (X3)50390.

result, the brigade for once sustained few casualties.

After suffering defeat at Fredericksburg, the Army of the Potomac set up winter quarters at Belle Plain on the outskirts of Washington. Gen. Joseph Hooker replaced Gen. Burnside as commander of the army. Hooker directed another reorganization of troops, shuffling corps commanders, trying to rebuild the army's sagging morale. One of the soldiers of the Iron Brigade aptly wrote of "re-inspiration." The winter of 1862–1863 was "spiced up occasionally with rumors of marching orders." Several times the rumors turned out to be true. Once two regiments of the Iron Brigade conducted a foraging raid into Virginia. It was mid-February, and the weatherman treated the troops harshly. But generally the time was spent in drilling, cooking, reading, writing letters, or "just plain talkin.'" While the Army of the Potomac rested at Belle Plain, Gen. Lee's Army of Northern Virginia wintered around Fredericksburg. Both commanders waited for spring and the resumption of hostilities.

On May 2–4, 1863, at the Battle of Chancellorsville, Lee gave Hooker and his staff a lesson in strategy. As in so many previous battles, the Union army fought bravely but was poorly served by its commanders. And, as at Fredericksburg, the main fighting took place along a different section of the line than that held by the Iron Brigade, which was primarily involved in skirmishing. When Gen. Hooker decided he had had enough, he withdrew from the battlefield and toward Washington. The Iron Brigade once again served as the army's rear guard, covering its retreat. It was a rainy and dismal day. "One hundred thousand miserable and discouraged men," wrote a veteran of the Iron Brigade, "wading through this terrible mud and rain." Lee did not pursue the retreating Union army; he too complained about the weather and mourned the loss of Stonewall Jackson, his strong right arm, who had died of wounds a week after the battle.

In the reorganization of the Army of the Potomac after Chancellorsville, the "men of iron" became the First Brigade of the First Division of the First Corps. (As one soldier explained, this meant that if the entire Union army were formed in line of battle, the Iron Brigade would be at the extreme right end of the line—a place of danger, and of honor.) As part of this reorganization Pres-

Headquarters staff of the Second Wisconsin at mess in northern Virginia, c. 1862. Lt. Col. Lucius Fairchild is at the center, fork in hand, facing the camera. (X3)11291.

ident Lincoln replaced Gen. Hooker with Major Gen. George Meade, a tough, irascible Pennsylvanian known behind his back as "that old snapping turtle."

Meanwhile Gen. Lee and his supremely confident army had once again crossed the Potomac and begun moving northward. Gen. Meade, with the Iron Brigade in the lead, maneuvered to keep his army between the Confederates and Washington. For days the two armies groped for each other among the fruitful hills and valleys of southern Pennsylvania. On July 1, 1863, just west of the crossroads town of Gettysburg, Union cavalry engaged a portion of Gen. A. P. Hill's corps of Lee's army. Hill's men were headed for Gettysburg where they hoped to get a new supply of shoes and pick up some provisions. What began as a skirmish soon escalated into a major battle. After an hour of hot fighting, the engaged Union

cavalry was forced back toward Gettysburg. Major Gen. John Reynolds, commanding the First Corps (of which the Iron Brigade was the leading unit), had hurried on ahead when he heard the firing. He climbed up into the cupola of a Lutheran seminary building on the extreme western outskirts of Gettysburg. After surveying the countryside and conferring with the Union cavalrymen who were bravely holding the Confederates at bay, Reynolds decided to hold the high ground along Seminary Ridge, just north and west of Gettysburg. He ordered up his corps double-quick from the south, with the Iron Brigade in the lead.

Reynolds was a professional soldier. He knew he would be badly outnumbered. But he had orders to keep the enemy out of Gettysburg, and he knew that a delaying action would give the rest of the Union army a chance to get to the battlefield. He also believed that, if his forces could not hold

Seminary Ridge, they could, perhaps, amply reinforced, hold the hills and ridges just south of Gettysburg. Reynolds' historic decision to commit his corps transformed the farmland around Gettysburg into one of the great battlefields of the Civil War.

The Second Wisconsin led the Iron Brigade into the fight, followed by the other brigades of the First Division which made up Reynolds' First Corps of the Army of the Potomac. It was late morning when the Second Wisconsin crashed head-on into several Alabama and Tennessee regiments in McPherson's Woods, just north of McPherson's Ridge and west of Seminary Ridge. The other four regiments of the Iron Brigade entered the fray. The "Black Hats" swept the Confederates back, sustaining heavy casualties but capturing numerous prisoners and temporarily halting the enemy advance. However, in this opening phase of the Battle of Gettysburg, the Confederates outnumbered the Union forces by three to one. Elsewhere along the extended battle line, superior numbers of Confederates gradually overpowered the Union forces. Before long, Gen. Reynolds fell dead, victim of a sharpshooter's bullet. The fighting increased in fury, with Confederate reinforcements relentlessly increasing the pressure. Overpowered, and with their ranks decimated, the Iron Brigade grudgingly began to withdraw toward Gettysburg, still fighting, still in coherent lines. Of the 1,883 men who had charged up McPherson's Ridge that morning, 1,212 had been killed or wounded. Late in the day, as the Union line crumbled, the remnants of the Iron Brigade retreated through the streets of Gettysburg and to the summit of Cemetery Hill, just south of town. On July 1st, Reynolds' First Corps as a whole sustained 6,000 casualties out of 9,400 troops engaged.

As dusk fell, the Union army halted and dug in, disorganized but defiant, awaiting a resumption of battle the next day. All through the night, reinforcements joined the armies of Lee and Meade until, by the third and climactic day of battle, more than 160,000 men would be locked in mortal combat.

The decimated Iron Brigade played little part in the battles of July 2 and 3. The fight for Little Round Top, a rocky hill that anchored the Union left, highlighted the second day's bloody work. On the third day, Lee sent 13,000 of his best

troops against the center of Meade's position on Cemetery Ridge. In the end, Pickett's Charge was repulsed with terrible losses. On the evening of July 4, the Army of Northern Virginia withdrew from the blood-stained battlefield and began its long retreat toward Virginia.

The North celebrated its great victory over Lee's army. There was much talk afterward about Pickett's Charge and the fight for the Peach Orchard and Devil's Den, for the Wheatfield and Little Round Top—places whose names would live forever on the field of Gettysburg. But no one could ever convince the men of the Iron Brigade that the first day's fighting was not the key to whatever followed. The Iron Brigade had sacrificed itself to give Meade time to occupy the heights of Cemetery Hill.

After Gettysburg, some eastern regiments were added to the battered First Brigade of the First Corps (meaning the Iron Brigade). New recruits were also brought up to fill up the ranks of the five old regiments in the brigade. In 1864 and 1865 the battles of the Wilderness, of Spotsylva-

Edward S. Bragg (1827–1912), colonel of the Sixth Wisconsin at Gettysburg. (X3)11286.

nia, Cold Harbor, Petersburg, Hatcher's Run, and Five Forks were written into the brigade's history and emblazoned on its flags. But the formal demise of the Iron Brigade really occurred at Gettysburg, where the unit reached its pinnacle of fame. The veterans who fought and died there on July 1, 1863, committed the opposing armies to fighting the crucial battle of the war. After Gettysburg, the brigade was no longer composed of only western troops; it had lost its distinguishing mark.

At war's end, when the final, awful cost of victory was counted, the Iron Brigade held pride of place. A greater percentage of its men had been killed or died of wounds than any other brigade in all the Union armies. Each of the brigade's five regiments ranked among the top fifty in percentage of deaths in combat; and the Second Wisconsin Infantry, which had lost 19.7 per cent of its men in battle, ranked first.

⊰ 14 ⊱

Wisconsin Troops at Gettysburg

NO BATTLE OF THE CIVIL WAR possessed the drama of the one fought on the hills and in the valleys near Gettysburg, Pennsylvania, on July 1–3, 1863. Six Wisconsin regiments, three belonging to the famous Iron Brigade, took part in the three-day encounter. The Wisconsin men of Company G of Berdan's U.S. Sharpshooters also played a role. In addition, although they were attached to other units, three Badger State soldiers played dramatic roles: Carl Schurz, once a Watertown resident, who commanded an army corps during the first day's fight; Alonzo Cushing, who commanded a battery and lost his life repelling Pickett's Charge; and Frank A. Haskell, a Madison lawyer who served as aide-de-camp to corps commander Maj. Gen. John Gibbon.

A confident Robert E. Lee led his Army of Northern Virginia northward into Pennsylvania late in June, 1863. The army consisted of three corps of infantry (128 regiments), sixty-seven batteries of artillery, and twenty-eight regiments of cavalry—about 75,000 men in all. Lee's "old war horse," James E. Longstreet, commanded the I

Corps; Richard E. Ewell, the II Corps (Stonewall Jackson's old command); and Ambrose P. Hill, the newly constituted III Corps. Lee's cavalry was commanded by the celebrated Maj. Gen. James E. "Jeb" Stuart, whose failure to keep track of the Union army was to cost Lee dearly.

The Union's Army of the Potomac was commanded by Maj. Gen. George G. Meade, newly appointed by President Lincoln to replace Joseph Hooker. Meade's seven corps of infantry numbered about 100,000 men.

Almost accidentally, the advance units of Lee's army (part of Heth's division of Hill's corps) stumbled upon the advance units of Meade's army in the form of Brig. Gen. John Buford's cavalry along the Chambersburg Pike about five miles west of Gettysburg. (A day or two earlier, when Buford learned that Confederates were west of Gettysburg, he had occupied the town and, in a way, had chosen the place for a major battle.)

Early on the morning of July 1, Heth's four brigades moved against Buford's cavalry, which fought dismounted behind behind fences and trees. Buford's troopers, though outnumbered, were armed with the new repeating rifles, and they held their own. Both sides wheeled in some field pieces and the fighting escalated. Knowing that Maj. Gen. John F. Reynolds' First Corps was on the way, Buford's men fought tenaciously, withdrawing to McPherson's Ridge to reform. Reynolds and his staff arrived by mid-morning. After conferring with Buford, Reynolds made the momentous decision to stand and fight west of Gettysburg. The skirmish had grown into a battle, and now it became a race with time. Around 11:00, the anxious Union generals saw the lead brigade of his division coming up from the south. It was the Iron Brigade: the First Brigade of the First Division of the First Corps. Reynolds shouted, "Forward men! Forward for God's sake, and drive those fellows out of the woods."

This was an awesome assignment for the Iron Brigade, a five-regiment outfit with a great record. Col. Lucius Fairchild, a native of Portage County but a Madison lawyer when the war began, commanded the Second Wisconsin; Col. Lysander Cutler, a native of Maine who was living in Milwaukee when the war began, commanded the Sixth Wisconsin; Col. John Callis of Lancaster commanded the Seventh Wisconsin. The other two regiments of this veteran brigade were the Nineteenth Indiana and the Twenty-fourth Michigan.

Gen. Reynolds quickly explained to Brig. Gen. Solomon Meredith, commander of the Iron Brigade, how he should deploy his five regiments. A fife-and-drum unit, playing "The Campbells Are Coming," piped the eager soldiers into line. Moving forward rapidly, and waving or wearing their distinctive black hats, the Iron Brigade shocked the Confederates who thought, at first, that they were merely engaging some Pennsylvania militia. The word spread among the rebels: "Thar comes them damn blackhats! It ain't no milishy! It's the Army of the Potomac!" The fighting rose in crescendo. Before long, Gen. Reynolds was killed, and command of the First Corps devolved upon Gen. Abner Doubleday.

By then the Iron Brigade was fully engaged in its biggest battle of the war. At first the brigade outnumbered and outfought the enemy in their front, even capturing a Confederate general as a prize. Then another Confederate brigade pressed back a portion of the Union line and drove eastward through an unfinished railroad cut, threatening the Union flank and rear. In this moment of crisis the Sixth Wisconsin came to the rescue. Rufus Dawes said, "We must charge." With a shout, the regiment rushed upon the Mississippians in the railroad cut, capturing their battle flag and 200 prisoners, and routing the rest.

Meanwhile, Gen. Lee arrived with reinforcements and ordered a general assault. Outnumbered and outflanked, Doubleday's men still fought bravely against heavy odds. Col. Fairchild was wounded and taken to a makeshift hospital in Gettysburg where his left arm was amputated above the elbow. The outmanned Union troops withdrew toward Gettysburg, leaving behind many dead and severely wounded. Among them was Col. Callis of the Seventh Wisconsin, who lay on the battlefield for more than forty hours. (He recovered after being rescued.) As the Sixth Wisconsin retreated through Gettysburg, they saw Col. Fairchild on a porch; he waved jauntily to them with his remaining arm. Then the Wisconsin troops moved southward with the rest of the Union forces to occupy the heights of Cemetery Hill and count their losses. The First Corps had paid a heavy price buying time for Meade's army. Of 9,400 troops engaged in the first day's fight, 6,000 were dead, wounded, or missing. The Iron Brigade was decimated.

Carl Schurz (1829–1906), a "political general" who served Wisconsin well. (X3)17937.

The Twenty-sixth Wisconsin, a predominantly German regiment attached to Maj. Gen. Oliver O. Howard's Eleventh Corps, also suffered heavy casualties in the first day's fighting. Howard's command had been deployed north of Gettysburg, astride three of the ten roads leading into town. Howard himself had charge of overall operations for a while, so Carl Schurz, a division commander, directed the Eleventh Corps most of the day. Before Schurz's troops were attacked, he placed a division, along with two batteries, atop Cemetery Hill south of town. Events were to prove this a propitious decision.

Early in the afternoon of July 1, a division of Gen. Ewell's Confederate corps launched an ill-coordinated attack against Schurz's troops along the Mummasburg road. It stalled with considerable Confederate losses. Another Confederate division then came up and entered the fray. (The first day's fighting at Gettysburg became what is known as a "meeting engagement.") As the numbers on both sides grew and the fighting heated up, Lee committed two more divisions, instructing them to dislodge Schurz's men. After about an hour of hard fighting, Schurz's troops, including the Twenty-sixth Wisconsin, cracked under relentless pressure and withdrew in disorder through the streets of Gettysburg to Cemetery Hill. Although the German regiments in Meade's army were frequently maligned by their fellow soldiers, the Twenty-sixth Wisconsin fought well at Gettysburg, helping to cover the division's retreat and suffering forty-one killed, 137 wounded, and thirty-two missing.

About 4:30 that afternoon, Maj. Gen. Winfield S. Hancock arrived on the field, sent by Gen. Meade to take charge in Meade's name. Hancock ordered a division of Doubleday's corps, including the Second and Sixth Wisconsin, to occupy Culp's Hill, a heavily wooded prominence on what would become the right of the Union line south of Gettysburg. Then, after conferring with his corps commanders, Hancock stated firmly, "Very well, I select this as the battlefield." As Union reinforcements poured in, Hancock put them in position here and there, forming the famous fish-hook-shaped line: Culp's Hill being the barb, Cemetery Hill the bend, Cemetery Ridge the shank, and two steep, prominent hills—Little Round Top and Round Top—the "eye" of the hook.

The Third Wisconsin regiment, part of the Twelfth Corps, did not reach the field until 7 o'clock that evening of July 1st. It was assigned a place to the right of the First Corps and instructed to be ready for the next day's fight. The Fifth Wisconsin (part of the "Light Division" of Maj. Gen. John Sedgwick's Sixth Corps) did not arrive on the field until the afternoon of July 2, the second day of the battle. It was promptly placed at the extreme left of Meade's three-mile line. Wisconsin's contribution to Berdan's U.S. Sharpshooters, Company G, was attached to Maj. Gen. Daniel Sickles' Third Corps. Most of Sickles' men also arrived about 7 o'clock on the eve of the first day's fight. Gen. Howard assigned them to a low-lying portion of Cemetery Ridge, just north of Little Round Top.

Gen. Lee, after stationing two of his corps along Seminary Ridge, faced Meade's lines. That night he decided to attack both flanks of the Union army the next day, saying something to the effect that "They are there, and I am going to whip them, or they are going to whip me."

On July 2, for a variety of reasons, Gen. Longstreet's troops did not begin their attack on the Union left until late in the afternoon. When he

Union batteries in action on Cemetery Hill, Gettysburg, from a contemporary engraving.
(X3)22925.

finally attacked, it was like a volcano erupting. Bloody engagements took place over the Peach Orchard, the Wheatfield, the Devil's Den, and Little Round Top (the crucial rocky hill which commanded the Union position). Longstreet hammered the Union left wing, virtually destroying Sickles' Third Corps, inflicting (and sustaining) terrible losses; but still the defenders clung to the high ground, bending but refusing to crack. Other Confederate forces were supposed to have launched their attacks on the Union center and right in conjunction with Longstreet's. Instead they delayed for hours after Longstreet engaged, and then their attacks on the Union center, on Cemetery Hill, and on Culp's Hill were disjointed and ill-coordinated. It was a case of too little, too late. The Union forces were hard-pressed, but their line held. As darkness fell, the Confederates had been thwarted all along the line, except where one of the Ewell's brigades had captured and held some Federal entrenchments on the south slope of Culp's Hill.

Some Wisconsin troops took part in the second day's fighting. The Second and Seventh Wisconsin—both badly crippled after the first day—were on Culp's Hill, where they were subjected to a terrible artillery barrage and suffered more casualties. The Sixth Wisconsin, also hurting, likewise had a hand in repulsing Ewell's attack. The Third Wisconsin engaged in some desultory skirmishing but was not heavily engaged on July 2. Portions of the Twenty-sixth Wisconsin also skirmished with the enemy. Company G of Berdan's Sharpshooters was posted near the center of the Union line on Cemetery Ridge and played a role in repelling Longstreet's attack late on the afternoon of July 2.

About midnight, Gen. Lee laid his plans for the next day's action. Following a massive artillery barrage to soften up the Union position, he would send three divisions, led by Maj. Gen. George Pickett's fresh troops, against the Union center near a prominent copse of trees on Cemetery Ridge. At the same time, Jeb Stuart's cavalry would strike the Union lines behind Culp's Hill. Despite the obvious strength of the enemy position and the doubts expressed by some of his subordinates, Lee was confident of success. Quite simply, he believed his men to be invincible.

Action began early on the morning of July 3 on the eastern slope of Culp's Hill, where the Confederates had gained a toehold the evening before.

After a hot morning's fight, Federal troops ousted the rebels. The rest of the morning was characterized by an eerie silence, with plenty of apprehension. Capt. Frank A. Haskell of Madison, a staff officer who was destined to play a dramatic role in the day's events, later recorded: "Eleven o'clock came. The noise of battle ceased upon the right; not the sound of a gun or a musket could be heard upon the field; the sky was bright, with only the white fleecy clouds floating over from the West. The July sun streams down its fire upon the bright iron of the muskets in stacks along the crest and the dazzling brass of the Napoleons [i.e. cannons]. The army lolls and longs for the shade, of which some get a hand's breadth from a shelter tent stuck on a ramrod."

About 1 o'clock the Confederate artillery broke the silence, pounding the point of attack in the Union line for two hours. The Union guns responded furiously. A pillar of gunsmoke rose high over Gettysburg, and the terrible drumming of the guns could be heard fifty miles away. The artillery duel took a toll on both sides. "Those guns are great infuriate demons, not of this earth," Haskell wrote, "whose mouths blaze with smoky tongues of living fire, and whose murky breath, sulfur-laden, rolls around them and along the ground, the smoke of Hades. . . ."

About 2 o'clock, Pickett's division, supported by the division of James J. Pettigrew and other Confederate units, began to move from their positions along Seminary Ridge, across the valley, and toward the Union center on Cemetery Ridge about a mile distant. As the artillery fell silent and the smoke drifted away, Capt. Haskell saw "a magnificent sight . . . a sloping forest of flashing steel." The Union artillery began to rain shot and shell upon the approaching foe; the breastworks "flamed" as Meade's infantry opened up. The "horde of gray" advanced as some fell, halting once to fire and reload. "[T]he enemy in front halts," Haskell wrote, "and his countless barrels blaze back at us. . . . The volleys blaze and roll; as thick the sound as when a summer hailstorm pelts the roofs; as thick the fire as when the incessant lightning fringes a summer cloud."

Despite their terrible losses, the leading Confederate troops penetrated the Union line. A Union brigade pulled back from the stone fence as fear and frenzy reigned. Frank Haskell, on horseback, "rode between the two lines, then swaying

Frank A. Haskell (1828–1864), chronicler of the Battle of Gettysburg. (X3)50396.

backward and forward under each other's fire, calling upon the men of the Second Division to follow him, and setting an example to the thousands who witnessed it." Alonzo Cushing of Wisconsin, with wounds in both legs, stayed with his battery, giving the approaching rebels "one more shot" before falling beside his smoking cannon. Perhaps 300 rebels broke through the Union line, but they were outnumbered and quickly killed or captured. Pickett's men began to retreat, their lines disintegrating. Jubilant, Haskell shouted, "See the graybacks run!" The Confederates had lost 7,500 men of the 13,000 who had set out across the broad valley half an hour before.

Pickett's assault, gallant but foolhardy, signaled the defeat of Lee's army. After dark on the following day the Confederate invaders began their long trek back to Virginia. Casualties had been very high on both sides: 28,000 Confederates killed, wounded, or taken prisoner; 23,000 Union men. But the tide of the war in the East had turned at Gettysburg.

Wisconsin troops participated in some of the third day's fighting. The Sixth Wisconsin helped to drive Confederates from Culp's Hill early in the morning, and the Twenty-sixth Wisconsin took part in some of the skirmishing—the total loss for that regiment over the three days was forty-one killed, 137 wounded, twenty-six taken prisoner, and six missing. Company G of Berdan's Sharpshooters played its small part well, exacting a toll on Pickett's men as they advanced on Cemetery Ridge.

Other Wisconsinites also made their marks at Gettysburg. Lucius Fairchild's empty sleeve helped him win an election—secretary of state in Wisconsin in the fall of 1863—and then three terms as governor, 1866–1872. Carl Schurz, a "political general" who did his best soldiering at Gettysburg, left Wisconsin for Missouri where he had an illustrious career as U.S. senator, organizer of the Liberal Republican party, and Secretary of the Interior, 1881–1884. Frank Haskell, during the month following the battle, wrote a long account of the battle as a letter to his brother which was later published under the title *The Battle of Gettysburg* and won enduring acclaim as a classic of battle-writing. After the war, Rufus Dawes wrote *Service with the Sixth Wisconsin*, one of the best regimental histories to emerge from the war. After returning to a farm in Wisconsin, Sgt. James P. Sullivan, also of the Sixth Wisconsin, wrote recollections of his wartime experiences as articles for the Milwaukee *Telegraph*. A century later, in 1993, Sullivan's account re-emerged as a book. And finally there was brave Alonzo Cushing, who had, quite literally, "stuck to his guns" in the face of the massive Confederate assault of July 3—thereby losing his life but earning a place in the pantheon of Union heroes.

⊣ 15 ⊢

The Cushing Brothers

INDIVIDUAL ACTS OF COURAGE during the Civil War numbered in the hundreds of thousands. Some men died so that their comrades might live; others, that their country and its ideals would survive. Acts of bravery occurred in every battle, and on both sides, for no state or section had a monopoly on courage. Every state of the Union and Confederacy could recite incidents which were a tribute to itself and its soldiers. Of course, not all of these varied deeds of valor were put into the written record. Often the hero died; sometimes the witness died as well. But among those heroes of the Civil War whose deeds were amply witnessed and memorialized by the press and public as well as by the army and government, none were more celebrated than the three Cushing brothers of Waukesha County, Wisconsin.

The story of the Cushing brothers is in part the story of the Yankee exodus and the westward movement. In 1838, Dr. Milton Cushing brought his wife to Wisconsin Territory by way of Massachusetts, New York, and Ohio. The eldest of the three sons whom the Civil War would transform into heroes was born in Milwaukee. Then Dr. Cushing moved to a farm near the Bark River, a short distance west of Delafield. Three more sons were born to the Cushings, though one did not

William B. Cushing (1842–1874), youngest of the three brothers. (X3)7698.

outlive early childhood. The family soon moved to Chicago, then Ohio. Upon the death of Dr. Cushing in 1847 the family drifted back to New York. But when war came in 1861 and the three Cushing brothers entered the service, their records listed them as natives of Wisconsin.

William B. Cushing (b. 1842), the youngest, had a most varied and colorful career. Like his brother Alonzo, he wanted to be a professional soldier. He spent several years as a cadet at the Naval Academy, where his practical jokes earned him demerit after demerit. When the faculty's Spanish teacher, on his way to an evening party, was doused by a pail of water placed atop a door, the mischievous Cushing "resigned" his cadetship during his senior year. A month later he boarded the U.S.S. *Minnesota* with the rank of acting master's mate. The frigate, assigned to help blockade the Carolina coast, captured a couple of Confederate merchant ships. Each time William B. Cushing, as prize-master, sailed the captured craft to a northern port. Once the "capture crew" took their ship to Philadelphia with William B. Cushing as the only Union man aboard. The daring and courageous youngster gained the respect and admiration of his superiors, who restored him to good standing in the U.S. Navy and gave him the rank of acting midshipman.

Within a year—at age nineteen—he had gained a lieutenant's bars and was assigned as executive officer aboard the *Commodore Perry*, part of the North Atlantic Squadron blockading the Confederate coastline. In the fall of 1862, while traveling downstream following the Battle of Franklin, Cushing's ship ran aground on the Blackwater River in Tennessee. When an enemy force tried to board the vessel, young Cushing shoved a howitzer out on the forecastle, discharging it point-blank at the Confederates. This turned the tide of the skirmish and saved the ship.

Assigned to command of the warship *Ellis*, Cushing exhibited an audacity that amazed his men. He captured prizes, destroyed a Confederate salt works, and even captured an enemy camp. His daring earned several compliments and citations. As commander successively of the *Commodore Barry*, the *Shokokon*, and the *Monticello*, he won more honors in 1863. But his most notable feats were yet to come.

Perhaps the most remarkable episode linked the name of William B. Cushing with the destruction of the *Albemarle*, a famous steam-powered Confederate ram, in 1864. That much-feared ship lay at anchor about eight miles up the Roanoke River in North Carolina, off a town she had captured. Young Cushing devised a daring but almost suicidal plan for attacking the ship. ("Another stripe or a coffin," Cushing joked before embarking on his adventure.) He equipped a small steam launch with an explosive "torpedo" on the end of a boom, and with fifteen volunteers set off under cover of darkness. They silently glided up the river to where the formidable ram was moored. But Confederate sentinels sighted the raiders as they neared their goal and let loose with devastating revolver and musketry fire. Cushing, nevertheless, ordered full steam ahead, directly toward the *Albemarle*. His launch crashed through the ring of logs rigged up to protect the enemy ship. Cushing, exposed to small-arms fire on the foredeck of the launch, succeeded in lowering the boom which held the torpedo just as his launch crashed into the hull of the *Albemarle*.

There was a tremendous explosion, and a geyser of water shot upward. Those of Cushing's crew who had survived the face-to-face fire of the Confederates jumped into the water and tried to swim to safety. Most of Cushing's men were killed, some were taken prisoner. Only two escaped: young Cushing (unhurt, but with his clothes riddled by bullets) and a lucky companion. The pair made their way through enemy lines and the surrounding swamps to report that their mission had succeeded. The mighty *Albemarle* lay at the bottom of the river, a gaping hole in her hull.

For this remarkable feat of daring, the federal government heaped honors upon young William B. Cushing. At age twenty-one he was raised to the rank of lieutenant commander. The Navy Department gave him its highest praise, and at President Lincoln's request, Congress tendered him its formal thanks. Testimonials, swords, and citations came in rapid succession. New commands and several brilliant exploits followed. But those were team victories, and young Cushing excelled in individual heroics.

William B. Cushing's participation in the capture of Fort Fisher was another daredevil accomplishment. Again he proved that he was a man without fear. Fort Fisher guarded the harbor of Wilmington, North Carolina. On January 15, 1865, Cushing led a company of volunteers, in-

Cushing's attack on the Confederate ram Albemarle, *from* Battles and Leaders of the Civil War.

cluding both sailors and marines, over a 300-foot strip of land while under heavy fire from the fort. With bullets tearing his clothing, he leaped sword in hand over the parapet and played a part in forcing the defenders to surrender. He was the only officer in the party to survive the assault. Again honors came his way, though he cared more for action than for honors.

The young officer spent the remaining months of the war removing Confederate "torpedoes" (floating mines) and capturing several more blockade runners. William B. Cushing's raw courage and heroic achievements were matched by his intelligence and sense of duty, and he ended the war one of the Union's most famous and highly decorated seamen. He continued in the U.S. Navy after the war, but his brilliant career was cut short by his untimely death in 1874, at age thirty-two.

William's older brother, Alonzo B. Cushing (b. 1841), also had a number of opportunities to show that he was both daring and fearless. Alonzo graduated from West Point in June of 1861, a month before First Bull Run. He received his commission as second lieutenant shortly before being assigned to the Fourth U.S. Artillery, and almost immediately he was promoted to first lieutenant. His first assignment was in the Washington area, where he drilled raw recruits and worked on the defenses of the capital. His artillery unit took part in First Bull Run. It was a harrowing experience, but on that bloody battlefield Alonzo B. Cushing learned that he was cool under fire and that the turmoil of battle brought out the best in him.

During the winter of 1862 most of his time was spent in camp. He considered his participation in the battles of 1862 as routine and without incident. Not until the Battle of Fredericksburg did he have a chance to shine. His gallantry in that disastrous battle won praise from his superior and earned him the brevet rank of captain. (A "brevet" rank meant "for the duration of the war.") He added to his honors at Chancellorsville and was breveted a major "for gallant and meritorious services," even though it was yet another lost battle for the Union army.

When Lee invaded Pennsylvania late in June of 1863, Cushing's artillery company accompanied the Federal army which moved in pursuit. Cushing's company did yeoman service on July 1 when

Alonzo B. Cushing (1841–1863), a hero of Gettysburg.
(X3)14030.

a major battle unexpectedly developed northwest of Gettysburg. He was cited for his "conspicuous gallantry" in the first day's battle. Cushing added to his laurels on the second day of the battle when his guns "shook the earth and inflicted punishment upon the enemy." But it was the events of the third day at Gettysburg that set Alonzo B. Cushing apart from most ordinary soldiers.

Cushing's battery of six guns was located in the very center of the Union line atop Cemetery Ridge, near an angle in a stone wall that was soon to become famous. Beginning about 1 o'clock on the afternoon of July 3, 1863, his battery took part in the prolonged artillery duel which preceded Pickett's Charge. The crest of Cemetery Ridge soon became an inferno of deafening explosions and screaming horses. Fragments of bursting shells pierced both of Cushing's thighs, yet the intrepid artilleryman stayed at his post, directing his men and setting an extraordinary example. After an hour's cannonading, only two of his guns were still serviceable. Then the artillery fire slackened and died away. Across the fields a mile to the west, Lee's splendid infantry, 13,000 strong, emerged from the woods and marshalled for the assault. Through ripening fields of grain and up the long, gradual slope came a wave of men in uniforms of gray and faded brown, brigade after brigade, in perfect order, their battle flags held high. This was Pickett's Charge—proof that valor and fortitude also characterized the Confederates.

Union artillery fire tore into the Confederate formations from the moment they stepped off. With a quarter-mile to go, musketry began to thin the advancing lines, but the attackers closed up and filled the gaps in their ranks. The brave men of Virginia and North Carolina leaned into the withering storm of fire, gradually converging on the center of the Union line, where Lt. Cushing, age twenty-two, smoke-blackened and severely wounded, helped his gunners load and fire round after round of canister—deadly blasts of iron pellets, as if from giant shotguns. As the range narrowed, the carnage was frightful. But those Confederates who survived the musket fire and the hail of canister surged forward, nearer and nearer to the Union lines. Some of the advancing rebels returned fire; the artillerymen began falling at their posts. A bullet pierced Cushing's shoulder. Gritting his teeth in agony, he called to his division commander, "I'll give them one more shot!"

From Battles and Leaders of the Civil War.

With help from his men he rolled a cannon forward to the stone wall. The big gun belched forth a hail of canister.

That "one more shot" was the last. As his gun recoiled, a bullet struck Cushing in the face, piercing the base of his brain. He fell forward, into the arms of one of his men, just to the right of his field piece. Seconds later the leading Confederates broke through the Union line. Gallant Gen. Lewis A. Armistead led the remnants of his Virginia brigade over the stone wall. In the smoke and din, Armistead reached Cushing's cannon and laid his hand on it for balance. The next instant he went down, mortally wounded, not far from Alonzo Cushing's lifeless body. There was a deadly swirl of hand-to-hand combat; then Union reserves overwhelmed the attackers. In moments it was all over. Pickett's Charge had failed; the "highwater mark of the Confederacy" had crested around the wreckage of Cushing's battery. Today, the markers honoring Cushing and Armistead stand within a few yards of each other inside the Angle on the crest of Cemetery Ridge.

The eldest of the three Wisconsin-born Cushings was Howard B. Cushing (b. 1838). His role in the Civil War is less well-known, but only because he did not have the same opportunities which befell his brothers. Howard was employed as a printer in Chicago when he volunteered for service in March, 1862. He served as a private in Company B, First Illinois Artillery, for six months. When he learned of his brother Alonzo's death at Gettysburg, he requested a transfer to his dead brother's battery. His superiors granted his wish, and Howard B. Cushing went east to join the Fourth U.S. Artillery. In November, 1863, he gained his first promotion, a second lieutenancy. For six months his artillery unit was kept in camp at Brandy Station, Virginia, while Lt. Cushing chafed at the bit. Then it was attached to the second division of the cavalry corps and engaged in

Howard B. Cushing (1838–1871), eldest of the three brothers.
(X3)10564.

several battles. Cushing's artillery company lost so heavily at the Battle of Yellow Tavern in May, 1864, that it was sent back to Washington to be reorganized and to recuperate. In the closing months of the war, Cushing was a member of a company guarding 12,000 Confederate prisoners confined at Elmira, New York.

When the war ended, he remained in the U.S. Army and was transferred to Arizona Territory to discipline the Apache Indians. There he was killed in action in 1871, ambushed by a war party led by Cochise. A fellow officer called Howard B. Cushing the bravest man he had ever seen: "I mean just that—the bravest man I ever saw!" At the time of his death, he was thirty-three years old.

Truly the Cushing brothers of Delafield were a heroic trio. Small wonder that Wisconsin claims them as her native sons!

16

Eight Other Regiments

BEFORE THE FIRST YEAR of the Civil War had come to an end, Wisconsin raised, equipped, and sent off to war eleven regiments. Three formed part of the Iron Brigade. The other eight served on a variety of battlefields—mostly in the western theater of war—and most earned and maintained excellent reputations.

Wisconsin's regiments were usually kept at full strength—roughly 700 officers and men. When death, disease, or desertion reduced the ranks of a Wisconsin regiment, new recruits were assigned to take the place of those missing. The army commanders appreciated this effort to keep regiments at full strength. Gen. William T. Sherman commented favorably on Wisconsin's policy and practice. "I remember," he wrote in later years, "that Wisconsin kept her regiments filled with recruits, whereas other States generally filled their quota with new regiments; and the result was that we estimated a Wisconsin regiment equal to an ordinary brigade."

Wisconsin troops took part in most major battles and fought on the soil of every Southern state except Florida. They chased Confederate guerrillas on the flats of southern Missouri and through the

Colonels George B. Bingham, John C. Starkweather, and Rufus King, all of the Iron Brigade. (X3)7930.

swamps and cottonfields of Arkansas. They campaigned in the bayous of Louisiana and under the broiling Mississippi sun. They helped Ulysses S. Grant capture Vicksburg and fought under Generals Buell and Rosecrans in central Tennessee. Some Wisconsin troops took part in every major battle near Washington and Richmond; others helped Sherman capture Atlanta and cut a wide swath "marching through Georgia." They were at Appomattox when Lee surrendered to Grant and with Sherman in North Carolina when Gen. Joseph E. Johnston's army laid down its arms.

The First Wisconsin, which had seen but little service in the Shenandoah Valley before its three-month term of enlistment ended, returned to Wisconsin to be mustered out and reorganized. Those who had tired of war returned to their homes. Most of the volunteers, however, accepted the thanks of the governor and reenlisted as three-year men. The depleted ranks were filled with new recruits, and Col. John C. Starkweather again took command. The regiment stayed at Camp Scott, Milwaukee, during its reorganization. Most of the veterans had a furlough before the reorganized First Wisconsin again departed for the front.

The War Department did not send the re-vamped First Wisconsin back to Washington. Instead, Col. Starkweather received orders to take his troops to Louisville, Kentucky, and then report to Gen. Sherman. The regiment spent most of the fall and winter repairing and guarding the railroad line between Louisville and Nashville, where rebel raiders had wrecked some bridges and torn up some tracks. The First Wisconsin repaired the bridges and tried to prevent further sabotage.

During the spring and summer, the First Wisconsin skirmished with "the rebels, the ague, and diarrhea." (The "ague" being a severe malarial fever.) On October 8, 1862, the regiment bore "a conspicuous and noble part" in the Battle of Chaplin Hills (or Perryville) in Kentucky. The First Wisconsin repulsed three separate attacks upon its line. Then, leading a bayonet charge, it turned the tide of the battle, breaking the Confederate line and capturing the colors of the First Tennessee. Gen. L. H. Rousseau, Union commander in the battle, cited the First Wisconsin for its "courage and achievements." "They drove the enemy back several times with great loss," he reported, "and until their ammunition gave out bravely maintained their position." The First Wisconsin's losses during the war totaled 235 dead, of whom 103 died of disease.

The Third Wisconsin received several citations and was unique in that it was one of the few western regiments which fought the first half of the war with the eastern army and the last half of the war in the West. It was organized at Fond du Lac under the immediate direction of Col. Charles S. Hamilton, a resident of the city. A West Pointer, Hamilton knew how to transform raw recruits into an organized unit. Its first assignment, previously mentioned, was to arrest the members of the seceding or "bogus" Maryland legislators at Frederick. After a term of duty at Frederick, the Third Wisconsin engaged in a sharp fight at Bolivar, Virginia. That minor battle became a Union victory because three companies of the Third Wisconsin engaged in a "heroic charge," boldly capturing an enemy field-piece and driving the Confederates from their position. Then the Third Wisconsin was transferred to the Shenandoah Valley, where it participated, with heavy losses, in the two battles occurring near Winchester in 1862. Later, as a part of Gen. Nathaniel Banks's corps, it was bested by Stonewall Jackson's troops in the sanguinary battle of Cedar Mountain. But even in defeat the Third Wisconsin fought well; the commander reserved special praise for "the men of the Third." Had the other regiments fought as well, the battle might not have gone into history as a Union defeat.

Starkweather's brigade distinguished itself at the Battle of Perryville, 1862.
From Battles and Leaders of the Civil War.

Charles S. Hamilton (1822–1891), commander of the Third Wisconsin. (X3)33926.

After the Third Wisconsin joined the main Union army near Washington, bloody battles followed one another in rapid order. The regiment played a prominent part in the Second Battle of Bull Run and suffered heavy losses at Antietam (twenty-seven killed, 171 wounded). It fought well in the Chancellorsville campaign and at Gettysburg. In the fall of 1863 the Third Wisconsin became part of the reorganized Twentieth Corps, which soon traveled westward across the mountains where it joined Gen. Sherman's command. The corps participated in all of the western campaigns, from Chattanooga to Atlanta and, after Atlanta fell to the Union forces, in Sherman's famous march to the sea. The Third Wisconsin thus saw more of the war than most Wisconsin regiments, and it represented its state nobly and well. In all, 247 men of the Third gave their lives for the Union.

The Fourth Wisconsin fought in fewer battles than either the First or Third regiments. It was, however, the center of more controversy. Midway through the war, the regiment was transformed from an infantry unit into a cavalry regiment.

The Fourth had a controversial beginning. It rendezvoused at Camp Utley, Racine. When it

came time to be mustered in as a three-year regiment, many of the enlisted men of Company H objected to the longer term of service and returned home. Since the company was reduced below the minimum, Governor Randall at once disbanded Company H and accepted another company, from Oconto County, in its place. Halbert E. Paine of Milwaukee, a former law partner with Carl Schurz, was named colonel and drilled the regiment daily until its departure from the state on July 15, 1861.

A second controversy developed while the Fourth Wisconsin was on its way to Washington. The regiment was temporarily marooned in Corning, New York, because railroad officials objected to travel of the troops over a rival railroad line. Col. Paine solved the problem by seizing a locomotive, coupling the engine to the sidetracked troop coaches, and proceeding to Elmira. Eventually the regiment reached Baltimore. The troops of the Fourth Wisconsin established "Camp Paine," built the "Wisconsin Barracks," and spent the several months on the outskirts of Baltimore. On February 19, 1862, the regiment embarked for Fortress Monroe, to join Gen. Benjamin Butler's expedition to capture New Orleans. After the Union navy succeeded in passing the rebel forts which barred the way to New Orleans, the Fourth Wisconsin took part in an expedition to strike at the rear of the forts. Soon after, the road to New Orleans lay open. The Fourth Wisconsin was the second regiment to enter New Orleans. "The expedition was conducted in a manner that elicited high praise," wrote a witness to the events, "both for the men of the Fourth and their commander."

Out of New Orleans the Fourth Wisconsin went on a number of side-expeditions. They chased guerrillas into a cypress swamp. They captured, then evacuated Baton Rouge. They took part in the siege of Port Hudson, where Col. Paine lost a leg in combat.

Throughout his military career, the impetuous colonel was involved in one argument after another with with his superiors. One controversy was concerned with fugitive slaves, or "contrabands" as they were called. On June 5, 1862, the brigade commander, Brig. Gen. Thomas Williams, ordered fugitive slaves turned out of camp and sent beyond the lines. Col. Paine, an abolitionist, countered with a letter saying that the Fourth Wisconsin would not return free men to slavery;

nor would he violate a federal law (enacted on March 15, 1862) which forbade Union troops to return "fugitives" to their self-proclaimed masters. Gen. Williams thereupon ordered Col. Paine arrested. Only the fortuitous death of Gen. Williams in battle and the need for Paine's regiment and services in a campaign against Baton Rouge saved Paine his reputation and his command.

Col. Paine soon became embroiled in another controversy, this time with Gen. Butler, commander of the Department of the Gulf. Butler had given Paine orders to burn Baton Rouge. The Wisconsin colonel, through a messenger, asked the temperamental Gen. Butler to rescind his order. Paine's arguments evidently were effective, for Gen. Butler changed his mind and spared Baton Rouge, which owed a debt of gratitude to a Wisconsin colonel whose firmness of mind and "sense of just humanity" saved it from destruction.

Amasa Cobb (1823–1905), who commanded both the Fifth and the Forty-third Wisconsin. (X3)2381.

The history of the Fourth Wisconsin Infantry came to an end on September 1, 1863, on which day a special order of the War Department converted it into a cavalry outfit, the Fourth Wisconsin Cavalry. As a cavalry unit, the regiment also had an interesting history, though one of less controversy and more accomplishment.

The Fifth Wisconsin Infantry added to the fame of Wisconsin soldiery. Col. Amasa Cobb of Mineral Point commanded the regiment when it entrained for Washington the day after First Bull Run. It spent the fall and winter in camp, occasionally partaking in a reconnaissance into enemy country.

This regiment became indelibly identified with the Army of the Potomac. Its baptism of fire occurred during the Peninsular campaign in 1862. In the battle of Williamsburg, one of the bloodiest of Gen. McClellan's campaign against Richmond, it helped to turn the tide. The commander of the army, pleased and impressed, paid a flowery tribute to the heroics of the Fifth Wisconsin: "My lads, I have come to thank you for your gallant conduct the other day. You have gained honor for your country, yourselves, your State, and the army to which you belong. *Through you, we won the day; and Williamsburg shall be inscribed upon your banner. . . .* By your action and your discipline, you have gained a reputation which shall be known throughout the Army of the Potomac. Your country owes you its grateful thanks. As for myself, I can never thank you enough."

McClellan's effusive words of praise helped Col. Cobb to win a seat in Congress in the fall of 1862. Cobb left the regiment for Congress, and Thomas E. Allen of Dodgeville took over the command of the regiment. Col. Allen went on to become one of the best soldiers Wisconsin contributed to the war. Under Col. Allen, the Fifth Wisconsin took part in the major battles of the Army of the Potomac. They were at "Bloody Antietam," Fredericksburg, Chancellorsville, and Gettysburg. The regiment welcomed Gen. Grant when he assumed command of the Union armies in the East; the Wisconsin soldiers trusted Grant, for he too was a westerner. The Fifth fought under Grant from Culpepper Courthouse to Appomattox, missing none of the bloodstained battlefields on the way. Its casualty list was impressive: ninety-eight men killed in action; seventy-one dead of wounds; and 116 lost to disease—a grand total of 285.

While the Fifth Wisconsin enhanced its reputation on eastern battlefields, the Eighth Wisconsin spread the name of Wisconsin over the battlefields of the West. The Eighth Wisconsin became nationally known because of its unusual mascot: the bald eagle named Old Abe. In 1861, a Chippewa County farmer named Dan McCann purchased a young bald eagle from an Indian who had shot the mother bird and chopped down the tree containing her nest. After taming the bird, McCann in turn sold the eaglet for $2.50 to Company C of Eau Claire, a newly formed militia company which soon became part of the Eighth Wisconsin Volunteer Infantry. Nicknamed after President Lincoln, the eagle was adopted by the regiment as its official mascot.

Old Abe was carried on a special perch, next to the regimental colors, at the head of the regiment. He attracted attention in parades and on the battlefield, where he might be seen soaring above the smoke, his shrieks mixing with those of screaming shells and bullets. The "Eagle Regiment," as it came to be known, was credited with taking part in twenty-two battles and sixty-odd skirmishes. A favorite target of Confederate soldiers, Old Abe lost some feathers, but he was never wounded. He not only survived the war but also served the Union veterans as a symbol of their victory. When he died in 1881, Old Abe was as famous as many generals and heroes of the Civil War.

The Eighth was the first Wisconsin unit to be assigned to trans-Mississippi duty. After reporting to St. Louis, where the regimental mascot attracted considerable attention, the Eighth Wisconsin was shipped down to Pilot Knob, Missouri. There it guarded railroad bridges and chased "bushwhackers" (guerillas), conducted foraging expeditions, and protected provisions and property. In the spring of 1862 it helped to capture Island No. 10, a Confederate stronghold on the Mississippi. Then the Eighth received orders to join the forces of Gen. Henry W. Halleck in front of Corinth in northeastern Mississippi. The regiment took part in the Battle of Corinth, where on October 3, 1862, it lost seventeen killed, eighty wounded, and eighteen missing in three hours of intense combat.

In the spring of 1863 the Eighth Wisconsin be-

Old Abe and the color guard of the Eighth Wisconsin Infantry, Vicksburg, 1863. (X3)11606.

came a part of Gen. Grant's forces which began the long and arduous campaign against Vicksburg on the Mississippi. At Holly Springs, Col. Robert C. Murphy of the Eighth (temporarily detached from his regiment) had his reputation tarnished. There Grant had piled up provisions for the army which he assigned Col. Murphy to protect. A Confederate force swooped down, captured the depot, and destroyed a million dollars' worth of stores. Unwilling to admit that he had failed to provide enough troops to protect the stores, Grant made Murphy the scapegoat and summarily dismissed the colonel of the Eighth Wisconsin. Col. Murphy retaliated with a request for a hearing, which Grant ignored, claiming such a trial or hearing was impractical during a campaign.

Under a new commander, the Eighth Wisconsin won more honors in the days that followed. The regiment took part in the capture of the Mississippi capital, Jackson, mounting a spirited bayonet charge which routed the enemy. The Eighth took part in a series of battles leading up to the siege of Vicksburg, the Confederacy's last remaining citadel on the Mississippi River. It participated in Grant's ill-starred "grand assault" of May 22, 1863, which produced heavy casualties but failed to capture the city by storm. Thereafter the regiment settled into siege warfare, holding the extreme right of the "band of steel" which Grant threw around Vicksburg. It took part in the victory celebration when the Confederates surrendered on July 4, 1863.

After the fall of Vicksburg, the Eighth Wisconsin—its eagle mascot by then a battle-tested veteran—participated in a variety of expeditions: to Meridian, Mississippi; to the Red River in Texas; to Missouri again, and to Arkansas; and finally to Tennessee, where it added to its honors in the Battle of Nashville on December 15, 1864—one of the few truly decisive battles of the war. The Confederate army was routed and destroyed, and the war in the West was nearly over. At Nashville, the Eighth Wisconsin captured a six-gun battery, took 400 prisoners, and seized two stands of Confederate colors. But of all the glory and the trophies of war they had won, the men of the Eagle Regiment perhaps prized most the tribute paid them by Gen. David Stanley, a West Pointer and winner of the Medal of Honor: "I had the Eighth Wisconsin, big burly fellows, who could march a mule off its feet, and who proved at Corinth, on the 28th of May,

1862, at Iuka, and again at Corinth, the 4th of October, that they could *fight* as well as march."

The Ninth Wisconsin spent all of its three years' service west of the Mississippi River and escaped the horrors of massive, set-piece battles like Antietam and Vicksburg. But its men served faithfully enough and brought no discredit upon Wisconsin's name. The regiment consisted almost wholly of German-Americans, mostly from Milwaukee and the Lake Michigan shore. Its first commander was also a German: Col. Frederick Salomon, brother of Governor Edward Salomon.

Cold weather harassed the Ninth while still in camp in Milwaukee; then the regiment was dispatched to Fort Leavenworth, Kansas, a sub-zero trip in cattle cars which tested the mettle of the men. Upon their arrival at Leavenworth, the troops took part in what was called "the Southwestern Expedition." During the campaign, Col. Salomon of Wisconsin and Col. William Weir of Kansas argued and disagreed. As senior officer of the expedition, Salomon felt compelled to arrest Weir, whose insubordination and stubbornness threatened the success of the expedition. He was packed off to Leavenworth. In mid-August, 1862, the regiment marched 350 miles in six days to intercept raiders in Missouri. But the regiment's long and arduous marches brought little in the way of recognition; the rebel raiders they chased away usually escaped to fight another day. The regiment even had several sharp skirmishes with Indians who had been organized into Confederate regiments. (The Battle of Newtonia, for example, remains a minor—and forgotten—fight in the records of the war, but it was a major one for the Ninth Wisconsin, which bore the brunt of the fighting.)

The Ninth eventually became part of a force assigned to Gen. Fred Steele, whose orders were to support Gen. Nathaniel Banks in his expedition up the Red River into Arkansas. When Steele learned that Federal commanders had called off the ill-fated Red River expedition, he ordered his army to retreat back toward Little Rock. At Jenkins' Ferry, on the Saline River, the pursuing Confederates caught up with Steele's rear guard. Although the ensuing attack was repulsed, the Ninth lost heavily—fourteen killed, seventy wounded. The regiment spent the remaining months of the war on guard duty, watching railroad lines and chasing guerrillas. Its men had the dubious honor of missing every major battle of the war. Still, the Ninth Wisconsin lost 175 men—seventy-five in combat and another hundred from disease and accidents.

The Tenth Wisconsin likewise learned that war could mean long marches, much suffering, and little recognition. The regiment left the state for field service on November 11, 1861. After arriving in Louisville, it guarded the Louisville & Nashville Railroad. An expedition into Alabama captured Huntsville, but the subsequent retreat from Huntsville to Nashville was one of great suffering: no rations, no blankets, no medicine, and no transportation.

In the Battle of Perryville, Kentucky (October 8, 1862), the Tenth was under fire for seven hours—from 11 o'clock in the morning until sundown. There the Tenth was part of the First Brigade of the First Division, commanded by Gen. Lovell H. Rousseau. The Tenth Wisconsin teamed up with an Indiana regiment to secure and hold a rise in the center of the Union line. The brigade commander praised the two regiments generously. "I am convinced," he wrote, "that both regiments would have suffered extermination rather than have yielded their ground. . . ."

In the months that followed, the Tenth participated in the battles of Murfreesboro, Chickamauga, Missionary Ridge, and Buzzard Roost near Chattanooga, suffering its share of killed and wounded but always losing more men to dysentery and assorted fevers. They were campaigning with Gen. Sherman near Atlanta when their original term of enlistment expired. Some men left for Milwaukee to be mustered out; those veterans who reenlisted were transferred to the Twenty-first Wisconsin. The Tenth Wisconsin ended its career with a total of 219 dead—ninety-three as a result of combat, 126 from disease.

The Eleventh Wisconsin, commanded by Col. Charles L. Harris of Madison, gained a measure of fame for the Badger State. The regiment was composed chiefly of farm boys—"a fine-appearing body of men." It spent the winter of 1861–1862 along the Iron Mountain railroad in Missouri. Before long it became part of Gen. Fred Steele's army of 8,000 men and received orders to march southward to effect a junction with Gen. Samuel R. Curtis' army, about 200 miles distant. The march was distinctly unpleasant. The roads were pitiful, the country rough, swamps numerous, rations and forage scarce, and water very bad. Malaria and various other "fevers" assumed epidemic proportions.

The Eleventh Wisconsin spent the rest of 1862 on guard duty, patrolling transportation routes, and chasing Missouri bushwackers—the tedious and often frustrating life of an army in the backwaters of the war. But early in 1863 the regiment received orders to join Grant's army, which had crossed the Mississippi River below Vicksburg and was engaged in a lightning campaign against the rear of the Confederate fortress, punctuated by the battles of Anderson Hill, Port Gibson, Champion's Hill, Big Black River Bridge, and finally direct assaults upon the Vicksburg fortifications. As one small unit in Grant's well-publicized assault of May 22, the Eleventh Wisconsin lost heavily. Then the Union army dug trenches and besieged the city.

After the fall of Vicksburg, the Eleventh helped Gen. Sherman capture Jackson, Mississippi, and soon thereafter received orders to proceed to New Orleans to operate in the Department of the Gulf. There it took part in expeditions into the Louisiana back country and to the coastal regions of Texas. When Charles A. Dana, Assistant Secretary of War, visited the area, he was apparently impressed with the qualities of the Eleventh Wisconsin and complimented the regiment for "the perfection of instruction discovered in their picket and guard lines."

The better part of the regiment reenlisted in February, 1864, and took part in expeditions into western Tennessee and northern Mississippi, where it skirmished with Gen. Nathan Bedford Forrest's cavalry. Then, in the spring of 1865, the Eleventh was in the operations against Mobile, Alabama. There, on April 9, 1865, it took part in the siege and capture of Fort Blakely, the last infantry battle of the war.

As far as the men of the Eleventh Wisconsin were concerned, malaria was more deadly than Confederate bullets. The regiment lost a total of 348 men in the war—262 of them to disease.

Taken all in all, the losses sustained by these first eleven Wisconsin regiments to leave the state were staggering. The three regiments of the Iron Brigade (Second, Sixth, and Seventh Wisconsin) reported total losses of 973 men. The eight other regiments described above—none of which achieved the fame of the "Black Hats"—lost a total of 2,146 men.

⋇ 17 ⋇

Wisconsin Troops in the Vicksburg Campaign

IN HIS MEMOIRS, Ulysses S. Grant stated that his Vicksburg campaign began on November 2, 1862. On that day he notified Washington that he was moving his army, based in southwestern Tennessee, against Grand Junction, about eight miles north of the Tennessee-Mississippi border. Grand Junction was a railroad center, crossed by an east-west railroad leading to Memphis and a north-south railroad line going through Holly Springs, Oxford, and Granada, Mississippi. Grant's plan was to follow the railroad line southward and, after capturing Granada, head westward to Jackson and then Vicksburg. Meanwhile, Grant's strong right arm, Gen. William T. Sherman, with a portion of Grant's army, would move down the Mississippi on transports, land somewhere above Vicksburg, and assault the city's defenses while Grant was engaging the Confederate troops fronting him.

Grant's plan was flawed. His supply lines were too long and were vulnerable to Confederate raiders; he needed twice as many troops as he had to undertake such a campaign; high water and rivers would prove troublesome; and Vicksburg's defenders were much stronger than he anticipated. As Grant's army began its southward advance, Gen. John Pemberton's Confederate forces were stationed at Grand Junction, Holly Springs, and in fortifications along the rain-swollen Tallahatchie River.

Still, Grant's campaign got off to a good start. He captured Grand Junction without too much trouble. He then moved on Holly Springs as Pemberton retreated. Grant then decided to make Holly Springs his supply base, collecting a huge store of food and ordnance before moving southward along the railroad line towards Lumpkin's Mill and Waterford. There were numerous skirmishes en route. Pemberton fought a series of small engagements and continued to withdraw, gradually extending Grant's lines of communication and drawing the Union general further into his web. Grant reached Oxford and cast his eyes westward, toward the state capital of Jackson.

The roof fell in on Grant in late December. Confederate Gen. Earl Van Dorn's cavalry swooped down on Grant's Holly Springs base, surprised and captured many of the Union defenders, carried away all the supplies they could, and burned the rest. By Christmas day, Grant's tenure in Oxford was untenable: if he stayed, he might be trapped deep in enemy territory. Worse soon followed. Gen. Sherman's attack against the northern environs of Vicksburg at Chickasaw Bluffs (December 27–29) was a disaster. A foolish frontal assault cost him 2,000 men, to the enemy's loss of only 207. With that, Grant's army withdrew as quickly as possible along the railroad line all the way back to Grand Junction. Phase one of Grant's campaign against Vicksburg ended ignominiously.

Twelve Wisconsin Wisconsin units took part in this two-pronged campaign. The Eighth, Twelfth, Fourteenth, Sixteenth, Seventeenth, and Eighteenth infantry regiments and the Sixth and Twelfth batteries of light artillery accompanied Grant on the way to Oxford and back. The Thirty-second and Thirty-third Wisconsin infantry accompanied Gen. Sherman when, prior to his repulse at Chickasaw Bluffs, he marched from Memphis to Oxford; the two regiments then rejoined their old brigades and participated in the withdrawal. The Thirty-third was the first regiment to enter Holly Springs after Van Dorn's raiders had captured the place, burned $1,500,000 worth of stores, and left as suddenly as they had arrived.

In the early stages of the campaign, the Eighth Wisconsin and its eagle mascot Old Abe were part of the second brigade of Gen. David S. Stanley's division. The regiment took part in periodic skirmishing but suffered no losses. After that there was little fighting, lots of building of railroad bridges and duty as the army's provost guard. The Twelfth, Fourteenth, Sixteenth, and Seventeenth Wisconsin regiments marched and camped and then countermarched and camped some more without tangling with the enemy on either the southward move or the northward retreat. The losses among these Wisconsin regiments were minimal; after all, in this farcical campaign, they were engaged in not even a good skirmish.

One Wisconsin soldier, however, had an exasperating experience. Col. Robert C. Murphy, detailed from the Eighth Wisconsin—which stayed with Grant's southward-moving army—was assigned to defend the Holly Springs stores with an inadequate force, less than 1,500 men. Gen. Van Dorn's Confederate cavalry, 3,500 strong, surprised Murphy's defenders, captured the entire garrison, and took off or burned the huge supply of food and ordnance. Gen. Grant believed that Murphy's troops should not have been surprised and should have put up a good fight. Furious, Grant wrote to a cousin: "The surrender at Holly Springs was the most disgraceful affair that has occurred in this Dept." Grant made Col. Murphy the scapegoat for the Holly Springs affair, and ordered him dismissed from the army. Murphy defended himself, saying that the enemy had twenty-two regiments of cavalry (10,000 men) and that it was impossible to hold the place with 500 effectives. To be sure, Murphy underestimated his force and overestimated the strength of the enemy; but Grant nonetheless deserved more of the blame for the fiasco than Wisconsin's disgraced colonel.

With Vicksburg still his goal, Grant next decided upon a down-the-Mississippi campaign. In late January, 1863, Grant took his army to Memphis, crossed the muddy Mississippi, and moved southward on the Louisiana side to Young's Point, assuming command of all the troops already there. During the remainder of the winter he engaged in a number of different projects to circumvent or isolate Vicksburg: dredging a canal across the base of the elbow on which Vicksburg was located in order to divert the river and leave the well-fortified city high and dry; devising a watery bypass via Lake Providence and the Red River around Vicksburg; building a passageway for gunboats through a slough and to the Yazoo River. There were other plans and projects, equally imaginative; and Wisconsin troops were used in one way or other in all of them. Every one of the plans failed—thwarted by Mother Nature or by the tenacious Confederates. (In his postwar years Grant justified these failed projects by saying that his real intention was to keep his troops busy during the winter months and until weather permitted the resumption of a real campaign.)

In the spring of 1863, with President Lincoln urging action, Grant devised another and even bolder plan. From Millikens Bend, where his troops were reorganizing, the army would march

Union gunboat of the type used in Grant's Vicksburg campaign. From Battles and Leaders of the Civil War.

downriver on the Louisiana side to a point below Vicksburg. There the army would halt and wait for the Navy's gunboats and troop transports to run downriver, at night, past Vicksburg's formidable batteries. Grant would then use the gunboats and transports to ferry his troops across the river—"getting the army on dry ground on the same side as the enemy," as he put it. This plan worked. On the night of April 16, eleven Union vessels successfully ran the gauntlet past Vicksburg; all were hit and a twelfth was sunk. In early May, Grant began the second phase of the campaign. After crossing the river, his troops first captured the fortified river posts of Grand Gulf and Port Gibson. Then the army moved swiftly north and east, living off the country, anxious to take on Pemberton's Confederate forces.

Grant's army consisted of four corps, commanded by generals William T. Sherman, John A. McClernand, James B. McPherson, and Cadwallader C. Washburn—the latter a Wisconsin man who became a Congressman and then governor after the war. The Union troops, numbering about 45,000, engaged the rebels at Raymond on May 12 and elsewhere before capturing Jackson on May 14. The state capital lay fifty miles directly east of Vicksburg; it was here that Grant turned westward, his eye trained on Vicksburg. On May 16, Grant's army tangled with the bulk of Pemberton's army at Champion's Hill, where some Wisconsin troops played a major role in seizing some key high ground. Defeated in this biggest and most important battle of the campaign, the Confederates retreated westward into the trenches surrounding Vicksburg. By May 19, Grant was ready to take the city by storm.

Thirteen Wisconsin infantry regiments and three batteries of light artillery took part in the campaign that bottled up Pemberton's army in Vicksburg. The Eighth Wisconsin, part of Sherman's corps, after rather heavy fighting, was one of the first Union regiments to enter Jackson. The Eleventh, part of McPherson's corps, helped to capture Port Hudson and pursued the retreating rebels after their defeat at Champion's Hill. The Twelfth and Fourteenth came upon the scene belatedly and took part in no engagement. The Sixteenth Wisconsin was assigned to the sidelines, guarding the rear of Grant's army; the Seventeenth arrived at Champion's Hill just as the rebels started to retreat and then took part in the

Cadwallader C. Washburn (1818–1882), one of Grant's corps commanders in the Vicksburg campaign. (X3)26348.

chase. The Eighteenth, with Gen. McPherson's corps, lost twenty men in the Battle of Jackson and six more at Champion's Hill. The Twentieth did not arrive in the Vicksburg area until Pemberton's army was already confined within Vicksburg's fortifications. The Twenty-third was on the fringe of several engagements before becoming involved at Champion's Hill, where it captured most of a Tennessee regiment and its colors. The Twenty-fifth and Twenty-seventh arrived in time to take part in the siege. The Twenty-ninth Wisconsin, part of Gen. McClernand's corps, won honors at Champion's Hill, being in the thick of the fight and helping to dislodge Confederate troops atop a key hill; the regiment suffered a loss of nineteen killed, ninety-two wounded, and two missing. The Thirty-third helped to take Snyder's Bluff north of Vicksburg. The three Wisconsin artillery units were engaged here and there in Grant's lightning campaign, and then settled into positions on the siege line.

After Pemberton's retreating rebels entered Vicksburg in rather disorganized fashion, the

Confederate commander faced the task of reorganizing his army in order to repel anticipated attacks by the Union forces. Grant brought up his four corps, putting them in a half-circle anchored at either end on the river, "a seven-mile-long line of steel around the city." Impatient after ten months of frustration, Grant decided to mount a general attack against the well-fortified enemy. A full-scale assault on May 19 failed to break the defenses, but Grant persisted—foolishly, as it turned out—in believing he could crack the Confederate lines. On the evening of May 21 he sent a directive to each of his four corps commanders: "A simultaneous attack will be made tomorrow, at 10:00 a.m., by all of the Corps of this Army."

This "grand assault" of May 22, undertaken in the face of ferocious rebel fire, took a heavy toll of the attacking soldiers in blue. Some units of each of the four Union corps succeeded in fighting their way up to the outer works, and some even planted their battle flags upon the ramparts, but at terrible cost. Nowhere did the Union troops breach the main rebel line of defense. After two hours it was evident that the attack was everywhere a failure, and Grant ordered a halt—but his army had suffered more than 3,200 casualties in the fruitless attack.

Several Wisconsin regiments took part in the assault of May 22. The Eighth Wisconsin lost five killed and twenty wounded and won a compliment from the commanding general. The Eleventh lost eleven men killed and "suffered greatly." The Twenty-third Wisconsin lost so heavily in the attack that at the time of Pemberton's surrender the regimental colonel could only count 150 effectives. But the Fourteenth Wisconsin paid the heaviest price on May 22. Of the 256 men who made the attack, 107 became casualties. (When, after the siege and surrender of Vicksburg, the brigade marched into the city, the Fourteenth Wisconsin was assigned to the right as the position of honor.)

Reporting to Washington on these assaults on the Vicksburg defenses, Grant concluded with a white lie: "Our losses were not severe." But he resigned himself and his army to a protracted siege.

Reinforcements brought Grant's army to 70,000. Guns of every caliber thundered away day and night. Union gunboats on the Mississippi lobbed mortar shells into the city. Small, local attacks gained a few yards of advantage—or failed. The sharpshooters on both sides exacted their daily toll. Men in blue and in gray—and women and children too, in Vicksburg—were wounded

Union entrenchments during the siege of Vicksburg, 1863, from a contemporary engraving.
(X3)12902.

or killed in the ongoing bombardment. Pat Chauncey Cooke, a Wisconsin boy from Buffalo County, wrote: "I lay with the flap of my tent back, watching the shells from a hundred mortars making a fiery half circle as rising like a flaming rocket, they circled and fell into the city. Then followed the explosion. How can these people sleep? There has not been an hour . . . but shells have been bursting in every part of the city."

Meanwhile, Grant's soldiers continually tightened their grip on the city, tunneling away like moles, inching their lines closer, digging galleries under the Confederate positions and planting dynamite charges. On June 25 Union troops exploded "an underground mine," consisting of more than a ton of gunpowder, under a portion of the Confederate line. Two infantry regiments then attempted a breakthrough, but the assault failed miserably. Wisconsin losses in this campaign totaled 651: seventy-nine killed, 538 wounded, and thirty-six taken prisoner. Army life hardened the soldiery. A Wisconsin artilleryman wrote a friend, "I thought no more of riding over a dead man than if it had been a dog." Sickness too took its toll. The commander of the Twenty-ninth Wisconsin, Col. Charles R. Gill, resigned because of "ill health" and returned home to Watertown.

But gradually the ceaseless pounding of the guns, combined with despair and the growing threat of starvation, accomplished what Grant's head-on assaults had failed to do. On July 4, 1863—the day after Lee's calamitous defeat at Gettysburg—Gen. Pemberton surrendered his 40,000-man garrison. By 3 o'clock that afternoon, Vicksburg was entirely in the possession of the Union army. The stars and stripes again flew over "the citadel of the West," and the Mississippi, in President Lincoln's words, flowed "unvexed to the sea."

The ordinary soldier's elation at Pemberton's surrender was illustrated in a letter written by Edwin Levings of the Twelfth Wisconsin to his folks back home: "If you have any gloomy, restless thoughts, put them away at once and rejoice with those that rejoice. Victory, victory, victory! . . . The rebels' stronghold is in our possession." After watching some rebel soldiers stack their arms, he added: "Most are fine looking fellows, but dirty and starved practically to death. They came outside to eat blackberries, make trades, etc. with us. The utmost good humor and pleasant

feelings prevailed—glad they are once more free from the authority of their officers and to get something to eat. We gave them all we had with us—our hard bread, meat, and coffee. . . . They realize as well as we how strange it is to be firing away at each other, to kill day after day, then finally meet in friendship as we have today."

Vicksburg was in Union hands, but there remained much work ahead for those Wisconsin soldiers who had participated in one of the Civil War's most memorable and decisive campaigns.

⚜ 18 ⚜

Wisconsin and the Gettysburg Soldiers' Cemetery

TWO WISCONSIN CITIZENS played a part in the establishment of the soldiers' cemetery at Gettysburg: Governor Edward Salomon and W. Yates Selleck, a Milwaukee insurance agent and political appointee. As governor, Salomon helped provide state funding for the eighteen-state cooperative venture. Selleck, for his part, assumed three responsibilities: he helped to promote the idea that Union soldiers whose bodies were still buried in ill-marked graves in various sectors of the battlefield should be reburied in a newly created graveyard atop Cemetery Hill; he served as Wisconsin's representative on the commission set up to organize and administer the new cemetery; and he served as an assistant marshal to supervise Wisconsin residents who marched in the procession and joined the audience at the dedication program of November 19, 1863. Indeed, Selleck was the only Wisconsin resident to have a reserved place on the speakers' platform during that impressive dedication program—and he was therefore witness to Lincoln's most famous and enduring speech, the Gettysburg Address.

The story of the Gettysburg soldiers' cemetery really goes back to the great battle that took place on July 1–3, 1863, in the area surrounding that small city of 2,500 residents. On July 4th, when the Confederate army began its retreat toward Virginia, Gettysburg citizens and soldiers scoured the far-flung battlefield to bury the more than 6,000 dead soldiers and the countless hundreds of

W. Yates Selleck, the Milwaukeean who played a key role in establishing the soldiers' cemetery at Gettysburg. (X3)19197.

horses whose bloated carcasses littered the fields and woods surrounding the town. It was a dreadful task to locate and bury them all. Because of the summer heat and the rapid decay of the bodies, many soldiers were interred in shallow, hastily dug trenches with at best a wooden marker which might read "35 Confederate dead." Some bodies were not even put into real graves; earth was simply shoveled over them in haphazard fashion where they lay. To make matters worse, heavy rains fell on July 4 and 5, washing away the fresh-turned earth. "I saw one entire skull above the ground," one witness wrote, "and in many instances hands and feet are sticking through." A Wisconsin woman who visited the battlefield wrote, "The atmosphere is truly horrible, and camphor and smelling salts are prime necessities for most persons, certainly the ladies." Worse than that, "hogs were actually rooting out the bodies and devouring them"—this in the sector of

the battlefield where the men of the Iron Brigade had fought so heroically.

W. Yates Selleck entered the picture as the state agent assigned to oversee Wisconsin troops in the Washington, D.C., area. His responsibilities included visiting wounded or sick Wisconsin soldiers in hospitals, distributing mail and goodies sent by relatives, arranging furloughs, reporting on the dead and wounded, overseeing the distribution of mail, and generally seeing that Wisconsin soldiers were taken care of.

Selleck was a Milwaukeean with insurance as a vocation and politics as an avocation. His work in the Republican vineyards in the election of 1860 earned him a clerkship in Washington, compliments of Congressman John F. Potter. After the Union defeat at First Bull Run, the Wisconsin legislature passed an act providing for "military state agents." Governor Salomon asked Selleck to be the caretaker of Badger troops in the Washington area. So Selleck resigned one appointment to accept another. Unlike many another political appointee, however, he was honest, conscientious, and hard-working. As the war went on and more Wisconsin soldiers took part in battles involving the Army of the Potomac, Governor Salomon assigned William P. Taylor as Selleck's assistant.

After the battle of July, 1863, Selleck and Taylor hurried to Gettysburg. Selleck visited hospitals to see to the needs of Wisconsin's wounded. He visited Col. Lucius Fairchild, whose left arm had been amputated above the elbow, in one of the makeshift hospitals. He made out lists of wounded and dead for his governor. Since needed supplies were meager, Selleck hurried back to Washington and Baltimore to bring back, among other things, "three bundles of crutches, five boxes of underclothing and other hospital stores."

In his work of mercy, Selleck became acquainted with David Wills, a Gettysburg attorney and spirited citizen with a similar appointment as agent for Pennsylvania's governor regarding that state's dead and wounded. When Pennsylvania relatives came to claim the remains of their sons or brothers, Wills helped them locate the graves and have the bodies shipped home. Selleck did the same for Wisconsin relatives who came to locate bodies of the dead. But he found it impossible to identify the bodies of a considerable number of members of the Iron Brigade.

Then an agent for Massachusetts suggested to

his governor that those among the state's soldiers who were still unclaimed and still buried on the battlefield be reinterred in a special graveyard atop Cemetery Hill, adjacent to Evergreen Cemetery, the existing local cemetery. Wills and Selleck discussed the possibility of doing the same for all the Union dead. Selleck was sure that his governor would be willing to have Wisconsin pay its share in an eighteen-state cooperative venture. When agents from other states also expressed an interest in the establishment of a battlefield cemetery, David Wills recommended the proposal to Governor Andrew G. Curtin of Pennsylvania. Curtin, in turn, asked Wills to take over the project, supported by the state legislature but also seeking the cooperation of seventeen other states that had lost sons at Gettysburg.

Wills promptly purchased seventeen acres atop Cemetery Hill. Then, after consulting with Wills, Selleck, and other agents, he drafted a telegram which he dispatched to all the relevant governors. His telegram to Governor Salomon of August 1, 1863, read: "By authority of Gov. Curtin I am buying ground on or near Cematary [sic] Hill in trust for a cemetery for the burial of the soldiers who fell here in defence of the Union. Will Wisconsin cooperate in the project for the removal of her dead from the field? Signify your assent to Gov. Curtin or myself and details [will] be arranged later."

Governor Salomon replied promptly. Yes, Wisconsin would cooperate. He would take the case to the legislature. Interested in details about the project, Salomon instructed Selleck, back in Washington again, to go to Gettysburg and "confer with Mr. D. Wills" in regard "to the detail of arrangements for the removal of the Wisconsin dead to the Cemetery grounds." Selleck did so, and he soon reported to his governor that Wills had purchased seventeen acres for $2,475.87, that Wills would let a contract for reburials at $1.59 per body, and that Wills had secured the service of William Saunders, a well-known landscape gardener, to come to Gettysburg and "lay out" the proposed cemetery.

It was time, Wills wrote Governor Salomon, to think about a dignified and appropriate ceremony to dedicate this national soldiers' cemetery. Wills did not want the reburials to begin until after the dedication. Wills wanted Edward Everett, the famous Massachusetts scholar and orator, for the

occasion, so he wrote promptly and asked him to take a leading part in dedication ceremonies tentatively scheduled for October 22, 1863. Wills then wrote another round of letters to the governors, reporting on progress.

Everett replied to Wills that he was willing to accept the role of orator, but he could not write and memorize a two-hour oration before November 19. Since Wills had his heart set on Everett as the orator, he reset the dedication date to November 19. This necessitated another round of letters to the governors. Wills's letter of October 13, 1863, to Governor Salomon stated some salient facts: Everett would be the day's orator; the dedication date would be November 19 rather than October 22; reburials, at Everett's suggestion, would begin "about" October 26; Secretary of War Edwin M. Stanton had promised a hundred coffins a day for the reburials; and each governor should name "a representative" to serve on an eighteen-state commission to finish cemetery plans and oversee its operation. Wills hoped that Governor Salomon, with a large Wisconsin delegation, would be present "to participate with the consecration exercises." Salomon promptly responded that Selleck himself should represent Wisconsin as the state's representative on the cemetery commission—so for a time Selleck wore two hats, that of cemetery commissioner as well as state military agent.

Wills asked President Lincoln's bodyguard, Ward H. Lamon, to serve as marshal-in-chief for November 19, supervising the procession and acting as master of ceremonies during the dedication program. Lamon, in turn, wrote to Governor Salomon (as well as the other governors), asking him to appoint an assistant marshal for the dedication procession and program. Governor Salomon, solicitous as always, asked Yates Selleck to represent the state in that capacity.

As a result, on Saturday, November 19, Selleck was seated with the President of the United States and other ranking dignitaries on the twelve-by-twenty-foot platform at Gettysburg. He listened as Birgfield's Band of Philadelphia played the opening program number, a dirge or funeral march. Then the Rev. Thomas H. Stockton, chaplain to the House of Representatives, recited a long invocation—"a prayer which thought it was an oration," as someone remarked at the time. Next, the U.S. Marine band played the traditional hymn "Old Hundred," performing admirably. Marshal-in-chief Ward Lamon then introduced Edward Everett as the day's orator. Everett spoke for two hours and performed adequately, "with his accustomed grace." A Baltimore chorus chanted a composition entitled "The Consecration Hymn." This drew tremendous applause and set the stage for President Lincoln's "few appropriate remarks"—a five-minute effort that drew polite applause but no more. Following the President's performance, a mixed chorus of Gettysburgers sang a doleful dirge composed especially for the occasion. The Rev. Harry L. Baugher, president of Gettysburg College, concluded the formal program with a brief benediction.

The first meeting of the Gettysburg soldiers' cemetery commission took place at in Harrisburg on December 17, 1863. W. Yates Selleck was there as Wisconsin's representative. The commissioners elected David Wills as president and Selleck as secretary, indicating his standing with his peers. The commissioners discussed plans for the protection and preservation of the grounds, including their proper adornment and care. They adopted five resolutions concerning the cemetery's completion and operation. They also arranged for the appointment of a committee "to procure designs of a monument to be erected in the cemetery."

After this meeting, Selleck returned to Washington to resume his duties as state military agent. He wrote a report on the cemetery commission's doings. The sum spent on the monument would be $25,000 instead of the $10,000 first proposed. It would cost about $65,000 to complete the cemetery project; Wisconsin's share of the $65,000 would be $2,523.18, or $420.53 for each of the state's six members of the House of Representatives.

In March of 1864 the reburials were completed. Wills wrote a lengthy report to his governor and for his state's legislature. He sent a copy to Selleck, who was still busy with soldier care in Washington. Selleck in turn reported to Governor Salomon. In all, 3,512 Union soldiers had been reinterred in the new cemetery. Of that number, seventy-three were Wisconsin men, and of those, twenty were buried as "unknowns." The Wisconsin legislature, at Governor Salomon's recommendation, passed a bill appropriating $2,523 to cover the state's share of the cost of the cemetery project.

State agent Selleck was busy, busy, busy in 1864 as Gen. Grant's army suffered heavy losses in its brutal, grinding campaign to defeat Gen. Lee and take Richmond. But with the Confederate surrender at Appomattox in April of 1865, four years of war at last came to an end. As Wisconsin troops were demobilized, Selleck tendered his resignation as state military agent, asking that it take effect on June 1, 1865. The editor of the Milwaukee *Sentinel* paid Selleck a compliment: "The duties of this office were performed with great faithfulness and tact, and many a hundred of the Badger State's 'boys in blue' will hold his name in grateful remembrance for the valuable service which he has rendered them, and will united with his friends in Milwaukee in wishing him success in the new horizon in which he is now to labor."

Selleck returned to Milwaukee early in June of 1865, accepting a job with an insurance company. He still served as Wisconsin's representative on the Gettysburg Soldier Cemetery Commission until he left the state after accepting an offer from the Travelers' Insurance Company which took him first to Hartford, Connecticut, and then to Philadelphia and Washington.

In 1865, before leaving for Connecticut, Selleck received David Wills's second, revised report on the cemetery. At the top of page 51 was "the official map" of the soldiers' cemetery—the plan originally drawn by William Saunders. It was designated "Map of the Grounds and Design for the Improvement of the Soldiers' National Cemetery, Gettysburg, Pa., 1863." Pencil in hand, Selleck drew a rectangle on that map marking the spot where the speakers' stand was located. Then, on a piece of paper, he wrote an explanation: "The stand on which President Lincoln stood in the National Cemetery at Gettysburg on November 19, 1863 when he delivered his ever to be remembered address was 12 ft. wide and 20 ft. long, and facing to the North West—it was located 40 ft. North East of the outer circle of Soldiers' Graves as shown by pencil mark on the Cemetery map in the book to which this memorandum is attached." After writing his holograph, he pasted it near the top of page 50, opposite the cemetery map.

There was a pot of gold at the end of Selleck's rainbow. He prospered as an insurance man, became well-to-do, and, in addition to other positions of trust, he even won appointment as American vice-consul at Bradford, England. Then, in the summer of 1906, he returned to Milwaukee to visit a daughter, a sister, and old friends. The editor of the *Evening Wisconsin* urged him to write his recollections about his role in the dedication of the soldiers' cemetery at Gettysburg and as a witness to Lincoln's famous address. Eventually Selleck wrote an 1,800-word account which the paper published in its edition of February 6, 1909. Wills's report (sent to Selleck in 1865) containing the cemetery map—with the square showing the location of the platform and the pasted-in holograph—eventually came into the possession of the Lincoln Museum in Fort Wayne, Indiana, whose director, the noted Lincoln scholar Louis A. Warren, used it to challenge the traditionalists who claimed that the platform once stood where the grand central monument now stands. The dispute over the precise location of the speakers' platform at Gettysburg continues to this day. W. Yates Selleck of Milwaukee, witness to Lincoln's famous address, never dreamed that his penciled rectangle and brief handwritten note would become a central issue in this ongoing saga.

⚜ 19 ⚜

The Wisconsin Supreme Court Thwarts the President

ON JANUARY 13, 1863, in a case entitled *In re Kemp*, the Wisconsin Supreme Court told President Lincoln that his suspension of the writ of habeas corpus dated September 24, 1862 (Gen. Order No. 141 of the War Department), was not "a legal and valid exercise of executive power under the constitution" and therefore was null and void. This decision rocked the Lincoln administration and put it in hot water.

The case had its roots in the Port Washington anti-draft riot of November 10, 1862, and the arrests that followed its suppression. Or rather it centered upon three of the 150 arrests made after the riots, as a result of which some fifty civilians supposedly involved were held prisoner at Camp Randall in Madison. (About a hundred others were freed.) W. D. McIndoe, special provost marshal headquartered in Madison, explained his in-

volvement to Brig. Gen. W. L. Elliott, commander of the Department of the Northwest: "I have the honor to inform you, in answer to your inquiries, that *Nicholas Kemp*, Joseph Hine, and Anthony Alheison [should have been Ablheisen] . . . were each arrested by my order [Kemp on November 12 and the others on November 15] in the village of Port Washington, county of Ozaukee, Wisconsin. The cause of the arrest of said Kemp and Hine was for viable resistance to the draft of the militia of this state. . . . The cause of the arrest of Alheisen was the use by him in public . . . of violent language discouraging volunteer enlistments into the army of the United States, and language opposing and tending to induce others to oppose the draft."

Those arrested by the state militia, under orders of Governor Edward Salomon, were turned over to "the Federal Army for trial by court martial." This action was taken under President Lincoln's order subjecting to martial law any civilians who resisted militia drafts—and suspending the writ of habeas corpus in such cases.

On December 4, 1862, Nicholas Kemp, through his attorney John Diedrich, petitioned the Wisconsin Supreme Court for a writ of habeas corpus. The petition stated that Kemp's imprisonment was illegal because it was not based upon a decision of a civil court, and because civilians were entitled to a fair and just trial under the Constitution of the United States. The court granted the writ. But Gen. Elliott declined to release Kemp from military custody, citing Lincoln's suspension of the writ of habeas corpus and Gen. Order No. 141. On the 22nd of December the petitioner, through his attorney Hugh Cunning, moved that the respondent (Gen. Elliott) be required to produce "the body of the petitioner" (Kemp) before the court, at a day and hour to be fixed by the court.

At this juncture, Edward G. Ryan, a constitutionalist who had written the so-called "Ryan Address" in 1862 and who continuously opposed what he viewed as the high-handedness of the Lincoln administration, volunteered his services on Kemp's behalf. Ryan prepared "an able and elaborate argument." He knew each of the three justices well—during the 1860's the state court consisted of only three justices, each elected for a ten-year term. Luther Dixon was the most moderate of the three; he was serving as chief justice and

Byron Paine (1827–1871), soldier and jurist of Oshkosh.
(X3)46860.

would seek reelection in April, 1863. Justice Byron Paine had gained some publicity in 1859 because of his involvement in the Sherman Booth cases, *Ableman v. Booth* and *U.S. v. Booth*. Both cases had eventually come before the United States Supreme Court, and the justices issued writs of error and asked the Wisconsin Supreme Court to send in the records of its proceedings. This the Wisconsin court refused to do. Booth also refused to cooperate, merely sending a pamphlet that contained the arguments of his former attorney, Byron Paine, before the Wisconsin courts. Paine was elected to the Wisconsin Supreme Court in 1859 largely because of the publicity he received for his argument against the constitutionality of the Fugitive Slave Law of 1850. The third justice, Orsamus Cole, had been elected in 1855 and had the reputation of being "a staunch Republican."

Appearing before the Wisconsin Supreme Court on behalf of the prisoners, Ryan contended that Lincoln's suspension of the writ of habeas

corpus was unconstitutional *because only Congress had that power.* Even if President Lincoln had possessed that power, Ryan argued, it could and should not be used to sanction illegal arrests. He closed his argument with an oratorical flourish: "I want to see this Court have the courage to set this brute law of the sword at defiance."

Each of three justices worked on his opinion for several weeks. The three announced their decisions on January 13, 1863. All three justices agreed that Kemp should be freed because Congress alone, and not the President of the United States, had the power to suspend the writ of habeas corpus. The court issued two notable statements. The first of them asserted: "The power of suspending the writ of habeas corpus under the first section of art. IX of the Constitution of the United States, is a legislative power, and is vested in congress, and the president has no power to suspend the writ of habeas corpus within the sense of that section of her constitution."

In its second statement, the court said: "Martial law is restricted to and can exist only in those places which are the actual theater of war and immediate vicinity, and it cannot be extended to remote districts, or those not immediately connected with the operations of the contending armies."

Each of the three judges stated his view that Congress, not the President, had the power to suspend the writ of habeas corpus. Chief Justice Dixon wrote: ". . . I think the president has no power . . . to suspend the privilege of the writ of habeas corpus. It is, in my judgment, a legislative and not an executive act." Justice Cole said the same thing in a more interesting fashion: "But although the order might have been, and doubtless was, issued with the purest intentions and for the most patriotic purposes, and perhaps might be vindicated upon high moral and public grounds, I still think it is technically illegal." Justice Paine, in an opinion twice as long as those of Dixon and Cole, said that "the constitution, with all its safeguards" must remain "undisturbed." "I must therefore say that martial law does not prevail in Wisconsin," he wrote, "and that the proclamation of the president cannot legally authorize a military officer to hold the prisoner in custody for trial by a military court."

Edward G. Ryan was jubilant, for the Republican-dominated court had accepted his arguments. Wisconsin Democrats celebrated, for, in effect, the court had ratified the "Ryan Address." Editor Stephen D. Carpenter of Madison's *Wisconsin Patriot* admonished his Republican critics either to "back down from treason charges against the Democrats or . . . move for the impeachment of the three judges."

There were long faces in Washington, where the Kemp decision shocked the administration and its allies. At a conference between Secretary of War Edwin M. Stanton and President Lincoln, the two decided to ask Senator Timothy O. Howe of Wisconsin to hustle off to Madison to obtain a transcript of the case record. Their intent was to appeal the case as soon as possible to the U.S. Supreme Court. But U.S. Attorney General Edward Bates advised against it; he feared an adverse decision from the nation's highest tribunal.

Timothy O. Howe (1816–1879), a "radical Republican" U.S. Senator. (X3)1547.

After all, in *Ex parte Merryman* (1861), Chief Justice Roger B. Taney had scolded the president for stepping on unconstitutional grounds and instructed him that suspending the writ of habeas corpus was a congressional and not a presidential right. The War Department may well have accepted Bates's recommendations, for the Kemp case was never brought to the chambers of the U.S. Supreme Court.

Instead, Lincoln's friends in Congress devised a bill that would authorize the president to suspend the writ; the decision of the Wisconsin court *In re Kemp* provided the stimulus. Both houses of Congress passed the bill and the president signed it into law on March 3, 1863. With that, the issue of the Kemp case became moot. Ryan's notable personal victory had a very short life.

⚜ 20 ⚜

Politics and the Elections of 1863

SUCCESS IN THE ELECTIONS of November, 1862, gave Democrats cause to look forward to the political campaigns of 1863. Democratic party hopefuls dreamed that victories at the polls might give them possession of the governor's chair, and they were anxious to regain control of the legislature. Republicans, on the other hand, were less anxious to argue their party's case in public. They recognized that widespread antipathy to the war, the lukewarm reaction to emancipation, and dread of federal conscription affected their political future.

Some supposed that the April elections of 1863 would serve as a weathervane—might point which way the gubernatorial election in the fall would go. Democrats who convened in Madison on February 25 to draft a platform and nominate judicial candidates emanated optimism. They recognized that 1863 might well be a golden political year. The apparent chance of success seemed to give them less need to present a united front. Like many Democrats before and since, the delegates soon fell to quarreling among themselves. One controversy revolved around the platform. Edward G. Ryan, a man of firm mind and strong political views, served as chairman of the resolutions committee. The previous September he had drafted a controversial platform (the "Ryan Address") for his party. Now he introduced a set of resolutions which disturbed some conservative Democratic delegates. One such resolution condemned the Lincoln administration for violating the Constitution and establishing a military dictatorship. Another committed the Democratic party to a radical position on the question of peace and compromise. This controversial resolution called for "an immediate armistice" and asked that a "convention of the States" be called to adjust "the difficulties" between North and South "on a peace basis." When the resolution drew a hostile reception—a straw vote indicated it was opposed by most of the delegates—Ryan and his committee grudgingly withdrew it and accepted a watered-down version. Ryan, however, forced the delegates to swallow the other controversial planks. This was bitter medicine, and it brought about much grumbling.

Then the Democrats fell to arguing about a nominee for the chief justiceship of the Wisconsin Supreme Court. Ryan, trying to dominate the convention, supported Luther S. Dixon, who had announced himself as "an independent candidate for reelection." Ryan extolled Dixon and the court for its decision in the Kemp case. Ryan claimed that Dixon was a good enough Democrat for him; he vowed he would support Dixon and no one else. Most Democratic delegates, however, wanted a tried-and-true party member as their candidate for the justiceship. They questioned the orthodoxy of Dixon's Democratic views; some supposed him an opportunist rather than one possessed of the Democratic faith. Furthermore, many of the delegates were tired of Ryan's theatrics and his dictatorial tactics. They supported the candidacy of Montgomery M. Cothren, a Mineral Point blueblood. Cothren nosed out Dixon by a vote of 70 to 68. Ryan snorted his disapproval and announced that he would vote for Dixon anyway. By his dogmatism and defiance, Edward G. Ryan widened the split already developing in the state Democratic party.

The Republicans, meanwhile, were in a quandary. If they nominated a partisan Republican for the high court, he was sure to be defeated if Dixon and Cothren stayed in the race. Some party strategists suggested that Republicans support Dixon; they preferred Dixon, the independent, to Cothren, the Democrat. Some, however, pointed out that Dixon's decision in the Kemp case was a rebuke to Republicans generally and to Lincoln in particular. Republicans solved their dilemma by declining to name a party candidate for the judgeship. Instead, and halfheartedly, they passed a resolution expressing confidence in Dixon's integrity.

Throughout the campaign, Democratic and Republican editors exchanged vicious arguments and charges. Democrats contended that Dixon was the "tool of railroad interests" and "a friend of the foreclosure lawyers." Republicans countered by calling Cothren a Copperhead, a drunkard, and a "pledged and partisan" candidate. Republican editors also reminded voters that Edward G. Ryan, the high priest of Copperheadism in Wisconsin, favored peace and that Ryan's pro-peace views had rubbed off on the Democratic party. Republicans concocted a strange syllogism which they circulated throughout the state: "The Copperheads are for peace; Benedict Arnold was for peace; therefore, the Copperheads are Benedict Arnolds."

While newspaper editors exchanged insults, Republican legislators took a bold step to aid Dixon and their party. They passed an amendment to the soldier voting-in-the-field act of 1862 which permitted soldier votes to be cast in judicial elections. Soldier votes thus could affect the outcome of the Dixon-Cothren contest.

At the time the amendment was passed, the State Supreme Court was hearing arguments in *Chandler v. Main*, a case involving the constitutionality of the soldier-voting law. Democrats considered the amendment to extend soldier voting to judicial contests a brazen attempt to bribe the court to give a favorable decision in *Chandler v. Main*. Democrats were not at all surprised when the court ruled that the soldier-voting act was not in direct conflict with the state constitution.

Republican strategy won the election of April, 1863, for Dixon and the party. The statistics told the story. Cothren, the "pledged" Democratic candidate, received a 5,000-vote majority of the home vote. The count stood: Cothren, 56,840 votes; Dixon, 51,948. But the soldier vote (1,747 for Cothren to 9,440 for Dixon) more than wiped out Cothren's home-vote margin and gave the election to Luther M. Dixon. Dixon's decision that soldier votes were valid—in *Chandler v. Main*—made his reelection possible. Without the soldier vote, Dixon would have been defeated. Democrats expressed outrage and indignation. They had been badly bested by Republican strategists.

Defeated but not dismayed, Democrats took steps to reunite their party and prepare for the far more important fall elections. They knew the complaints of the populace and they catered to the fears and prejudices prevalent among Wisconsin voters. They tried to capitalize upon the widespread fear of federal conscription. Democratic spokesmen therefore argued that the federal draft act discriminated against the poor. In advancing that argument, they pointed to the provision which allowed a man to "buy his way out" with a $300 commutation payment or by hiring a substitute. "The blood of the poor man," stated the Democratic editor of the *Sheboygan Journal*, "is worth as much as the blood of the rich man; this is discrimination against the mechanics and working men of the country." Although Democratic orators and editors denounced federal conscription as "unfair," "unnecessary," and "unconstitutional," they still advised citizens to obey the law and avoid violence. "Obey the law," advised one Democratic editor, "but record your disapproval by casting your votes for the Democratic candidates."

There were some cases, nevertheless, where the enrolling officers received a hostile reception. On May 18, the first day of the enrollment in Milwaukee, an Irish-American hit the enrolling officer in the face with a spade. Some women then joined in the attack and pelted the hapless official with stones. There was violence elsewhere, as well; but it was of a minor character. A mob of "infuriated rebels" assailed an enrolling officer in Dodge County. In that same county someone shot and wounded the official charged with listing the eligible citizen-soldiers. In Washington County, a defiant "rabble" chased and insulted the enrolling official. In Fond du Lac, persons unknown jostled and insulted the list maker. The enrolling officer in Brown County complained about the rude treatment accorded him by the citizenry. But firm action by sheriffs and local officials prevented such incidents from assuming major proportions and evolving into full-scale riots. Indeed, Adjutant Gen. Augustus Gaylord expressed satisfaction that the enrollment was completed with so few incidents. Some credit should also have gone to the

Democratic leaders who urged obedience to the law. Democrats claimed that their party, traditionally, was one that had always emphasized law and order.

The modest advantage which fear of federal conscription gave the Democratic party was more than offset by Gettysburg and Vicksburg. These major Union victories undercut Democratic charges that the war was a failure and seemed to make liars out of Democratic leaders who had argued that the South could never be conquered and that the Lincoln administration was linked only to military defeats. Republican leaders, of course, made a deliberate attempt to parlay the Union victories into Republican votes.

While reports and accounts of the battles of Vicksburg and Gettysburg still circulated in the newspapers, Democratic and Republican politicians prepared for their respective state conventions. Democratic delegates met in state convention in Madison on August 5, 1863. The delegates, despite some opposition, readopted the "Ryan Address" and then nailed a peace plank onto their platform. The Democrats selected Henry L. Palmer of Milwaukee, a straitlaced Democrat, a prominent lawyer, but a lackluster candidate, to head their slate of officers.

Matthew H. Carpenter of Beloit, an opportunist who was anxious to bolt the Democratic party, took the lead in discrediting the action of the Madison convention. Carpenter was a bitter personal enemy of Edward G. Ryan; there was hardly room for both men in the same party. Carpenter, quite naturally, felt uneasy in a party of which Edward G. Ryan was the "fountain of knowledge." Calling himself a "War Democrat" and a patriot, Carpenter criticized the "Ryan Address," the compromise plank, and the "Peace Democrats." He declared: "I am for the Government, right or wrong—for the Government, howsoever and by whomsoever administered." He labeled the "Ryan Address" "treasonable" and he called Ryan's followers "Copperheads."

Carpenter was joined by forty-five "bolters" in calling for a Milwaukee meeting to put the Democratic machine back on the track—"to determine the true course for Wisconsin Democracy." Carpenter's appeal to the spirit of nationalism brought forth more bolters. Even such a long-time Democrat as Charles D. Robinson of the Green Bay *Advocate* joined Carpenter's growing list of

Matthew Hale Carpenter (1824–1881), an outstanding lawyer and orator of the Civil War era. (X3)50398.

"War Democrats." Carpenter's personal animosity toward Ryan and the bolt of the "War Democrats" helped to split the Wisconsin Democracy and presaged its defeat in the November election.

While Democrats quarreled among themselves, Republicans took steps to cement their control of the machinery of state government. The Republicans also held their state convention (August 10, 1863) in Madison. To catch unwary Democrats and to appeal to Matt Carpenter and his growing body of bolters, the Republicans wisely designated their state session a "Union" convention. Moderates felt that Governor Edward Salomon had done a creditable job and deserved the nomination. He had made military appointments upon merit, had exhibited considerable forthrightness and efficiency. But the "Madison Regency," headed by Elisha W. Keyes, had decided to discard Salomon. Keyes's crowd pointed out that Salomon had vetoed a railroad farm mortgage measure, had supported emancipation halfheartedly,

and had generally outgrown his usefulness. Salomon had also failed to gain the support of German-Americans, who persisted in casting Democratic ballots. Boss Keyes, the Madison postmaster, supported James T. Lewis of Columbus as his gubernatorial choice. Lewis was a late convert to Republicanism—some still called him a "War Democrat"—and secretary of state. Keyes argued that Lewis would draw the votes of Democratic bolters and that he alone could win the election for the Republicans.

A straw vote indicated that Salomon would gain the nomination; the informal poll showed Salomon, 134; Lewis, 122; and scattering, 9. Therefore Boss Keyes and his faithfuls resorted to ballot-stuffing to invalidate the formal vote. The secretary to the convention reported that the vote stood: Lewis 135; Salomon, 134. The secretary added, however, that the total vote of the two contenders exceeded the number of certified delegates by four! The convention chairman therefore ruled the ballot null and void; wherupon Boss Keyes and his crowd asked for an adjournment until 8 o'clock that evening. In the interim, Keyes and other members of the "Madison Regency" buttonholed delegates and gathered up a dozen more votes for Lewis. When the delegates reconvened in the evening, they named Lewis to head their state slate. The official vote gave Lewis 143 votes to Salomon's 119, with 2 votes scattered.

The conventioneers also adopted resolutions pledging support of the Lincoln administration and expressing a determination "to crush the Southern rebels." With its slate of officers and through its carefully worded platform, the Republican convention bid for the support of those who had bolted the Democratic party.

Matt Carpenter rose to the bait. He helped to arrange for a meeting of "War Democrats" at Janesville on September 17. At that splinter session, Carpenter gave a patriotic address. He compared the Democrats of 1863 with the Federalists of 1814. He compared the Madison convention (of Democrats) with the Hartford convention. He asked for support of the Lincoln administration and the war. He hoped that petty partisanship would be shelved during the war. That patriotic plea drew a round of applause. But the bolters made no attempt to perfect an organization at Janesville. Theirs was only a protest meeting—

proof that the Democratic party was hopelessly divided.

Republican partisans found another ally during the fall campaign of 1863. War prosperity visited Wisconsin, erasing memories of the 1861 depression. Farmers received good prices for wheat, barley, and pork. Butter brought three times as much in October of 1863 as it had in October of 1861. The price of corn also rose threefold. As farm prosperity developed, the Lincoln administration gained new supporters. Rising farm prices helped to salve the wounds of war.

Democrats tried futilely to rally their divided and decimated ranks. They tried to downplay the importance of Vicksburg and Gettysburg, claiming that war prosperity was little satisfaction to fathers whose sons were dying on distant battlefields. They tried to disregard the wave of nationalism which Republicans and flag-waving patriots engendered. They tried to overlook the peace plank which Edward G. Ryan had written into their platform.

That very same peace plank gave Republicans an excuse to wage a campaign of abuse against the Democratic party. Republicans publicly distinguished between the "dishonorable Peace Democrats" like Ryan and Palmer and the "honorable War Democrats" like Carpenter and Lewis. Flag-waving Republicans claimed that the Wisconsin Copperheads belonged "down in Secessia." They appealed to all "red-blooded" Americans to rally "to the cause which merits the support of all true patriots." And they stigmatized the "Peace Democrats" as cowards, traitors, and secessionists.

Defiant Democrats hurled back abuse in full measure. They were as adept at name-calling as their Republican opponents. "Brick" Pomeroy of the La Crosse *Democrat* led the way. He stated the views of the bitter-enders: "Abraham Lincoln is a traitor. It is he who has warred against the Constitution. We have not. It is his policy—his Administration—which has prolonged the war. We have not. It is his proclamations—not our editorials—which have disgusted the country. . . . Abraham Lincoln was elected President by the people; he has been President but for the Republican party. He has broken his oath—lent himself to corruptionists and fanatics. . . ."

Those Democrats who were not as self-righteous and defiant as Pomeroy soon found themselves on the defensive during the gubernatorial campaign of 1863. The surge of nationalism, war prosperity, Republican charges and stratagems, and Union military victories favored the party in power. Those forces and factors caused the Copperhead high tide to ebb and give way to a Republican ascendancy.

The home vote gave Lewis (Republican) a 14,000-vote majority over Palmer (Democrat). The soldier vote increased Lewis' margin to nearly 25,000 votes. Republicans gleefully noted that their gubernatorial candidate received fourteen of every fifteen soldier votes cast. The soldier-voting machinery was becoming devastatingly efficient.

Not only did the Republicans retain control of the governor's chair, but they also seized a firm grip upon both houses of the legislature. In the next session they would hold twenty-three of thirty-three senate seats and seventy-five of 100 seats in the assembly.

While Republicans staged victory rallies and drank toasts to their party leadership, the Democrats groped blindly for explanations of their stunning defeat. Some partisan Democrats, ignoring the facts of the case, blamed their defeat upon "black and damnable frauds." They talked of "greenbacks," "coercion," and "fickle voters." There was a move, in some circles, to blame the soldier-voting scheme. Others blamed the bolters and cursed Matt Carpenter openly. "Many of our forces," wrote the disillusioned editor of the Madison *Patriot*, "have deserted to the enemy, and have received, if not the thirty pieces of silver, at least what is only fifty percent discount, for their treachery." That Democratic editor was thinking of the many appointments which had gone to men who had once called themselves Democrats. Some had accepted posts in the government; some had taken commissions in the army; some, favors and government contracts. The Democratic analysts conveniently overlooked such forces as nationalism, prosperity, and Gettysburg. They reluctantly admitted that their divided and disjointed party had contributed much to its own defeat. The crevice of 1862 had become a chasm by 1863, and the chasm had engulfed the party. "Brick" Pomeroy explained the Democratic demise in his own colorful way: "The Democratic ticket . . . defeated itself by the adoption of measures which none but the most ultra Democrats could ask for. It died of political gluttony. It died of cramming. It choked on words which could be doubly construed."

⚜ 21 ⚜

From Stones River to Missionary Ridge

THE MILITARY CAMPAIGN of 1863 that cleared south-central Tennessee of rebel troops opened the gateway to Atlanta and helped to seal the fate of the Confederacy. Wisconsin troops were involved in the year-long campaign that began with the bloody battle of Stones River and ended on the crest of Missionary Ridge at Chattanooga.

When the new year dawned in 1863, Gen. William S. Rosecrans' Army of the Cumberland had already fought Gen. Braxton Bragg's Confederate troops for two days near Murfreesboro, Tennessee. (The Battle of Stones River or Murfreesboro opened on December 30, 1862, and ended January 2, 1863.) Early in the contest the rebels had an edge but failed to take advantage of the situation. On January 2 the Union troops turned back a final Confederate assault and Bragg then decided to withdraw to Tullahoma. By holding the contested field at the end, Gen. Rosecrans could claim victory in what he boasted was "one of the greatest battles of the war." In fact, although both armies fought gallantly and each sustained some 12,000 casualties, the battle proved indecisive.

Five Wisconsin regiments of infantry—the First, Tenth, Fifteenth, Twenty-first, and Twenty-fourth—took part in the bloody encounter, and some suffered heavy casualties. In addition, Wisconsin soldiers manned three batteries and they were heavily involved during the four-day battle.

The First Wisconsin belonged to a division in reserve—"being engaged in supporting batteries, skirmishing with the enemy, and making rifle pits." Its casualties were minimal.

The Tenth Wisconsin saw heavy fighting on the first day of battle, being "exposed to a hot fire, until they reached and occupied a rocky ridge covered with timber," where the regiment "got into a terrible fire in front and on the flank, but they sheltered themselves behind the rocks and trees, returned the fire, and held their ground until ordered to retire, to prevent being cut off from the rest of the army." During the last two days at Stones River, the Tenth saw little action.

The Fifteenth Wisconsin "put up a good fight for a while," but it was outflanked and forced to retreat after its colonel was fatally wounded. It saw little action during the last two days, but it suffered rather heavy casualties during the first day's struggle.

The Twenty-first Wisconsin redeemed some of the honor it had lost at Perryville. At Stones River it was actively engaged at the front throughout the four-day battle. The brigade commander, in his report some days later, praised the Twenty-first and its colonel, Harrison C. Hobart of Milwaukee.

The Twenty-fourth Wisconsin, with young Arthur McArthur as adjutant, helped save an Indiana artillery battery from capture during the first day of the battle. On the second day (Wednesday, December 31), when the regiment was caught in a deadly crossfire, the men broke and ran for the rear (or "skedaddled" as they put it). In a letter he wrote back home, Lt. Robert J. Chivas expressed his disgust: "The fact that the 24th Regiment broke and ran, and that a good number of the line officers disgraced themselves, has pained me more than anything else. . . . All the officers of Company C . . . are cowards and so is the color bearer who rolled up the colors tight and hid behind a tree." During the remainder of the battle the Twenty-fourth was not engaged.

Among the regiment's many wounded was Sandford B. Williams, who was carried to a log house which served as a makeshift hospital. Later he wrote: "The roar of the artillery makes the ground shake, and the moans of the dying mix with the other sounds. It is awful, and they die fast. The bodies are carried out and the wounded brought in to take their places. Hundreds lie outside and have no shelter." One of those who died was a young Milwaukeean named Frank A. Hale—a great, great nephew of Nathan Hale of Revolutionary War fame. After receiving a mortal wound, he took his mother's last letter and placed it on his chest, evidently hoping that someone would read the letter, identify him, and send him back to Milwaukee to be buried in Forest Home Cemetery. At Stones River the Twenty-fourth Wisconsin lost 175 of its 400 men: twenty-one killed, fifty-eight wounded, and ninety-six missing (most of whom were taken prisoner).

Both sides were battered and somewhat disorganized after the battle. Rosecrans remained in the vicinity of Murfreesboro; Bragg, his adversary, withdrew southward to Tullahoma. Licking their wounds, neither army seemed anxious to fight again. But during the early months of 1863, Washington put pressure on Rosecrans to begin another offensive. He procrastinated, wanting more reinforcements (especially cavalry), more ordnance, and more provisions. The First Wisconsin Cavalry was transferred from Missouri to become part of Rosecrans' reorganized army, which totaled 50,000 by the middle of June.

Late in June, the Army of the Cumberland began its southward advance toward Shelbyville. Bragg's Confederate army was in and around Tullahoma in a carefully fortified position. By a series of brilliant maneuvers, Rosecrans forced Bragg to evacuate Tullahoma without a major engagement. "No better example of successful strategy," one of Rosecrans' division commanders wrote, "was carried out during the war than the Tullahoma campaign."

Bragg's army of about 30,000 retreated to Chattanooga, near the Georgia border, and established itself there south of the Tennessee River. Moving his headquarters to Winchester, fifteen miles south of Tullahoma, Rosecrans planned his next move against Bragg and Chattanooga, fifty miles away. In another series of skillful maneuvers, Rosecrans forced Bragg to evacuate Chattanooga and sent him on the road toward Lafayette, Georgia. Rosecrans' Army of the Cumberland claimed Chattanooga as its prize on September 9, 1863.

Then disaster loomed. Reinforced by Gen. James Longstreet's veteran corps from Lee's army in the East, Bragg suddenly turned on Rosecrans' scattered corps. Rosecrans pulled them together hurriedly and by September 19 the two armies collided in the two-day Battle of Chickamauga, some ten miles south of Chattanooga. The first day's fighting was a draw. The second day's honors went to Bragg; Longstreet's corps pierced the cen-

Assault by the Fifteenth Wisconsin at Chickamauga, 1863, from a painting by Alfred Thorson.

ter of the Union line and sent Rosecrans' army reeling back toward Chattanooga. Only a resolute stand by the corps commanded by Gen. George H. Thomas prevented a calamity. Chickamauga, fought at close quarters in rugged, heavily wooded country, was one of the bloodiest battles of the war. The Union army suffered 16,000 casualties; the Confederate, 18,000. Some 28 per cent of the troops involved were killed, wounded, or missing.

The Battle of Chickamauga cost Wisconsin dearly. The First Wisconsin, part of Brig. Gen. John C. Starkweather's brigade (he was a Milwaukeean, once colonel of the First Wisconsin), fought well until forced to retreat. Starkweather, wounded in the leg by a piece of shell, stayed with his troops until they retired to Chattanooga. The regiment had many casualties: thirty-four killed, seventy-nine wounded, plus some missing.

The Tenth Wisconsin did well on the first day at Chickamauga but badly on the second, when it was cut off and twelve officers and 111 men were captured.

The Fifteenth Wisconsin, a predominantly Scandinavian regiment originally raised and commanded by Col. Hans Christian Heg of Waterford, fared badly. During the first day's battle, an Illinois regiment mistook them for Confederate troops and fired on them. Placed between the galling fire of friend and foe, the regiment disintegrated into an "every man for himself" situation. The following day the regiment's commanding officer, Col. Ole Johnson, made a frantic attempt "to gather up" his scattered soldiers and reorganize the troops. Along with three-fourths of the army, the Fifteenth Wisconsin took part in next day's fight and subsequent retreat. Brave Col. Heg, commanding a brigade, "was shot through the bowels and died the next day." After the troops were safely ensconced within Chattanooga's defenses, Col. Johnson took roll call rather despairingly; his regiment was reduced to seventy-five men.

The Twenty-first Wisconsin also suffered at Chickamauga. During the first day's fight it recaptured the guns of an Indiana battery that had fallen into Confederate hands. But next day the regiment was caught up in the general retreat of Rosecrans' army and had the misfortune to be cut off by the enemy. As a result, Col. Hobart, about seventy men, and the regimental colors fell into enemy hands.

The Twenty-fourth Wisconsin, on the extreme right of Rosecrans' line, fought well on the first day; it held its position until nightfall, then fell back about 200 yards to a wooded area where it bivouacked for the night. Next day it held its own until the Union center gave way; it was then swept up in the disorganized retreat into Chattanooga.

The First Wisconsin Cavalry saw action on both days. On September 19 the regiment had an engagement with rebel cavalry four miles south of Crawfish Springs, driving the enemy back across Chickamauga Creek. On September 20 the unit was active on the extreme right of the Union line, withdrawing when Rosecrans' right and center gave way. Several days later the tired horse soldiers crossed the Tennessee River and set up camp along the north bank.

The three Wisconsin artillery units also took part in the fight and the retreat. The Fifth and Eighth Artillery escaped with few casualties and saved all their guns. But the Third Wisconsin Artillery unit was badly mauled by the enemy and ended up leaving five of their six guns on the field.

Too many of the Union dead and wounded were left behind during the disorganized withdrawal from the field. Many of the fatally wounded were not buried for months. In the confusion of a lost battle, strange and ironic events took place here and there, as illustrated by the adventures of a Wisconsin officer, Capt. Charles H. Ford, who could not keep up with his retreating company. He told his men to go ahead—he would follow. When safe within the confines of Chattanooga, he recorded his remarkable escape in his diary: "After resting a moment, I went on. It was now dark and I had done but a short distance when I heard rebels in front of me. I turned in another direction and found a friendly Rebel who told me where they [his troops] were and how to get out."

Dismayed by the turn of events, Gen. Rosecrans reported to Washington: "We have met with a serious disaster. . . . Enemy overwhelmed us, drove our right, pierced our center, and scattered them. Thomas, who had seven divisions, remained intact. . . . It seems that every available man was thrown against us." But Washington had little patience for his explanations and excuses; for Gen. Rosecrans, the war was all but over. He was relieved of command and sent to St. Louis. On October 20, 1863, command of the

A Wisconsin artillery unit encamped at Chattanooga in 1864, not long after the successful battles of November, 1863. Lookout Mountain is in the distance, at left. (X3)31660.

Army of the Cumberland passed to Gen. Thomas, "the Rock of Chickamauga."

Gen. Bragg, not wanting another bloody battle, decided upon a siege, hoping for the starvation and surrender of the Union army that had taken refuge within Chattanooga's fortifications. He deployed his army on the high ground along Missionary Ridge overlooking the city and placed a few brigades on Lookout Mountain. From these heights he could observe every move the Union forces made. But the Confederate government in Richmond made a mistake in sending Longstreet's corps back to Virginia and Gen. Simon B. Buckner's division on a wild-goose chase to Knoxville. Annoyed at this strategic bungling, Gen. Nathan Bedford Forrest took his crack cavalry elsewhere. Thus, although it occupied a commanding position, Bragg's army had been reduced to two corps—and in the meantime, reinforcements were being sent to the Union army.

In Washington, the War Department consolidated three military districts into one and put Ulysses S. Grant in overall charge. Aggressive as always, Grant planned to break the siege of Chattanooga by mounting an offensive against Bragg's encircling army. His plan was simple. Gen. Joseph Hooker's corps would assault the Confederate left on Lookout Mountain while Gen. Sherman's troops would attack the Confederate right. Anticipating that Bragg would draw troops from the center to repel the dual Union assaults, Grant would then strike the enemy's center with Gen. Thomas' 20,000 men.

Hooker's and Sherman's forces moved forward on the morning of November 24, 1863. After a brief engagement (the so-called "Battle Above the Clouds"), Hooker's men took Lookout Mountain and planted the Stars and Stripes on the highest point of the ridge. Bragg's three brigades put up only token resistance as they withdrew to Missionary Ridge. Sherman's corps, meanwhile, got halfway toward their objective and then, without good reason, paused for the night.

The next day, November 25, both Hooker and Sherman resumed their attacks against Bragg's left and right, respectively. About two o'clock in the afternoon, Thomas' troops assaulted the enemy's center, sweeping the Confederates from their rifle pits near the base of Missionary Ridge. Then, spontaneously, without orders, they continued furiously upward, toward the crest of the ridge. They clambered up the stony hillside in heroic fashion, seemingly unstoppable. Astonished, the Confederate defenders began to waver. Suddenly, as Hooker put pressure on the left and Sherman on the right, Bragg's center collapsed. As the Confederates withdrew in disorder, their captured field pieces were turned on them. Consternation gave way to flight, and then to utter rout. Bragg could not rally his army until it had fled into Georgia. That night Missionary Ridge blazed with Union campfires.

Six Wisconsin regiments of infantry and two batteries were part of Grant's victorious army. The First Wisconsin was part of a brigade held in reserve, but it took part in chasing the retreating Confederate troops. During the assault against the enemy's center, the Tenth Wisconsin acted as support for a Union battery. The Fifteenth Wisconsin was in the thick of the action. It helped to drive enemy forces out of the rifle pits in the Confederate center, and "with a yell and a cheer, started up the Ridge, drove the enemy back, [and] captured all his artillery and a great number of prisoners." Casualties were surprisingly light—only six wounded. The Eighteenth Wisconsin took part in the assault and the pursuit. Its casualties also were negligible. The Twenty-first Wisconsin, decimated in the battle of Chickamauga, saw no action; after the battle, and throughout the winter of 1863–1864, it manned an outpost atop Missionary Ridge.

The Twenty-fourth Wisconsin won a share of the glory by driving the enemy off the ridge. It faced heavy enemy fire while clambering up the steep, rocky slope, and some men fell wounded. Lt. Robert J. Chivas stopped on the way up to help a wounded comrade and then again moved forward "waving his sword and shouting encouragement to the others." Soon after, a bullet hit him in the chest. His men stepped over him as

they moved forward and upward. (Chivas recovered from his wound and related the incident in his diary.) Lt. Arthur McArthur, only eighteen years of age, seized the regimental flag from an exhausted color bearer and led the wild charge of the Twenty-fourth to the top of the ridge. His brave action earned him a Medal of Honor and gained him a commission as major—and not long afterward as lieutenant colonel. (He became known as "the boy colonel" and in later years was the father of Douglas MacArthur.) The Twenty-fourth Wisconsin sustained five killed and thirty wounded in its headlong assault.

The Twenty-sixth Wisconsin also was engaged "in the brilliant action at Mission Ridge, and, on the 26th [of November] joined in the pursuit of the enemy."

The battle had repercussions. The victory on the heights above Chattanooga in November, 1863, marked the beginning of the end for the

Young Arthur McArthur (1845–1912), winner of the Medal of Honor at Missionary Ridge. (X3)1799.

South. It opened the gateway to Atlanta and tightened the noose around the Confederate armies in the field. Grant's name made headlines again and Lincoln recalled him to Washington and assigned him overall command of the war. From that point on, the western army would experience only success, victory, and glory. The Wisconsin troops in both the eastern and western theaters would gain their fair share of all three.

⊰ *22* ⊱

More Regiments, More Heroics

IN ALL, Wisconsin furnished fifty-two regiments of infantry to the armies of the Union. (Actually, fifty-three different regiments were authorized, but the Fifty-third Wisconsin was only partially recruited when it was consolidated with the Fifty-first, and neither outfit saw action.) In addition to these fifty-two regiments of infantry, Wisconsin also furnished four regiments and one company of cavalry, twelve batteries of light artillery, one regiment of heavy artillery, one company of sharpshooters, and three brigade bands. Finally, the state contributed 133 men to the Navy and 165 to the United States Colored Troops, and was represented in various companies of scouts. In sum, Wisconsin furnished 91,379 men to the war: 79,934 volunteers, plus a total of 11,445 draftees and substitutes. The quota imposed on the state by the federal government was 90,116 men, so Wisconsin proved its patriotism by furnishing 1,263 men in excess of federal demands.

To be sure, some men may have been counted twice or even three times in that list of 91,379. The terms of enlistment varied, from three months to three years. If, for example, a man enlisted for a three-month term with the First Wisconsin Volunteer Infantry in April, 1861, and then reenlisted in the reorganized First Wisconsin for a three-year term in October, 1861, he was counted in the state records as two men. When the three-year term of the reorganized First Wisconsin ended in October, 1864, some of the veterans returned to action as members of still other regiments—so

Officers of the Twenty-first Wisconsin atop Lookout Mountain, Tennessee, early 1864. (X3)12221.

these few would have counted as three men in the statistics.

A Union regiment at full strength usually numbered around a thousand officers and men. (The authorized strength was a maximum of 1,025; the minimum, 845.) But 2,000 different men might have served in the ranks of a given regiment before the war was over. When a Wisconsin regiment lost men due to death or desertion, its depleted ranks were frequently restored to full strength by new recruits; many men therefore entered older regiments as replacements. Some regiments needed few replacements; others many. On balance, it seems reasonable to estimate that approximately 82,000 Wisconsin residents served in the war in one way or another—some for four days, others for four years.

Nearly every regiment from the First to the Fifty-second could point to some encounter or assignment which gave it special recognition. The three Wisconsin regiments which formed part of the Iron Brigade had a distinctive history which was well-preserved and has been told many times. Each of the remaining forty-nine regiments carried out its assignments as best it could, some covering themselves with glory in battle, others silently wasting away from disease and monotony far from the sound of the guns. It is not possible to relate separately each regiment's story. But several regiments received special recognition and won applause from the folks back home.

The Fourteenth, Sixteenth, and Seventeenth Wisconsin regiments performed heroically at Shiloh. The Fourteenth helped to capture a Confederate battery, and the Sixteenth and Seventeenth received their baptism of fire in that bloody encounter. Gen. Grant gave high praise to the Fourteenth for its gallantry. Those same three regiments also distinguished themselves at the Battle of Corinth on October 3–4, 1862. The brigade commander cited the Fourteenth as "the regiment to rely upon in every emergency; always cool, steady, and vigorous." The "Fighting Seventeenth" possessed a large number of Irish-Americans. At Corinth, the men of the Seventeenth led a bayonet charge with the Gaelic battle cry *Faugh a ballagh!* ("Clear the way!"). They earned the plaudits of the commanding general, who called it "the most glorious charge in the campaign."

The Fifteenth Wisconsin also claimed a special distinction. It was composed almost exclusively of Norwegians; 115 of its men were named Ole. Col. Hans C. Heg, who before the war was twice elected commissioner of the state prison, resigned that post to take command of the "Norwegian Regiment." The regiment took part in twenty-six engagements and came to be called "The Fighting Fifteenth." It won a citation "for bravery and coolness under fire" at Stones River; at Chickamauga it again exhibited "true courage" on the field where its old colonel gave his life. One of the regiment's many Oles—Ole C. Johnson—succeeded Col. Heg, and he led the Fifteenth throughout the Atlanta campaign.

The Eighteenth gained special recognition at Allatoona Pass in Georgia in October, 1864. There the Eighteenth was part of the force defending a vital Union supply depot and commanded by Gen. John M. Corse. A large Confederate force attacked the defenders and Gen. Sherman hustled to send reinforcements to aid the outmanned Union troops. Sherman sent word to Gen. Corse, begging him to hold his position. "I have lost an

Hans C. Heg (1829–1863), colonel of the Fifteenth Wisconsin. (X3)1336.

ear, part of a cheek and am wounded in one arm," replied colorful Gen. Corse, "but I will hold the Fort until Hades freezes over." Sherman's reinforcements arrived in time and the Confederates judiciously withdrew. Gen. Corse heaped praise on the Eighteenth for its part in defending the stores and the fort.

The adventures of Harrison C. Hobart helped bring publicity to the Twenty-first Wisconsin he commanded. This regiment took part in the battles of Perryville, Stones River, and Chickamauga in rapid order. At Chickamauga, when the enemy broke the center of the Union line, the Twenty-first was cut off and lost many of its men as prisoners of war. Col. Hobart was among those captured. He and some other officers were sent to the dreaded Libby Prison in Richmond, Virginia. There, on the night of February 9, 1864, a group of officers, Col. Hobart among them, organized the escape of 109 prisoners through a long tunnel they had made. Hobart, in charge of the exodus, was the last to crawl out and head for the woods. Confederates recaptured twenty-eight of the fugi-

Harrison C. Hobart (1815–1902), colonel of the Twenty-first Wisconsin. (X3)50392.

Col. Joseph Bailey (1826–1867), savior of a Union expedition on the Red River. (X3)21063.

tives, but Hobart was among the eighty-one who made good their escape.

Two Wisconsin regiments—the Twenty-third and the Twenty-ninth—played the major role in helping to save a federal gunboat fleet when it became entrapped on the Red River in central Louisiana in 1864. The two regiments were part of an army of 27,000 men which Gen. Nathaniel P. Banks led up the Red River Valley in the spring of 1864, supported by a fleet of gunboats and transports. But Gen. Banks encountered bad weather and suffered military reverses at Sabine Cross Roads and Pleasant Hill. He found the Red River as great an obstacle as the enemy. The treacherous nature of that "crooked, narrow, and turbid stream" and high banks which "furnished the most favorable positions for artillery and for the deadly sharp-shooter" prompted authorities to abandon the expedition. By the first of May, while the fleet was above the rapids at Alexandria, the water level fell, entrapping the gunboats and transports, some of which drew seven feet of water. Confederates on the banks rubbed their

hands in glee as they anticipated capturing a marooned Union fleet.

Col. Joseph Bailey of the Fourth Wisconsin Cavalry (once the Fourth Infantry) happened to be serving as an engineering officer with part of Banks's force. He devised a plan to free the stranded vessels. Reluctant superiors scorned Bailey's plan, but they acquiesced because no other suggestions were offered and the alternative was to abandon the fleet. Bailey asked for permission to assign the Twenty-third and the Twenty-ninth Wisconsin to work on his project, as well as some soldiers from Maine regiments. These were men who had worked in the pineries and knew how to handle an ax; some had ridden logs downriver in the spring drives.

Bailey proposed to build a log-based dam at a point where the river was 750 feet wide, raise the water level above the dam, and take the boats downriver by opening the dam. The loggers set to work, day and night, and within a week had dammed the river. Several vessels made it downriver on May 8 before part of the dam washed out. The resolute Bailey and his men then built two wing dams and on May 13 "washed" the remaining boats through the boiling chute to deeper water downriver. Although its ordeal was not entirely over, the fleet was spared from capture and destruction—and so was $2 million worth of federal property. Admiral David D. Porter, who commanded the naval component of Banks's army, frankly stated that his fleet owed its safety and escape to Col. Bailey's "indomitable perseverance and skill." The officers of Porter's fleet presented Bailey with a ceremonial sword and a loving cup. The Navy Department complimented Col. Bailey, and Congress voted him the nation's highest award: the Medal of Honor. Bailey, in turn, always gave special credit to the woodsmen of the Twenty-third and Twenty-ninth Wisconsin, who had done the hard and dangerous work that saved the fleet.

By contrast, the Thirtieth Wisconsin participated in no campaigns, saw no Confederate soldiers, and recorded no unusual experiences. In a way it typified the regiments which saw little actual action, but always begged for active duty. After the Sioux uprising of 1862, the War Department ordered the Thirtieth to proceed to Minnesota and eventually to Dakota Territory, where it did little more than perform guard duty and help quiet the nerves of the jittery settlers on the frontier. Several men died in the service, but from scurvy and Sioux arrows rather than Confederate bullets.

The Thirty-fourth Wisconsin had a similar history. It was composed of drafted nine-month men. It performed guard and garrison duty at Columbus, Kentucky. Thirty of its men gave their lives for the Union—but all were victims of disease, not enemy action.

In the summer of 1864, with his armies successful on every field, President Lincoln issued a special call for some 100-day troops. These special troops were supposed to relieve veteran regiments for battlefield duty while the Union made an all-out drive to end the war. Three Wisconsin regiments joined the army under this special call: the Thirty-ninth, Fortieth, and Forty-first. These 100-day recruits served garrison and guard duty—protecting railroads, convoying supplies, and keeping communication lines open. They were in Memphis when the Confederate cavalry of Gen. Nathan Bedford Forrest made a daring raid on the city (August 21, 1864). Although they won no laurels, each member of the three regiments received a special card of thanks from President Lincoln at the expiration of his 100-day term.

The war was about over when the men of the Fiftieth Wisconsin Infantry were sworn into federal service. Nevertheless, they remained in the army for almost a year. They were sent into Dakota Territory to intimidate the Sioux and to man the frontier forts. They saw many prairie dogs, few Indians, and no Confederates. Of the forty-three fatalities sustained by the regiment, only one was the result of combat. On September 16, 1865, Pvt. Theodore P. Putnam was killed—perhaps by an Indian—a full five months after the Civil War ended.

Wisconsin also furnished one company of sharpshooters, a specialized infantry unit. This company belonged to a federal regiment known as Berdan's Sharpshooters. In the fall of 1861 the War Department gave Col. Hiram Berdan of New York special permission to recruit a company of sharpshooters from each loyal state. W. P. Alexander, a noted marksman living in Beloit, recruited Company G for Col. Berdan. Alexander had specific instructions to accept only men who could, "when firing at rest, at *two hundred yards*, put *ten consecutive shots* in a target, the average distance not to exceed *five* inches from the center of the bull's eye." Alexander, serving as Captain of Company G, accompanied the recruits to Washington where they received their .52-caliber Sharps rifles and further instruction in riflery and combat. Alexander, being unable to take the field because of lameness, turned the captaincy over to Edward Drew (a New Yorker) and returned to Wisconsin for more recruits. By mid-November the company numbered 107. In March, 1862, Berdan's Sharpshooters—clad in dark green uniforms—became part of the Army of the Potomac. They played only a minor role in the Peninsular campaign, but Company G lost their captain at Gaines's Mill where the Wisconsin men were "among the last to cross the Chickahominy" during the retreat. Indeed, the Peninsular campaign took a heavier toll in Company G of the Sharpshooters than did any other battle—although Antietam, Gettysburg, and the Wilderness also were later to be inscribed upon the company's banner.

Friedrich Holdmann of the Second Wisconsin Cavalry—a far cry from the plumes and brass buttons of the pre-war militia! (X3)15263.

In addition to the fifty-two regiments of infantry and the company of sharpshooters, Wisconsin furnished four first-class regiments of cavalry. The First Wisconsin Cavalry served a couple of years in western Missouri and later saw service in Tennessee and Georgia. The regiment gained nationwide publicity for sharing in the capture of Jefferson Davis, the Confederate president, and his cabinet as they attempted to escape in the closing days of the war.

The Second Wisconsin Cavalry was organized and commanded by Cadwallader C. Washburn—in postwar years, governor of Wisconsin and a millionaire miller in Minneapolis. When the war broke out in 1861, Washburn had served three terms in Congress and was one of the best-known

Republicans in the state. But he was tired of debate and craved action. He found action aplenty as colonel of the Second Cavalry. His regiment served first in Missouri, then in Arkansas, where, during one expedition, it traveled 400 miles, losing not a man and returning with 150 prisoners. It later distinguished itself at Vicksburg, then in Louisiana and Texas.

The Third Wisconsin Cavalry had a less colorful record than Col. Washburn's regiment. It was commanded by ex-governor William A. Barstow and served in Missouri, Kansas, and Arkansas. It chased guerrillas, tangling a number of times with bushwhackers and Confederate raiders. The Fourth Cavalry, which had started its career as the Fourth Infantry, had a "dashing career" in

Louisiana and Texas. Col. Joseph Bailey, who saved the flotilla entrapped on the Red River, was a member of the Fourth Cavalry. This remarkable Wisconsin regiment served continuously from June 6, 1861, to June 16, 1866—longer than any other volunteer regiment in the war.

In addition to the infantrymen and the cavalrymen, Wisconsin furnished some soldiers to man both field pieces and heavy ordnance—meaning the cannons which did so much of the killing in the Civil War. Soon after First Bull Run, Company K of the Second Wisconsin Infantry was converted into a company of heavy artillery. During 1863 and 1864, eleven other companies of artillerymen were recruited in Wisconsin. These twelve companies constituted the state's only regiment of heavy artillery. In the main, this regiment served in the Army of the Potomac, although three of the companies were detached for a time to serve in the West and Southwest. In addition to the regiment of heavy artillery, Wisconsin contributed men for thirteen batteries of light artillery. Most of these batteries saw service in the western theater of war with Grant, Sherman, or Rosecrans.

For every nine persons living in Wisconsin, the state furnished a soldier—roughly 20 per cent of the entire male population, or one recruit for every two voters in the election of 1864. Of course, not all those who went to war were heroes; the desertion rate among Wisconsin troops was forty-three per thousand—nothing to be proud of, but lower than the desertion rate for the Union armies as a whole (sixty-two per thousand). And most Wisconsin troops showed they would fight; they suffered forty-two killed or dead of wounds per thousand, compared to thirty-five for the Union armies as a whole.

After reviewing the muster rolls of every Wisconsin regiment at war's end, the state's adjutant general reported in 1866 that 10,868 Wisconsin soldiers had died in the service of their country—about one of every seven who went into the service. Some were killed on the battlefield; many died lingering deaths from wounds suffered in combat. About twice as many died of disease as from combat, with malaria, typhoid fever, and dysentery taking the heaviest toll. (For example, of the last eight regiments Wisconsin sent to the war, 223 men died of disease, one in an accident, and only one in action.) A substantial number died as prisoners of war in Confederate hands; the single word "Andersonville" follows the name of many whom the records list as "Died of disease."

Union artillerymen, 1862, from Battles and Leaders of the Civil War.

Many of those who were wounded recovered—though frequently minus arms, legs, hands, or eyes. Lucius C. Fairchild, who lost an arm on the first day at Gettysburg, became the state's best-known amputee and also its first three-term governor.

Wisconsin residents could point with pride to the contribution they had made to winning the war. "No citizen of Wisconsin will ever have occasion to blush," wrote a historian in later years, "for what his state did in support of the general government in the great Civil War. No state in the Union, in proportion to population, made a better record."

⚘ 23 ⚘

Wisconsin's 353 Black Soldiers

THE RECORDS of Wisconsin's adjutant general show that 353 black men fought as Wisconsin soldiers in the Civil War. But at the very time these soldiers were marching and dying, they were still not regarded as citizens, for they did not have the right to vote in state elections. Indeed, there remained prominent citizens, principally Democrats, such as Edward G. Ryan and Peter V. Deuster, who wanted to pass laws excluding blacks from emigrating into the state. And since Wisconsin's black soldiers did not fight with state regiments, but instead belonged to separate units labeled United States Colored Troops, they have generally been ignored in books dealing with Wisconsin's role in the Civil War. This is irony, and more.

During the 1840's, the white population of Wisconsin Territory—soon to become the state of Wisconsin—increased ten-fold, from 30,749 in 1840 to 304,756 in 1850. In that same decade, the black population increased from 196 in 1840 to 635 in 1850. The following decade witnessed another increase in both whites and blacks. The white population (which, under federal census regulations, included Indians) increased to 774,710 by 1860; the black, to 1,171. This meant that, in 1860, blacks comprised less than one-fifth of 1 per cent of the state's total population. But during 1862 quite a number of new black residents moved into the state; they came from various "contraband camps," especially the one in Cairo, Illinois.

Wisconsin's blacks lived in a kind of no-man's land. They had to pay taxes if they owned property, and they could testify in the courts; but they could not vote in elections or join the state militia companies. Therefore they were not deemed "citizens." The views of many state residents were echoed by Deuster (himself an immigrant from Germany in 1847), editor of Milwaukee's German-language *See-Bote*, who said, "The North belongs to the free white man, not to the Negro."

Although blacks had fought in both the Revolutionary War and the War of 1812, neither state nor federal authorities would accept them as soldiers in 1861. Nor could black men serve in the state's militia, for they were excluded by a territorial enactment of 1836, and no subsequent laws had changed that measure.

After President Lincoln's call for 75,000 three-months' men on April 15, 1861, Gov. Alexander Randall called for organized militia companies to volunteer their services in order to meet the state's quota of one regiment: "All good citizens, everywhere, join in making common cause against a common enemy." This excluded blacks, for they did not have the status of citizens.

A Madison black man, William H. Noland, wrote to Governor Randall asking if he would accept "a company of colored men" for either state or federal service "on an equal footing with other soldiers." As Noland said, he wanted to disprove the popular supposition that blacks were neither brave nor loyal nor reliable. A portion of his letter read: "Notwithstanding they are deprived of the Election Franchize and many other Civil Rights they are not unmindful of the fact that they enjoy the protection of the laws in their persons and property, and that their Altars and firesides are held sacred, and to maintain a government guaranteeing these rights, and to defend it against such wicked attempts as the present, they would pledge their lives, their fortunes, and their sacred honor." The governor evidently ignored Noland's letter, for there is no record of a reply in Randall's correspondence.

In June of 1862, Congress authorized the president to employ blacks as laborers "or in whatever capacity they are competent" in the army. Until late in 1864, this congressional action served as the basis for raising black troops for the war.

*Peter D. Thomas of Oakfield (Fond du Lac County), who
soldiered with the Twenty-first Wisconsin Infantry.* (X3)21061.

However, many ablitionists strongly believed that
the war "was being waged for the black man, and
thus he should be a part of it." James R. Doolittle,
one of Wisconsin's two U.S. senators, stated that
since Southerners were already using blacks as
"soldiers" (principally as drovers in army transportation and for building fortifications), the
North should do likewise. The North, in good
conscience, Doolittle said, "should employ the
same class of persons to fight against the rebels
which they employ against us." Some Republican
newspapers like the Milwaukee *Sentinel* and the
Oshkosh *Northwestern* endorsed Doolittle's suggestion. "We shall soon find it not well to reject
even the assistance of blacks," the *Northwestern*
editorialized, "if we want to put down this rebellion."

On the other hand, Democratic leaders like Edward G. Ryan and "Pump" Carpenter of Madison's *Wisconsin Patriot* took a strong stand against
Doolittle's suggestion. Conscripting blacks, Car-

penter said, would make whites less likely to volunteer. It was, in Carpenter's view, "a cowardly
suggestion." Carpenter, however, did offer a way
to get rid of Sherman M. Booth, Wisconsin's best-
known abolitionist, who in 1859 had been charged
with seducing his fourteen-year-old babysitter.
After ridiculing Rhode Island's proposal "to raise a
Negro regiment," Carpenter sarcastically suggested that Booth go to that state to take command of that black regiment—"If the negroes do
not object."

Carpenter was not the only Democratic editor
to raise an objection to using blacks as "soldiers'
helpers." Flavius J. Mills of the *Sheboygan Journal* held the same views. So did the editor of the
West Bend Post, who said that using black troops
was "too great a humiliation upon white Americans by putting preservation of their institutions
in the hands of colored soldiers."

Nevertheless, some of Wisconsin's black residents doggedly continued to seek a way to aid in
the Union war effort. Cornelius Butler, a black
cook living in Kenosha, hoped to raise "a company or two" in the state and have them join
black companies in other states to make up an all-
black regiment or brigade. He expressed that hope
in a letter to Governor Salomon on July 29, 1862:
"I wish to lay before your excellency the hope and
desire of the colored men of this State to do something to aid the government at this time. If it shall
meet your approbation and receive the cooperation of the public authorities, we can raise a company perhaps two in the State to be joined to any
regiment of our race to fight the country." Although no evidence exists that the governor responded to Butler's letter, it appears it did at least
prompt Salomon to raise the issue with Secretary
of War Edwin M. Stanton in Washington. He
asked, in effect, whether Wisconsin should encourage the organization of black companies.
Since, at that time, President Lincoln had no plan
to arm blacks, Governor Salomon was told that
they were unacceptable as soldiers.

As the question of the use of black troops
rested in limbo, the Wisconsin legislature debated
two other related, though opposing, issues. One
would exclude the migration of more blacks into
Wisconsin. The other would give the suffrage to
the state's black residents. In the spring session of
the state legislature, Satterlee Clark, a state senator from Dodge County, introduced a resolution

that would deny blacks the right to come into Wisconsin after August 1, 1862. (Similar exclusionary laws existed in other midwestern states.) The bill came to a vote in the senate on June 10, 1862, and was defeated.

The issue of black suffrage dated back to the territorial days. When the constitution drafted in 1846 was presented to the state voters, a referendum proposing black suffrage also went before the electorate. It was rejected by 14,615 to 7,664. But that did not stop some Republican legislators from introducing black suffrage resolutions time and again. The issue came up once more in the legislature in 1862, and again it went down to defeat.

The question of black exclusion came up in the legislature once again in 1863. Peter V. Deuster, the Democratic editor who had been elected to the state assembly in the fall of 1862, introduced an exclusion resolution on January 28, 1863. The measure was endorsed by such Democratic editors as Mills of the Sheboygan *Journal*, Carpenter of the *Wisconsin Patriot*, and Jere Crowley of the Manitowoc *Pilot*. They pointed out that Illinois and Ohio had such exclusion laws and that a considerable number of blacks were coming to Wisconsin from "contraband camps." Deuster's bill went down to defeat by a narrow margin, but it continued to be an issue throughout the rest of the war.

On the national level, the issue of using black troops was finally resolved. Lincoln's Emancipation Proclamation of January 1, 1863, opened the door. One sentence of that famous document read: "And I further declare and make known that such persons [i.e. freed blacks] of suitable condition will be received into the armed service of the United States to garrison forts, positions, stations, and other places, and to man vessels of all sorts in said service." Several Union generals—James H. Lane, David Hunter, and Benjamin F. Butler—had already experimented with black troops in 1862. In January, 1863, the governor of Massachusetts received permission from Secretary of War Stanton to raise a black regiment and count it against the state's quota. (As the Fifty-fourth Massachusetts, the regiment became famous for its gallant assault on Fort Wagner, South Carolina, in July, 1863.) The same right was soon granted to other states. The Conscription Act of March 3, 1863, opened the door wider, because it did not exclude blacks from enrollment.

Finally, the president actually encouraged the recruitment of blacks for the Union army. The federal government established a Bureau of Colored Troops in May; only authorized individuals or agencies might recruit blacks for federal service. The Bureau of Colored Troops authorized Governor Salomon to enlist black troops on July 31, 1863. But he was slow in moving in that direction. Finally, in late October, state authorities announced plans for raising "colored troops" to form one or two companies.

Black troops credited to Wisconsin served in six different infantry regiments of the United States Colored Troops—the Fifth, Twelfth, Fourteenth, Twenty-first, Twenty-ninth, and Forty-ninth. (Company F of the Twenty-ninth U.S. Colored Troops was the only *unit* credited to Wisconsin.) In addition, a few blacks credited to Wisconsin served in the U.S. Navy, and four were part of the Twelfth United States Heavy Artillery.

William Bross, financial editor of the Chicago *Tribune*, gave support to the raising of a black regiment in which his younger brother John would be a lieutenant-colonel. John Bross received permission to recruit an all-black company in Wisconsin to help fill out his regiment; there would be white officers, of course, and those joining the all-black company would be credited toward Wisconsin's quota. Lewis Isbell, a black barber living in Chicago, became the company's chief recruiter, and his efforts received the endorsement of the Milwaukee *Sentinel*.

Company F was mustered into the Twenty-ninth United States Colored Troops for three years' service on July 8, 1864, in Quincy, Illinois. The regiment was promptly dispatched to Washington, then southward (and without adequate training) to join Gen. Grant's army, which was besieging the city of Petersburg, Virginia. When the troops arrived on July 22, Union "moles" were nearly finished digging tunnels under the largest rebel fort in Lee's formidable defense line. Four tons of black powder were placed in the underground galleries. All was in readiness for the mighty explosion, set for five o'clock on the morning of July 30. Grant massed four corps for the assault. The Ninth Corps (of which the Twenty-ninth U.S. Colored Troops comprised one small cog), commanded by Gen. Ambrose E. Burnside, would lead the assault into the breach in the Confederate defenses. The Seventeenth Corps would offer support for the Ninth Corps, while the Second Corps on the right and the Tenth

Black troops rushing forward into the maelstrom of "The Crater" at Petersburg,
from Battles and Leaders of the Civil War.

Corps on the left were expected to advance after the explosion.

Characteristically, Gen. Burnside fumbled his plans. At first he wanted his black troops (including the Twenty-ninth U.S. Colored) to lead the charge. He rationalized that these were fresh troops and that the battle-weary white troops had lost their edge. Furthermore, a successful assault by the blacks would vindicate the faith of those who believed that blacks made good soldiers. But other white officers argued that if blacks led the charge it would seem that they were being wantonly sacrificed. So Burnside altered his original plans, and there was some last-minute shuffling of regiments and brigades. Company F and the others making up the Twenty-ninth U.S. Colored Troops were relegated to a supporting role, and the Thirty-seventh and Thirty-eighth Wisconsin were among the troops assigned to lead the charge after the explosion of the mine.

Historian William D. Love, in his book *Wisconsin in the War of the Rebellion* (1866), described the scene that ensued: "At ten minutes before five o'clock, there was suddenly a tremor, then an earthquake rumbling and shaking, next a conical mountain upheaving from the earth and reaching toward the heavens, with streaks of lightning

flashes along its sides. An instant it hung in the air, filled with timbers, guns, cannons, men, and human limbs, and sank down in a mass of confusion. Three South Carolina regiments were . . . hurled to the dead. Then one hundred cannons from the Union lines poured in a thunderstorm of shot and shell such as history as seldom known."

The crater created by the explosion was more than 150 feet long, fifty wide, and twenty to thirty feet deep. As intended, it created an enormous breach in the Confederate line. But due to the drunkenness of one Union general and the incompetence of another, the Union troops delayed their assault by an hour, giving the rebels a chance to recover from their shock and consternation. By the time the attack came, the Confederates had ringed the crater with field guns and riflemen who raked the Union troops with a heavy fire. The crater was soon filled with a swarm of disorganized soldiers; they were, in effect, in a trap. There was no way for the reserve troops to pass through to assault enemy positions. Nevertheless, three divisions of the Ninth Corps made assaults, one after the other. The enemy rained death on them, and three times the Union troops fell back. Then a division of black troops, of which the Twenty-ninth U.S. Colored was a part, was sent forward to do what three others had failed to do. They too were repelled with heavy loss. By the time the attack was called off, Union losses approached 4,000 men. Gen. Grant, who had seen his share of bungled attacks, later termed the so-called Battle of the Crater the saddest he witnessed during the entire war. Company F of the Twenty-ninth paid its share of the bill; of its eighty-five men, eleven died in action.

Wisconsin, like other states, sent recruiters southward to sign up newly freed blacks or "contrabands" to be counted as state troops. This recruiting plan was not very successful, for Wisconsin offered no bounty to such recruits. (Some states offered as much as $500 to entice ex-slaves into the army.) Gov. James T. Lewis said that he did not like to send his recruiters to Gen. Sherman's army, which was then moving on Atlanta. "Our forces," Lewis said, "need all the darkies they can get to do work on fortifications." One recruiter, George Brockway, signed up eleven black recruits near Adairsville, Alabama. Shortly thereafter, Confederate cavalrymen captured the train on which Brockway and his recruits were traveling. The recruits promptly fled into the nearby woods, never to be seen again. All in all, Wisconsin's efforts to recruit blacks in the South had rather pitiful results.

In the end, 353 black men were officially credited to Wisconsin's roster of military service. Some argued that, by serving the state as soldiers, they had earned the right of suffrage; and in 1865, as the war was ending, the legislature finally passed a bill allowing black male residents of Wisconsin to vote. At the same time, efforts by legislators to introduce black exclusion laws also ended. This by no means spelled an end to racial bigotry and intolerance. But by war's end, black residents of the state of Wisconsin could at least claim the same rights, if not always the same privileges, as those long enjoyed by the white majority.

⊱ 24 ⊰

War Measures

IN JANUARY of 1864 Governor Edward Salomon, weary of the responsibilities which the war had placed upon his shoulders and dispirited because his party had thrown him overboard, turned the governorship over to his successor. Members of the "Madison Regency," which had prevented Salomon's nomination by means of back-room maneuvers, praised Salomon in public for his contributions to "good government." In private, Boss Keyes suggested that Salomon be given "a first class clerkship" in Washington because he was "terribly down on the regency."

However, Keyes's friend Horace Rublee of the *Wisconsin State Journal* wrote a kind valedictory, praising Salomon's war work and thanking him for the soldier-voting law, which had paid the Republican party handsome dividends. When he bowed out, Salomon returned to Milwaukee to practice law. Hurt and disenchanted, he soon thereafter deserted Milwaukee for New York City, where he practiced law for many years, trying to forget how Wisconsin's Republicans had mistreated him. Because of his wife's ill health, he decided in 1894 to return to Germany, where he survived until 1909.

James T. Lewis succeeded Salomon in the governor's chair. He proved to be a popular politician, for he had passed a long and successful apprenticeship in the workshop of politics. The editor of the *Wisconsin State Journal* praised Lewis to the skies, boasting that "there is not a blot or blemish upon him." Lewis wore well with those who knew him. When running for secretary of state, he received every single vote cast in his home town of Columbus. He possessed the quality of gaining the confidence of everyone who came to plead a cause; he was a good listener and bent a sympathetic ear to every visitor. Yet he could be firm if need be and he often steered an independent course. He was financially well-to-do, so he was not dependent upon favors or promises.

Some Democrats believed that Lewis was a political opportunist. Before the war he had been a professed Democrat. When the political winds shifted, he reset his sails. Some Democrats pointed to his record as a land speculator. When Lewis first came to Columbus in 1854 to practice law and seek his fortune, he invested heavily in land. As the tide of settlement pushed back the frontier and land prices rose, Lewis disposed of his vast holdings at tremendous profits. Perhaps his success in business prompted him to desert the Democrats and join the new party dominated by ex-Whigs. Republicans contended that Lewis was too perceptive, too prosperous, and too popular to re-main a Democrat. At any rate, Republicans pre-sented him with bait and he seized the chance to become secretary of state—a largely meaningless post but one which frequently held the promise of higher office. Two years later, he moved up to the governorship. Republican strategists, of course, recognized that Lewis was an eleventh-hour con-vert, but they needed his help. Their pact pro-duced mutual benefits.

After taking his oath of office in January of 1864, Governor Lewis set to work with zest. It was his duty to help to keep the stream of Wis-consin soldiers flowing toward the battlefronts. Gen. Grant's bloody battles before Richmond used up troops in a hurry, and Gen. Sherman's re-lentless campaign through the Deep South was likewise putting pressure upon the recruiting ser-vice. Throughout the year, President Lincoln is-sued a succession of calls for more troops: on Feb-ruary 1, for 500,000; March 14, for 200,000; July 18, for 500,000; and December 19, for 300,000—a total of 1.5 million new recruits for the armies of the Union. So Governor Lewis was busy re-plenishing old regiments and raising new ones. Al-though the federal government had taken over the odium of managing the machinery of the draft, state officials still had much to do. They tried to encourage volunteering, appointed the regimental officers, and maintained a favorable climate in which conscription could function.

Governor Lewis' name was associated with the organization of eighteen Wisconsin infantry regi-ments—from the Thirty-fifth to the Fifty-third. The Thirty-fifth was half filled at the time Lewis took office; regimental organization was com-pleted on February 27, 1864. It was hurried out of the state and shipped down to New Orleans. When the Thirty-sixth and the Thirty-seventh were projected, the quotas were filled in thirty days. The Thirty-seventh and the Thirty-eighth followed in rapid order —the men were mustered in and the regiments were soon on their way to the front.

In the spring of 1864, Governor Lewis joined the governors of Illinois, Iowa, and Indiana in urging President Lincoln to raise a large force of short-term volunteers to strike a prompt and deci-sive blow to end the rebellion. The four governors suggested that "the North-western States" raise a force of volunteers to serve for 100 days. These green troops would garrison towns in the backwa-ters of the war, maintaining order and guarding transportation and communications. The result would be to free up experienced and battle-tested troops for the final campaigns against the Confed-eracy.

President Lincoln reacted favorably to the gov-ernors' suggestion. In the ensuing call for 100-day troops, the War Department assigned Wisconsin a quota of three regiments. However, although Lewis had assured Lincoln that Wisconsin could readily furnish 5,000 "hundred-day troops" within thirty days, the governor had trouble rais-ing even three regiments. The last of the three reg-iments of the 100-day troops left the state with its ranks but little more than half full. In June, 1864, the War Department ordered these three regi-ments—the Thirty-ninth, the Fortieth, and the Forty-first—to Memphis, Tennessee.

Under President Lincoln's call of July 18 for 500,000 men, Wisconsin raised and sent nine more regiments to the field—from the Forty-second to the Fifty-first. The last of these nine was not at full strength, but it was shipped off to St. Louis nonetheless. In the closing months of the war, Adjutant Gen. Gaylord recruited for the state's last two regiments, the Fifty-second and the Fifty-third. Only five companies of the Fifty-second were fully recruited, and they were ordered to St. Louis com-pany by company. The Fifty-third had a short life; only four companies were organized when the War Department requested the discharge of all unmustered recruits. The four companies of the Fifty-third were dispatched to Kansas, where they were transferred to the Fifty-first Wisconsin. None of these regiments played much of a role in the war.

In addition to raising eighteen infantry regi-ments during Governor Lewis' administration, the state furnished twelve companies for the First Wis-consin Heavy Artillery. The state also received credit for raising a company of soldiers for the Twenty-ninth United States Colored Troops. Counting the recruits sent to replenish the depleted ranks of the veteran regiments and the 6,000 veter-ans who reenlisted, Wisconsin raised a total of 38,618 troops from January 4, 1864, to April 30, 1865. Governor Lewis was justly proud of the troop-raising record of his administration. In his second annual message he noted: "Amid the gloom which has surrounded the nation, our noble State

Officers of the Forty-third Wisconsin, 1865. Col. Amasa Cobb is seated third from left.
(X3)12680.

has never faltered. She has always and promptly responded to the call of the Gen. Government."

On the other hand, those who administered federal conscription in Wisconsin may not have agreed that Wisconsin had set such a fine example. The draft, in practice, produced few soldiers. Threat of the draft, however, may have prompted many to volunteer and get the bounties offered. On December 31, 1864, Adjutant Gen. Gaylord reported that of the 17,537 drafted in the state, only 3,439 were actually mustered into service—about one in four. The state adjutant general noted that 6,724 of those drafted received discharge—that is, they failed to qualify as soldiers—and another 7,367 men failed even to report. (Four other men avoided service by paying commutation money.) Small wonder that critics of the Lincoln administration contended that the draft was a miserable failure.

Nor would Secretary of War Stanton have been ready to compliment Wisconsin for prompt and cooperative action in furnishing its quotas. Gover-

nor Salomon and the Secretary had argued stubbornly about quotas and credits, and Governor Lewis took up where Salomon left off. Believing that the quotas assigned to Wisconsin were out of line with the state's population and that promised quota adjustments had not been made, Lewis took prompt action by dispatching the state adjutant general to Washington to obtain a "correction." Ultimately his persistence and inflexibility paid dividends, for the Wisconsin quota was reduced by 10,683.

In addition to assisting in the raising of troops, Governor Lewis worked hard at being "the soldiers' friend" and "the good Samaritan." He visited many Wisconsin soldiers in field hospitals and army camps. In 1864 he secured the establishment of two more federal hospitals in Wisconsin: one in Milwaukee and the other in Prairie du Chien. Then he took a long and exhausting trip to Washington, coastal Virginia, Mobile, and New Orleans. He wanted Wisconsin soldiers transferred from hospitals in the war zone to "home hospitals" in Madison, Milwaukee, and Prairie du Chien, believing, as he said, that these convalescents would get better care and would recover more rapidly in the state's "bracing and invigorating atmosphere."

In the wake of several major battles, Governor Lewis hurried to the battlefield area to supervise the distribution of military supplies and the delicacies contributed by the folks back home. He kept close tab on the state commissioners appointed to look after the welfare of Wisconsin regiments in the field. He was anxious to let the soldiers know how deeply the state appreciated their service and sacrifice.

Governor Lewis also took an active interest in the Gettysburg battlefield-cemetery project. That project, a cooperative venture of states whose soldiers had fought and died there, took shape shortly after the battle ended. When the cemetery was dedicated on November 19, 1863, Wisconsin had a large delegation in attendance.

Governor Lewis also recommended that an appropriate monument be erected in the state capital to honor the war dead—"the noble heroes of Wisconsin who have fallen in defense of the liberties of the Nation." He recommended the establishment of homes for soldiers' orphans and for disabled veterans. Subsequently, the Soldiers' Orphan's Home was built in Madison and the Harvey Hospital was enlarged. Governor Lewis, through his many humanitarian activities and welfare proposals, earned the appellation "the soldiers' friend."

In February, 1865, the governor submitted the proposed Thirteenth Amendment (which freed the Confederacy's slaves) to the Wisconsin legislature for its ratification. That amendment had earlier received the necessary two-thirds vote in both houses of Congress. Governor Lewis urged the legislature to take swift and favorable action. He wanted Wisconsin to be one of the first states to ratify the amendment which promised liberty and freedom for all. In part, his message to the legislature read: "Upon its adoption hangs the destiny of nearly four millions of human beings, and it may be, the destiny of the nation. I trust, and doubt not, the Legislature of Wisconsin will record its decision firmly, and I hope unanimously, in favor of the amendment. Let us wipe from our escutcheon the foul blot of human slavery, and show by our action that we are worthy of the name of free-men."

The legislature heeded the governor's advice and promptly approved passage of the Thirteenth Amendment to the Constitution of the United States.

25

From the Wilderness to Petersburg

FOLLOWING GEN. GRANT'S victory at Chattanooga and the conclusion of his campaign in Tennessee, President Lincoln recalled him to Washington and put him in charge of all military operations. As Lincoln said, whatever Grant's faults, "He fights." Congress cooperated by creating the commission of lieutenant-general (four stars) so Grant would outrank all other generals. Grant, in turn, put Gen. Sherman in charge of operations in the West and brought Gen. Phil Sheridan with him to take charge of cavalry operations in the East. Although Gen. Meade, the victor of Gettysburg, remained as commander of the Army of the Potomac, Grant made his headquarters with that army and actually ran the show.

Early in May, 1864, Grant's army of about 120,000 crossed the Rapidan River in northern Virginia as the start of its campaign against Richmond. It was basically an all-eastern army with a limited number of western regiments involved in the opening phase of the year-long campaign. In this major campaign, which was supposed to end the war in the East, Grant was opposed by Robert E. Lee and the Army of Northern Virginia, numbering about 62,000. The two armies fought four major battles in the months that followed: the Wilderness, May 5–7; Spotsylvania, May 8–12; Cold Harbor, June 3; and the prolonged siege campaign against Petersburg, which extended into the following year.

Only four Wisconsin regiments of infantry were with Meade's Army of the Potomac when it was reviewed by Grant and his staff in April of 1864. Three of the four were part of the Iron Brigade—the Second, Sixth, and Seventh Wisconsin. Rufus Dawes had charge of the Sixth on the day of the review. A dreary and incessant rain dampened spirits, but the Wisconsin boys were anxious to see their new commander, who like them was a westerner. Col. Dawes noticed that each regiment gave Grant a cheer as he rode past but that Grant made no discernible response to the ovations. Somewhat disrespectfully, Dawes said, "As Grant does not seem to think our cheering worth notice, I will not call for cheers. Maintain your position as soldiers." So the Sixth Wisconsin stood silently at attention as Grant reviewed the men and the color-bearer dipped the regimental flag. Grant, who well knew the reputation of the Iron Brigade, thereupon took off his hat and bowed to the men of the Sixth. The men appreciated the general's tribute. As one perceptive private blurted out afterward, "Grant wants men, not yawpers."

The Iron Brigade, decimated at Gettysburg and reduced to about 600 men (of the 5,000 originally enlisted in the five regiments), lost its all-western characteristic when the 167th Pennsylvania was added as a sixth regiment. The 800 members of the 167th Pennsylvania were nine-month men (also some draftees) and soon claimed that their term of enlistment was up. Of course they were scorned by the proud veterans who pointed with pride to the names of battles inscribed on their regimental banner. When the Pennsylvanians were sent home, their place in the Iron Brigade was taken by four companies of the First New York Sharpshooters and the Seventh Indiana.

Grant's campaign against Richmond was supposed to be a two-pronged affair. Gen. Benjamin Butler with an army of 40,000 men (including the Nineteenth Wisconsin) was instructed to move against Richmond via the James River and the Peninsula while Grant and the Army of the Potomac attacked from the north. Butler botched his part of the dual movement, getting himself "bottled up" in the swamps that interlaced the area. One Wisconsin soldier in Butler's army had a strange story to relate. Col. Rollin M. Strong, away from camp one foggy evening, was taken prisoner by four rebels belonging to a Tennessee regiment. But the Tennesseeans, confused as to directions in the thick fog, did not know in which direction to go with their prisoner. Col. Strong, offering his services as guide, led the unwary rebels to where his own regiment was encamped. He then shouted "Attention!" and his men claimed four more prisoners. Was this not a mean Yankee trick?

Grant's army, meanwhile, crossed into an area

Col. Rollin M. Strong of the Nineteenth Wisconsin. (X3)12873.

known as the Wilderness for its thick underbrush, scraggly pines, and meager roads. The heavy woods in this rugged area virtually neutralized Grant's artillery, and the Confederate forces, under Lee's astute leadership, made the most of it. As a part of Gen. James Wadsworth's division, the Iron Brigade reached Old Wilderness Tavern at dusk on May 4. The next day the division moved in a westerly direction, entered the woods, and encountered an entrenched enemy. Wadsworth's division was soon engaged in a furious fight. Edging their way forward through the scrub pine and heavy underbrush, Wadsworth's troops drove back the enemy until, in turn, the rebel lines were reinforced. The Union troops then retreated. Corporal George A. Smith of the Second Wisconsin brought back the colors of the Forty-eighth Virginia, which he had captured during the initial assault.

Wadsworth's division fell back to its original position, reformed, and then went to assist the II Corps, engaged on the left. The men lay on their arms during the night. The battle resumed next morning, and Wadsworth's division took part in a grand charge against fortified rebel troops. "The 7th Wisconsin," wrote historian Edwin B. Quiner in his famous military history, "was the only regiment that succeeded in holding, for a short time, the enemy's first line of breastworks." But a Confederate counterattack forced Wadsworth's division, including the regiments of the Iron Brigade, to fall back. Doggedly, the division assaulted the enemy line twice more. Gen. Wadsworth was struck by an enemy bullet and killed. Lysander Cutler, once the colonel of the Sixth Wisconsin, took over command of the division. Once again, Grant had attacked fortified positions—and once again his army paid a heavy price in the Wilderness. The three Wisconsin regiments of the Iron Brigade counted their losses with heavy hearts.

The Fifth Wisconsin, under Col. Theodore B. Catlin, took part in the later phases of the battle as part of the VI Corps. In the early fighting on May 5, the right wing of Grant's army found the enemy's left exposed and companies D and G of the Fifth Wisconsin attacked and captured nearly the entire Twenty-fifth Virginia, including the regimental colors. Hot and heavy fighting resumed the next day in front of the VI Corps, but a reinforced enemy again repulsed the Union attackers. The Fifth Wisconsin's losses were heavy: 142 killed or wounded. Grant's army sustained 17,000 casualties in the Battle of the Wilderness; Lee's, approximately 7,700.

Grant, undeterred by his losses and aggressive as ever, moved his army southward and leftward to the vicinity of Spotsylvania Court House, hoping to turn Lee's right and get between the Confederate army and Richmond. But Lee reacted swiftly, and his army was entrenched when Grant began his next general advance. For five days Grant hammered the Confederate position at Spotsylvania in a series of bloody attacks which bent but did not quite break the enemy's lines. The Iron Brigade participated in the battle, and its Wisconsin regiments again suffered heavy casualties. On May 11 the three regiments were engaged in heavy skirmishing, and Confederate artillery made life miserable and occasionally caused casualties. Since the Second Wisconsin was by then reduced to less than 100 effectives, it was detailed as provost guard of another division in the V Corps, thus ending its connection with the Iron Brigade.

The Fifth Wisconsin advanced to the vicinity of

Spotsylvania Court House on May 8 and fought in rifle pits all that afternoon as well as the next two days. On the evening of May 10 the regiment attacked and captured an enemy battery; but its success was not supported and it was "compelled to fall back under a flank attack, the regiment losing heavily." One member of the Fifth, Alvah Burgess, had a rather unique experience. While trying to capture an enemy flag, he was taken prisoner and ordered to lie down in a ditch. Striking up a friendly conversation with the rebels, he soon learned that their food supplies had been inadequate. Pvt. Burgess suggested that his captors would have good food and good care if they would walk into the Union lines. He offered to guide them there. Surprisingly, they accepted his suggestion, and he conducted his willing-to-be-prisoners back to his old company, where his former captors surrendered.

Spotsylvania was at best a drawn battle; Grant had once again sustained heavy losses without defeating Lee's army. But Grant did not withdraw. On May 11 he cabled Washington that he proposed "to fight it out on this line if it takes all summer." He then moved his army to the left again, seeking a way around Lee's flank. The engagement that followed became known as Cold Harbor (June 3, 1864).

The Iron Brigade was involved in a week of skirmishing before taking an entrenched position in the woods near Bethesda Church, but a short distance from the reformed lines of Lee's army. Here the Sixth and Seventh Wisconsin regiments remained during the Battle of Cold Harbor, exposed to occasional fire of artillery and musketry. In the campaign dating from May 5 to June 10, the three Wisconsin regiments of the Iron Brigade lost heavily: the Second Wisconsin reported ten killed and seventy-three wounded; the Sixth, forty-three killed and 110 wounded; and the Seventh, which suffered the most, ninety-two killed and 184 wounded.

The Fifth Wisconsin arrived in the Cold Harbor area about June 1. The men were fatigued and short on clothing and other supplies. Nevertheless, they were promptly thrown into the fray, and performed admirably. Elsewhere, however, Grant's army fared badly. As in so many earlier battles of the war, the army which occupied strong, deeply entrenched positions enjoyed a distinct advantage over an opponent who repeatedly attacked across open ground. For the third time in a little more than a month, Lee's outnumbered forces bested the Army of the Potomac.

Three additional Wisconsin regiments—the Thirty-sixth, Thirty-seventh, and Thirty-eighth—joined Grant's army as reinforcements to replace the casualties. The Thirty-sixth, organized at Camp Randall in late March of 1864, was commanded by Frank A. Haskell, chronicler and one of the heroes of Gettysburg. The regiment left the state for Washington on May 10 and was then sent to join Grant's army, being assigned to the 1st Brigade of Gibbon's Division of II Corps. On June 1 it saw its first fierce action, four companies leading an attack across an open field against the entrenched Confederates. More than half of the 240 that attacked were killed, wounded, or captured. It was a less than pleasant start for Haskell's green regiment. Two days later, the Thirty-sixth Wisconsin took part in an ill-advised "grand assault" which lasted no more than a quarter-hour. It proved one of the worst debacles of the war. In that brief time, Grant lost 7,000 men, including Col. Haskell, who was killed leading his regiment. By June 12, when the fighting sputtered out around Cold Harbor, the Thirty-sixth Wisconsin had lost sixty-four killed and 126 wounded.

Only six companies of the Thirty-eighth Wisconsin were sworn into service in Madison in late April of 1864. The six companies were shipped off to Washington and then southward to Grant's army. They reached the Cold Harbor area on June 11 and were immediately assigned to the first brigade of Wilcox's Division of IX Corps. Their first chore was to guard prisoners and partake in picketing, and they saw little action in the pitched battle.

Breaking off his futile attack at Cold Harbor, Grant moved to his left once more, crossing the James River on transports and across the longest pontoon bridge ever built. When his army came to the Petersburg area, he annexed Gen. Butler's army to his own. Petersburg, a vital road and rail hub twenty-three miles south of Richmond with a population of 20,000, now became Grant's target. The enlarged Army of the Potomac missed a chance to defeat the Confederate defenders, commanded by Gen. P.G.T. Beauregard, before Lee was able to shift his army from the Cold Harbor area to Petersburg. The pugnacious Grant lost nearly 12,000 men in four days of futile assaults

against an entrenched enemy before settling into a siege which extended into the spring of 1865 and in many respects foreshadowed the deadly, static trench warfare of World War I.

Eight Wisconsin regiments took part in Grant's ten-month campaign against Petersburg. The Second Wisconsin, serving as provost guard to a division, disintegrated when the term of the famous infantry regiment expired. Most of the veterans, feeling that they had done their share, returned to Wisconsin; the remainder were incorporated into an independent battalion which was eventually melded into the Sixth Wisconsin on November 30, 1864.

The Sixth Wisconsin, weary and worn out from its long service, took part in Grant's general movement from Cold Harbor to Petersburg. "The almost continual fighting since spring, and so many defeats and disappointments had a depressing effect on the hilarity of our fellows," wrote Pvt. James P. "Mickey" Sullivan, "and we trudged almost in silence." The regiment took part in half a dozen bloody encounters, including Hatcher's Run, Weldon Railroad, and Dabney's Mills (February, 1865), where the regiment lost eight officers and 136 enlisted men out of nine officers and 180 men who went into battle. Joseph McCoy of Valley (Vernon County) was one of the casualties. Wounded severely in the leg, he was being carried off the field when a cannonball flew between the two stretcher-bearers and decapitated him. He left behind a wife as well as a son whom he never saw.

Afterward the Sixth Wisconsin took part in some severe skirmishing prior to the battle of Five Forks in early April. It claimed a part in the pursuit of Lee following the fall of Petersburg and celebrated his surrender at Appomattox Court House on April 9, 1865. After taking part in the grand review in Washington at war's end, the Sixth Wisconsin was mustered out on July 14, 1865. "Its history," one writer stated, "forms one of the brightest pages in our national records." Its losses in the entire war totaled 308: 163 men were killed in action, seventy-three died of wounds, eighty-nine of disease, and three in accidents.

The Seventh Wisconsin fought in the same brigade and division as the Sixth, so it took part in the same battles. Then, on March 5, 1865, the decimated Seventh became part of the 1st Provisional Brigade, a unit which took part in the hottest part of the Battle of Five Forks and engaged in the final pursuit that preceded Lee's surrender. The Seventh was mustered out on July 2, 1865, and headed for Madison where the men were paid off and the regiment was disbanded. The Seventh Wisconsin, too, had its claim to fame: no Wisconsin regiment involved in the Civil War had sustained higher casualties. It suffered 179 killed in action, ninety-nine dead of wounds, and another 130 of disease.

The "Old Fifth" was mustered out of service in late September of 1864 when the enlistment terms of the veterans expired, but it was reorganized with the help of Gov. Lewis. Its seven companies left for Washington on October 2 and joined a battalion in Winchester. Its new colonel was Thomas S. Allen of Dodgeville, a veteran; its first assignment was in Alexandria; then it joined Grant's army in the trenches around Petersburg on December 4. The regiment saw action at Dabney's Mills and participated in Grant's general attack of March 25, 1865. After Lee evacuated Petersburg and withdrew westward, the Fifth Wisconsin joined in the chase, getting its fingers badly burned at Sayler's Creek on April 7. The pursuit of Lee continued to Appomattox. The so-called "Fighting Fifth" was mustered out in Madison on June 16. Col. Allen was breveted a brigadier for "gallant and meritorious service." The casualties of the Fifth Wisconsin, old and new, totaled 308: 116 men were killed in action, sixty-four died of wounds, and 125 died of disease. Desertions numbered 105.

The Nineteenth Wisconsin, which had been part of Ben Butler's army until it was fused with Grant's, saw some action during the siege of Petersburg. On February 6–7, 1865, the regiment fought the rebels for two days at Dabney's Mills, where it suffered heavy casualties. The Nineteenth then took part in the pursuit of Lee's army after he abandoned Petersburg. Of the regiment's 156 total casualties, 112 were attributable to disease.

Most members of the Seventeenth Wisconsin took part in the grand review when Grant's and Sherman's armies marched down Pennsylvania Avenue. George W. Fosmot of the Baraboo area was one who could not take part in the memorable march. He was recovering in a hospital in Lookout Point, Maryland. He had enlisted on February 22, 1862, exactly fifteen years and two months in age. He recovered and, after returning

to Wisconsin, became a fixture at the regiment's reunions, where tales of bravery and the death of friends were favorite topics.

The Thirty-sixth Wisconsin took part in the general movement of Grant's army when it tramped from Cold Harbor to the Petersburg battlefield on June 14, 1864. Four days later it was part of a general attack against a portion of Lee's line. Col. John A. Savage bravely led his troops into a breach in the rebel works. Ahead of his troops and the regimental colors, he scaled the enemy breastworks shouting, "Three cheers for the honor of Wisconsin! Forward my brave men!" Seconds later he was dead, felled by an enemy bullet. Without adequate support, the regiment retired under cover of night. On June 22, during another engagement, nearly half the brigade was captured by the enemy, the Thirty-sixth Wisconsin escaping by a narrow margin. On August 25, at Reams's Station on the Weldon railroad, the regiment was again entrapped by the enemy; and this time, only forty-five men and three officers escaped of the 175 men and eleven officers who went into the fight. With depleted ranks, the regiment was again involved in Dabney's Mills on February 6 and at Hatcher's Run on March 29, 1865. After the fall of Petersburg the Thirty-sixth Wisconsin was involved in the pursuit of Lee's army. At war's end a few weeks later, the regiment counted its blessings—and its losses. The Thirty-sixth had suffered 296 casualties in all, with seventy-nine men killed in battle, fifty-three dead of wounds, and another 164 of disease.

The Thirty-seventh Wisconsin took part in Grant's movement across the James River to a position in front of Petersburg. It was in action here and there, but was best known for its role in the Battle of the Crater (July 30, 1864). The Thirty-seventh was one of the lead regiments that dashed forward into the breached enemy line following the explosion of the massive underground mine. But the Federal assault turned into a disaster, and the huge crater proved a death trap for the attackers, including many members of Company K, which included quite a number of Menominee Indians in its ranks. Among the dead were Corp. Semour Hahpahtonwahiquette and Pvts. Meshell Kenosha, Joseph Nahwahquah, Dominekee Jeco, Felix Wahtahnotte, and Amable Nashahahappah. The wounded included Jerome Katapah, Meshell

Shaborwahshaka, Meshell Mamaquette, and Jacob Pequachewahnahno. After the Crater fiasco, which accomplished nothing, the regiment was relieved of front-line duty and set to building fortifications during the rest of the year. It was back in action in March of 1865, losing thirty men in the assault on Fort Mahone at Petersburg. After Lee's surrender, the Thirty-seventh Wisconsin took part in the grand review in Washington and then returned to Wisconsin to be mustered out. It recorded 223 casualties: ninety-eight killed in action, forty-six wounded, and seventy-eight fatalities from disease.

Col. James Bintliff of Monroe began the organization of the Thirty-eighth Wisconsin in March of 1864. But the government discontinued the payment of bounties and Col. Bintliff was only able to organize four companies (A, B, C, and D), most of whose members were recruits from other companies. The four companies were sent to

Capt. James Bintliff (1824–1901) served with both the Twenty-second and Thirty-eighth Wisconsin regiments.
(X3)39230.

Washington on May 3 while Col. Bintliff remained in the state to recruit other companies, under Lincoln's call of July, 1864. Company E was organized in July and sent onward to join the other five companies somewhat later, arriving near Petersburg on October 1.

When the first four companies of the Thirty-eighth Wisconsin arrived in Virginia, they were organized as a battalion and assigned to forwarding supplies to Grant's army. Then came a stint of trench-digging and picket duty. The first fight for the battalion took place along the Norfolk and Petersburg Railroad; casualties were heavy, totaling fifty. Company E arrived just four days before the five companies of the Thirty-eighth led the charge into the Crater, where Capt. Newton E. Ferris fell at the head of his troops. The brigade of which the five companies were a part remained in the Crater for almost twelve hours before they retired. They lost seven dead, thirteen wounded, and nine missing.

After the other five companies arrived on October 1, 1864, the Thirty-eighth Wisconsin was finally at full strength. The newly reorganized regiment participated in an encounter at Hatcher's Run (October 27) and in Grant's attack against Fort Mahone (April 2, 1865). The regiment suffered heavily in the attack on the fort, but several days later, pursuing Lee's army, captured quite a few prisoners. The Thirty-eighth Wisconsin was one of the lead regiments in the grand review of the Army of the Potomac down Pennsylvania Avenue. During the trial of Lincoln's assassins, the regiment was on duty at the arsenal where the trial was held. On July 26 it was mustered out of service and entrained for Madison. Its casualties totaled 108, including thirty-one killed in action and twenty-five dead of wounds.

Overall, the eight Wisconsin regiments that fought with the victorious Army of the Potomac in the final campaign of the war proved that Wisconsin men made good soldiers. Their losses were heavy because, in Grant's grinding war of attrition, they constantly attacked entrenched rebels. Finally, it is worth noting that, in the Battle of the Crater at Petersburg, Wisconsin's black troops (represented by Company F of the Twenty-ninth U.S. Colored Troops) and Wisconsin Indians (Company K of the Thirty-seventh Wisconsin) paid a heavy price for their part in a white man's war.

26

From Atlanta to the Carolinas

THE ATLANTA CAMPAIGN of 1864, it has been said, "stabbed the Confederacy in the heart." When Gen. Grant was called to Washington early in 1864 to take overall charge of the war, he put his trusted subordinate, Gen. William Tecumseh Sherman, in charge of the western theater. He ordered him to strike at Atlanta, the capital of Georgia and key to the Confederate heartland. Grant's orders were "to get into the interior of the enemy's country as far as you can, inflicting all the damage you can against their war resources. . . ." Sherman's army of about 100,000 veteran troops had triumphed over adversity in Tennessee and were now beginning to scent victory. Opposing him was a Confederate army of about 65,000 men led by Lt. Gen. Joseph E. Johnston, a master of defensive strategy.

The Atlanta campaign began on May 7, 1864. It quickly became a cat-and-mouse game. Flanking movement followed flanking movement as Sherman's larger army edged southward from Chattanooga. Every time Sherman thought he had an advantage, the wily Confederate general withdrew to new lines of fortifications. Once Sherman remarked, "I've got Joe Johnston dead," but he was mistaken, and the Confederates slipped away again.

Major battles were fought at Resaca, Dallas (or New Hope Church), and Kenesaw Mountain, and sometimes Sherman's army got the worst of it; but always Sherman continued his remorseless advance. In July, after a succession of battles around Atlanta, Sherman laid siege to the city. In the meantime, Confederate authorities had removed the wily Johnston from command and replaced him with John B. Hood, a brave but overly aggressive general from Texas. This proved to be yet another Confederate mistake.

Outmaneuvered and outnumbered, Hood and his army withdrew from the confines of Atlanta on September 1, and the blue-clad Union soldiers entered the city in time to have an effect upon the presidential election of November 8, 1864.

After dispatching Gen. George H. Thomas to Tennessee with two corps (where he eventually fought, and utterly destroyed, Hood's army) Gen. Sherman set off for Savannah on November 15 with his army of 60,000 men. The ruthless campaign which ensued became known as "the march to the sea." Sherman's men engaged in an orgy of destruction, destroying railroad lines and bridges, burning plantations and crops, killing livestock and looting homes. "Georgia has a million inhabitants," Sherman had written earlier to Grant. "If they can live, we should not starve." There was much plundering and brutality as the troops scoured the countryside for provisions. Sherman's famous observation ("War is hell") certainly applied to his campaigns in Georgia and the Carolinas.

Sherman captured Savannah "as a Christmas present for Lincoln," and then headed his army northward, into South Carolina. Charleston fell on February 18 and the stars and stripes were once again hoisted over Fort Sumter. The burning of Columbia, the capital of South Carolina, on February 17, 1865, was witnessed by Wisconsin troops. One Union general put the blame for the fire upon whiskey, observing, "A drunken soldier with a musket in one hand and a match in the other is not a pleasant visitor to have about the house on a dark, windy day. . . ." Like many another Union soldier, Pvt. Edwin Levings of River Falls believed the burning of Columbia was proper. In South Carolina, Levings wrote, "was passed the first ordinances of secession, . . . and now she must be punished . . . for the curse of God was upon her."

By then the end was not far off. Toward the end of March, 1865, after a brutal siege, Lee abandoned Petersburg and attempted to slip westward, hoping to link up with Gen. Johnston's army in North Carolina. (Johnston was by then back in command of the Confederates facing Sherman.) Richmond, the Confederate capital, surrendered to elements of the Union army on the night of April 2-3; but by then Grant and the bulk of his mighty host were off in ruthless pursuit of Lee's ragged, half-starved army. During the succeeding week, the Confederates fought a series of delaying actions, staving off the inevitable by a few days here, a few hours there. The end came on April 8, roughly seventy miles west of Petersburg, when Grant's encircling army cut off all retreat. The following day, at Appomattox Court House, Lee accepted Grant's terms and surrendered his Army of Northern Virginia.

On April 26, 1865, Gen. Johnston was brought to bay and compelled to surrender his weary, defiant army to Gen. Sherman in Raleigh, North Carolina. Four years and two weeks after the first shots were fired at Fort Sumter, the Civil War was over.

Sixteen Wisconsin infantry regiments participated in one way or another in Sherman's victorious campaign of 1864–1865. They were the First, Third, Tenth, Twelfth, Thirteenth, Fifteenth, Sixteenth, Seventeenth, Eighteenth, Twenty-first, Twenty-second, Twenty-fifth, Twenty-sixth, Thirty-first, and Thirty-second. In addition, there were two Wisconsin batteries of artillery (the Fifth and Eighth) and the First Wisconsin Cavalry.

On January 13, 1864, Gen. John C. Starkweather (the first colonel of the First Wisconsin infantry) was ordered to Washington to serve court-martial duty, so Col. George B. Bingham led the First Wisconsin throughout the Georgia and Carolina campaigns. It was involved in the maneuvers about Dalton, Georgia, and was part of a brigade repulsed in an attack against fortifications at Resaca (May 13–16, 1864). After the Confed-

erate forces withdrew from Resaca, the First confronted the enemy at Pumpkin Vine Creek and held its own. In an engagement on August 30, the regiment helped to drive "the enemy from the brigade front, and held the position until dark." Then came the siege of Atlanta and Hood's withdrawal from the coveted city. When the regiment's three-year term of enlistment expired, all its men were transferred to the Twenty-first Wisconsin, where they served to the end of the war. Those veterans who returned home were met "with an enthusiastic reception" in Milwaukee. The regiment's losses totaled 235. Ninety-seven men were killed in action, forty-five died of wounds, and 120 died of disease.

After spending two years with the Army of the Potomac, the Third Wisconsin was sent to the Tennessee sector where it became part of Sherman's campaign against Atlanta. Its first serious battle there was at Resaca. "Our men reserved their fire until the rebels were in easy range," one participant wrote, "and then opened so hotly that they [the enemy] soon wavered and retired in disorder, our men following up, and taking about

Headquarters of the Sixteenth Wisconsin, somewhere in Tennessee, c. 1864. (X3)12875.

forty prisoners." In action near Dallas, the officers and men of the Third "displayed a heroism never excelled by any troops." But the casualties in this encounter were heavy—thirteen killed, ninety-seven wounded. Like other Wisconsin soldiers, men of the Third celebrated the capture of Atlanta. The regiment then engaged in foraging, wrecking railroads, and seeking out the enemy on the march from Atlanta to the sea. Near Savannah, the Third Wisconsin captured an armed tender, *The Resolute*, "with its entire crew and a huge supply of stores." There were skirmishes aplenty as they army began a northward trek, with battles at Averysboro and Bentonville in South Carolina. Their opponent, Joe Johnston, was astounded by the efficiency and relentless energy of the troops that he faced. "I made up my mind," he wrote, "that there has been no army in existence like this since the days of Julius Caesar." Eventually Sherman's army reached Raleigh, the capital city of North Carolina. There Johnston surrendered, and the Wisconsin soldiers gloried in the end of the war. The Third passed through Richmond on the way to Washington and there took part in the grand review before being sent to Madison to be mustered out. The regiment's casualties totaled 259: 101 were killed in action, fifty-three died of wounds, and 105 died of disease.

The Tenth Wisconsin, after sustaining heavy losses in the Chattanooga campaign, received eighty-five new recruits early in 1864. Then it took part in Sherman's southward advance. The names of Dallas, Resaca, Kenesaw Mountain, and Peach Tree Creek were added to the regimental colors. After the capture of Atlanta, the regiment was stationed "on guard" at Marietta, Georgia, and then in their old entrenchments at Kenesaw Mountain. On October 16, the recruits and veterans who reenlisted were transferred to the Twenty-first Wisconsin; the veterans who did not reenlist were sent home, to be mustered out in Milwaukee on October 25. The regiment's casualties numbered 247: seventy-one killed in action, twenty-seven died of wounds, 145 died of disease, and four died in accidents. The final toll included members of the regiment who had been taken prisoner at Chickamauga and interned in rebel prisons at Salisbury, Millen, and Andersonville. The emaciated survivors were freed at war's end.

The Twelfth Wisconsin, perhaps, saw more action and had more casualties during Sherman's campaign than any other regiment from the state. After taking part in Sherman's successful foraging expedition to Meridian, Mississippi, in February, 1864, the veterans of the Twelfth left for Wisconsin and a thirty-day furlough. They reported back to Sherman's army at Ackworth, Georgia, on June 8, during the opening phase of the Atlanta campaign. At Kenesaw Mountain, a detachment of 150 men of the Twelfth Wisconsin made the usual "heroic charge" but were forced back—an action which won praise from the brigade and division commanders. The men of the Twelfth fought well at Peach Tree Creek and Bald Hill, a portion of the outer defenses of Atlanta. In describing the second day of the battle of Bald Hill, Pvt. Edwin Levings wrote, "For six hours the battle raged furiously.... We checked the rebels, threw up a new line facing south.... We had not half finished it when the rebels charged ... came up five deep ... some of them actually got inside our works—but never got out. They could not take our position." Following the capture of Atlanta, the regiment continually engaged in foraging, destroying railroads and bridges, and skirmishing with the ever-present enemy. After Savannah was taken, the army headed into the Carolinas, with skirmishing and minor battles here and there. The Twelfth captured a garrison flag in a heavy skirmish near the Salkehatchie River and witnessed the burning of Columbia. After the surrender of the Confederate army at Raleigh, the Twelfth Wisconsin marched in the grand review of Sherman's army in Washington. After returning to Wisconsin for mustering out, the final cost of its service was added up: 310 dead in all—fifty-eight were killed in action, thirty-five died of wounds, 214 died of disease, and three in accidents.

The Thirteenth Wisconsin took part in no major battle during the Atlanta campaign and spent most of its time in protecting military bases, building entrenchments, guarding railway lines, and marching from one assignment to another. The major engagement with the enemy took place at Point Rock Bridge where the Thirteenth beat off an attack by a rebel force of 400—but lost thirty-six men as prisoners. The regiment was encamped at Jonesboro, Tennessee, when the war ended. Throughout the war only three soldiers of the Thirteenth were killed in action; on the other hand, 192 men died of disease and seventy-one deserted. After its heroics at Missionary Ridge, the Fifteenth Wisconsin (Hans Christian Heg's old regiment) was part of the army sent to relieve the Confederate siege of Knoxville. The 110-mile march brought some hardship and fatigue, for there was a shortage of food and shoes and clothing. Sent from one place to another in Tennessee, the men expressed their disgust by not reenlisting when their three-year enlistment ended; only seven veterans signed up again. Belatedly assigned to Sherman's army, the reorganized Fifteenth saw some action at Rocky Face Ridge, Resaca, Kenesaw Mountain, and during the siege of Atlanta. The regiment did not accompany Sherman on his march to the sea, being assigned instead to guard some bridges near Chattanooga. The Fifteenth Wisconsin was then disbanded and its recruits and veterans were transferred to the Twenty-fourth

William H. Pomeroy, drummer with the Thirteenth Wisconsin. (X3)19141.

(and later to the Thirteenth) Wisconsin. The regimental casualty list totaled 299, of whom forty-nine were killed in action, thirty-three died of wounds, and 217 died of disease.

The Sixteenth Wisconsin, which had lost 149 men in the Battle of Shiloh early in the war, was reassigned in May of 1864, becoming part of Sherman's army and the XVII Corps. After a march of 320 miles, the Sixteenth reached Sherman's army on June 8. In the weeks of campaigning that followed, it helped to turn the enemy's right at Kenesaw Mountain, drive the rebels off Bald Hill, and assist in the siege of Atlanta. The regiment took part in destroying railroads, seizing stores, and skirmishing on the way to Savannah. Together with the rest of its corps, the Sixteenth Wisconsin helped capture Goldsboro and then moved on to Raleigh, North Carolina, where the battle-weary Confederate army surrendered. Then came the long trip home via Richmond, Washington (and the grand review), Louisville, and Madison. The regiment's record: 393 casualties, including 141 men killed in battle or dead of wounds, 247 dead of disease, and 115 desertions.

The Seventeenth Wisconsin, involved in Grant's siege of Vicksburg, also took part in Sherman's Atlanta campaign. After a long march, the regiment joined Sherman's army at Ackworth, Georgia, on June 8. It took part in several engagements before being involved in the siege of Atlanta; it participated in the bloody fight at Bald Hill and another at Lovejoy. After the capture of Atlanta there was the march to the sea, when the names of Savannah, Beaufort, Goldsboro, and Raleigh became part of the Seventeenth's lore. The regiment, like all others in Sherman's army, participated in the grand review in the nation's capital before it was sent home to be mustered out. The Seventeenth Wisconsin reached Madison on May 17, 1865, where it was "publicly received and welcomed." Of the regiment's 220 casualties, 177 were due to disease; only twenty-two soldiers had actually been killed on the field of battle.

After participating in the Vicksburg and Chattanooga campaigns, the Eighteenth Wisconsin was assigned to guard duty at Whitesburg, Alabama, from May 1 to June 19, 1864. Next it was sent to reinforce the garrison holding Allatoona. On October 5, a large rebel force attacked, an artillery duel preceding the assault. Three companies of the Eighteenth were stationed at a nearby blockhouse, and

Martin Norda of the Fifteenth Wisconsin. (X3)12869.

although the rebel attack was eventually repulsed, the Wisconsin troops were captured. Soon after, the survivors of the regiment were incorporated into the Ninety-third Illinois and some of the furloughed veterans became part of a provisional division, mustered in at Louisville and sent to Goldsboro, North Carolina, to reinforce Sherman in his final campaign. These soldiers witnessed Johnston's surrender to Sherman at Raleigh and later took part in the grand review in Washington before being mustered out. The Eighteenth Wisconsin lost 240 men: twenty-three killed in action, sixteen dead of wounds, and 195 of disease. One black mark against the regiment was its 208 desertions.

The Twenty-first Wisconsin, organized at Oshkosh, took part in the battles of Stones River—where it behaved badly because of the incompetence of its colonel, Benjamin J. Sweet—and Chickamauga, where its colonel, Harrison C. Ho-

bart, was captured. The regiment was a part of Sherman's army during the Atlanta campaign. The Twenty-first took part in engagements at Rocky Face Ridge, Dallas, Pumpkin Vine Creek, Kenesaw Mountain, and Peach Tree Creek before the Union army captured Atlanta. Then came the march to the sea and the trek into the Carolinas that ended at Raleigh. After taking part in the grand review, the regiment was sent to Milwaukee to be mustered out. Its losses were quite heavy, totaling 295. Sixty-nine men were killed in action; forty-seven died of wounds, 177 of disease, and two in accidents.

The Twenty-second Wisconsin, after taking part in the Chattanooga campaign, became part of Sherman's army as it moved against Atlanta. Skirmishing was commonplace, and the regiment took part in the sharp fighting around Resaca, where it suffered heavily, "many of the men being killed inside the enemy's works." Then came the Battle of Kenesaw Mountain where the Twenty-second was again hotly involved, "repelling a furious charge by the enemy." After the encounter at Peach Tree Creek, Union troops entered Atlanta, the Twenty-second Wisconsin being one of the first regiments to go into the city. As part of Gen. Henry W. Slocum's left wing of Sherman's great army, the Twenty-second saw little fighting all the way to Savannah. Then it was on to Goldsboro and Raleigh and Johnston's surrender. After the grand review, the regiment went to Milwaukee to be mustered out. Casualties were listed at 226: thirty-five men killed in action, thirty-two dead of wounds, and another 159 of disease.

The Twenty-third Wisconsin was mustered into service at Camp Randall in Madison on August 25, 1862, under Col. Joshua Guppey, former colonel of the Tenth Wisconsin. The regiment was sent to Kentucky on September 15 and subsequently was attached to Gen. Sherman's command in Grant's campaign against Vicksburg. In December, 1862, after crossing the Mississippi, the Twenty-third fought battles at Port Gibson, Champion Hills, Black River Bridge, and took part in the siege of Vicksburg, which ended on July 4, 1863. Continual skirmishing and occasional battles took their toll, but the effects of climate and disease were far worse; in the first four months of 1863 the regiment lost 150 men, almost all from sickness. In August of that year, the regiment campaigned in Louisiana and east Texas and, early in 1864, was attached to Gen. Nathaniel Banks's ill-starred Red River expedition. On April 8, at the Battle of Sabine Cross Roads, the Twenty-third held the extreme left of the Union position against heavy odds and was badly mauled in the process, losing seven killed, fourteen wounded, and forty-three taken prisoner. Thereafter the regiment soldiered on along the Gulf coast of Louisiana and Alabama, alternately skirmishing and marching, to the end of the war. The Twenty-third was mustered out on July 4, 1865. Of the 1,117 officers and men who served in the regiment, 287 died—all but thiry-eight of them from disease.

The Twenty-fourth Wisconsin, which had won honors at Chickamauga, likewise became part of Sherman's invasion of Georgia. The regiment saw action at Rocky Face Ridge, Resaca, Adairsville, Dallas, Kenesaw Mountain, Peach Tree Creek, and in the battles before Atlanta. On June 4, 1864, two days after his nineteenth birthday, Arthur McArthur was promoted to the rank of lieutenant-colonel. The Twenty-fourth did not take part in the campaign against Savannah, instead being sent northward to Franklin, Tennessee. It was there, on November 30, 1864, that the regiment took part in a bloody counterattack and recaptured at bayonet point a line of trenches the rebels had carried. (Col. McArthur was seriously wounded in the encounter.) After an assignment of repairing railroad lines near Blue Springs, the Twenty-fourth Wisconsin was in camp when word came of Lee's surrender and Lincoln's assassination. Of the regiment's total losses of 175, sixty-one men died in battle, thirty-six of wounds, and seventy-seven of disease.

The Twenty-fifth Wisconsin, organized at Camp Salomon in La Crosse on September 24, 1862, helped suppress the Sioux uprising in Minnesota before taking part in Grant's Vicksburg campaign and Sherman's campaign against Atlanta. The names of Resaca, Dallas, Decatur, and Atlanta were inscribed on the regiment's flag. Then it was on to Savannah and the sea. During the subsequent campaign northward, the Twenty-fifth was hotly engaged near the Salkehatchie River in South Carolina, where a shell decapitated Col. Jeremiah Rusk's orderly and grazed the head of the colonel's horse. After the grand review of Sherman's entire army, the regiment was mustered out and the men entrained for Milwaukee and Madison. For his "meritorious service," Col. Rusk was promoted to brigadier general. (He later won election to Congress and was governor of Wisconsin, 1882–1889.) No Wisconsin regiment sustained more casualties

than "the glorious 25th," but unfortunately most were the result of disease. Of 422 men who died in the war, only twenty-seven were killed on the field of battle, and another sixteen died of wounds. The balance (381) died of illness or accidents.

After taking part in the bitter fighting at Gettysburg and Missionary Ridge in 1863, the Twenty-sixth Wisconsin took part in Sherman's Atlanta campaign. The regiment fought in battles at Resaca, Dallas, Kenesaw Mountain, Peach Tree Creek, and in the siege of Atlanta. Then came the march to the sea and the final campaign in the Carolinas. Following the triumphal review in Washington, the regiment entrained for Milwaukee. There it took part in a parade, following which it proceeded to Turner Hall, where "a splendid banquet was prepared by the German citizens." The Twenty-sixth Wisconsin was one of the few "all-German" regiments that fought with distinction in the war, and it did so in both theaters of the war. Indeed, the regiment suf-

Poster for the Twenty-sixth Wisconsin touting the state bounties for veterans and new recruits. (X3)44246.

fered more men killed on the battlefield than any other regiment in the western theater. Of its 249 total casualties, 128 men were killed in action and another fifty-six died of wounds.

The Thirty-first Wisconsin was mustered into service in Prairie du Chien on October 9, 1862. After service around Nashville during 1863, it was sent to join Sherman's army. On the way, a train carrying the regiment ran off the track, killing one soldier and severely injuring a dozen others. It suffered eighteen casualties in the Atlanta campaign. Then it was on to Savannah and the Carolinas. On March 19, 1865, the men of the Thirty-first Wisconsin assaulted a well-entrenched Confederate force at Bentonville, North Carolina, where they paid a heavy toll: ten killed and forty-two wounded. The sixty-five-day, 200-mile march through the Carolinas wore down the troops, a tenth of whom were barefoot by the time they reached Goldsboro and the end of the war. After the grand review in Washington, the regiment was mustered out in Madison on July 20, 1865. The Thirty-first Wisconsin sustained losses of 114 in its

thirty-three months of service: thirteen men dead in action, nine of wounds, and ninety-two of disease.

The Thirty-second Wisconsin was mustered into service at Camp Bragg in Oshkosh on October 20, 1862, and campaigned in Mississippi before becoming part of Gen. Sherman's army. Its most memorable day in combat occurred near Courtland, Tennessee, where it surrounded and defeated a force of 400 rebels, taking forty-nine prisoners. The regiment took part in the siege of Atlanta, Sherman's march to the sea, and the invation of the Carolinas. In the campaigns of 1865 the Thirty-second saw sporadic fighting but much hard marching before reaching Raleigh and ultimate victory. Following the grand review in Washington, the regiment was sent to Milwaukee, where it was paid off and disbanded. The regiment lost 287 men—thirty-eight as a result of combat, the rest victims of malaria and dysentery.

Between Savannah and the end of the war in North Carolina, Sherman's great army had marched and fought over 400 miles in fifty days. A historian of the war would later say, "As a triumph of physical endurance and mechanical skill on the part of the army and of inflexible resolution in the general, it stands unrivalled in the history of modern war. . . . " Still, for some Wisconsin soldiers, the campaigns of 1864–1865 held their share of fun and frolic. The fall of Atlanta and the historic march to the sea involved constant foraging and a good deal of looting and pillaging—traditional pursuits of veteran troops. Some soldiers took pleasure in destroying rebel railroads and plantations and in putting the torch to Atlanta and Columbia. There was also a pervasive sense of companionship and adventure: "Tenting on the Old Campground" and "Marching Through Georgia" became favorite songs at veterans' reunions for many years afterward. On the other hand, Sherman's victorious march through the Southern heartland was also a test of endurance for his men, who sometimes went barefoot and made do with scanty rations. Incessant rain or broiling sun produced misery, and the pestilential swamps of the Carolinas brought on diseases that killed three times as many soldiers as did Confederate bullets. As in any war, the victors as well as the vanquished paid the bill.

Richard Crowe, Co. F, Thirty-second Wisconsin Volunteer Infantry. (X3)46636.

27

Wisconsin Women and the Civil War

WOMEN PLAYED IMPORTANT ROLES in the story of Wisconsin and the Civil War. As mothers and wives, as sisters and sweethearts, they were interested in the welfare of the soldiers and in the winning of the war. No story of the war is complete without giving considerable attention to the aid and relief programs in which women played the chief part.

In countless ways, women became involved in the enlistment and the welfare of Wisconsin's regiments. Alexander Randall, the first of the state's four wartime governors, recognized that women were destined to have an important role in morale and in wartime activities. Shortly after he responded to President Lincoln's first call for volunteers, Governor Randall issued a proclamation addressed to the "Patriotic Women of Wisconsin." In part, his proclamation of April 22, 1861, read: "It is your country and your government as much as theirs [i.e. the men's] that is now in danger, and you can give strength and courage and war sympathies and cheering words to those who go to do battle for all that is dear to us here. Bitter as the parting may be to many, I am assured that you will bid them go bravely forward for God and Liberty, to 'return with your shields, or on them.' I commend the soldiers to your kindness, encouragement and prayers, with full confidence that when occasion calls, many, very many Florence Nightingales will be found in our goodly land."

The women of Wisconsin followed Governor Randall's advice. They entered into the multitiude of activities which women could do during the war. They scraped lint and made bandages, wrote letters, organized aid societies, and sometimes even encouraged men to enlist.

Women as well as men attended the hundreds of war meetings. These meetings—or war rallies, as they were in fact—built up patriotism and bestirred men to volunteer. The typical rally featured martial music, patriotic speeches, cheers for the Union, and the eventual invitation to the young men to join a volunteer company. Occasionally young women, carried away by the emotionalism of the hour, would add their powers of persuasion. Their boyfriends had no alternative, for patriotism brooked no excuses.

The spirit of patriotism was well illustrated at a war rally by an elderly Madison woman who was both wife and mother. She already had five sons in the service and her sixteen-year-old was begging her for permission to enlist as a drummer boy. Her husband, too, had placed his name on the muster rolls and would soon leave for the front. Just as the speaker arose to address the rally, this proud wife and mother proposed three cheers for "the good old flag." She then walked up and kissed the flag displayed on the speaker's platform. Needless to say, the rally produced more than the quota of volunteers needed.

That same spirit of patriotism was exhibited by a woman in Vernon County who accompanied her husband to enlistment headquarters and watched him sign the enlistment sheet. When he laid down the pen, she picked it up and wrote after his name: "God bless and protect you, my husband."

It remained for an elderly Waukesha matron to top them all. At a war rally, the martial music and the patriotic orations moved her. Anxious to testify that the fires of patriotism had seared her soul, she climbed the steps to the speaker's platform and proudly announced that her husband was already in the service. "And if I had another husband," she proclaimed in a firm voice, "I would send him also."

When companies or regiments held formal drills, many young ladies gathered to watch both the men and the maneuvers. When regiments paraded down the streets of cities or towns, many of these same young ladies waved handkerchiefs from doorways and windows. The presence of pretty girls in crinoline encouraged soldiers to do their best. "We marched along Racine's most aristocratic streets," wrote a soldier stationed at nearby Camp Utley, "and every man did his best, for the walks were filled with the belles of that fair city." One observant company commander noticed that when "a bevy of admiring maidens" were spectators, his men "stood up straighter and taller" and did their "best work."

Goodies and delicacies, as well as attention and sympathy, were contributed by women to maintain soldier morale. Mothers and sweethearts either sent or brought cookies, pies, and homemade candies to soldiers in training at the state army camps, or to train depots as they departed for the war. Commandants of camps often found it necessary to post guards to keep the soldiers in and the visitors out.

When the First Wisconsin barracked in Camp Scott, in the first month of the war, Milwaukee women baked a huge cake for each of the ten companies in the regiment. Company B, formerly the Milwaukee Light Guards, received not only a giant-sized cake but also a big bouquet accompanied by a note which read: "Flowers may fade, but the honors of the brave never." This was a sentimental age, and few shrank from expressing their emotions about courage, honor, duty, and the like.

Men who happened to be stationed at Wisconsin camps on Thanksgiving Day or at Christmas time usually enjoyed special feasts prepared by women of the nearest city. Racine women, for example, furnished the men in Camp Utley with an awesome Thanksgiving dinner: 175 roast turkeys, 500 pies, and 1,200 doughnuts. "We had cold turkey, roast chicken, apple, pumpkin, and mince pies, sponge cake, pound cake, and indeed everything the most fastidious could wish for," wrote one of the appreciative soldiers, "and above all, the ladies seemed to take a special delight in smiling upon us, while we were eating."

Women also assumed the responsibility of sewing the company and regimental banners. (Their flags, or "colors," were extremely important to Civil War regiments.) The regimental banners were ordinarily made of silk, and sometimes groups of women (often headed by the wife of the colonel) held special banner-making sewing bees. The formal presentation of the regimental colors always attracted a large audience and took place at a special program. A crowd of 5,000, for example, gathered to witness the formal dedication of the banner of the First Wisconsin. Mrs. George Walker, wife of one of the co-founders of Milwaukee, presented the regimental flag to Col. John C. Starkweather in the presence of all the troops at Camp Scott on May 8, 1861. Governor Randall and the mayor of Milwaukee were among the dignitaries present. The regiment, formed in a hollow square, heard Mrs. Walker make a stirring presentation speech. "In confiding this banner to be upheld by your strong arms and dauntless hearts," she concluded, "we feel that you will

never permit a hostile or traitor's flag to assume the place of the glorious and unsullied stars and stripes, which have been, with the blessing of God, and ever shall be, a symbol of our national glory."

As soon as Wisconsin troops left the state, relatives and sweethearts expressed concern for their welfare. On April 19, 1861, a number of Milwaukee women met in a schoolroom to organize a soldiers' aid society. They founded the Ladies' Association of Milwaukee, selecting officers and discussing a program of action. The movement spread to other cities and the participants talked of establishing a state organization with auxiliary units in every city and town. Mrs. Joseph S. Colt of Milwaukee took charge of creating the Wisconsin Aid Society and reorganizing the Ladies' Association of Milwaukee as a local unit. Mrs. Colt accepted the position of corresponding secretary of the Wisconsin Aid Society and was its guiding light throughout the war. Dedicated, able, and energetic, she became one of the best-known women in Wisconsin because of her war work.

Before the end of the war, Mrs. Colt had helped to establish 229 local units or auxiliaries. As corresponding secretary of the state organization, she gave advice and encouragement to the far-flung local units. The women who belonged to the state or local aid societies performed a variety of chores. They aided the families of soldiers and found suitable employment for disabled veterans who had been honorably discharged. They sent vast quantities of delicacies to camps and hospitals. "Mitten fever" swept the state during the first winter of the war. Women made quilts, blankets, and comfort-bags for the soldiers in winter camp. They scraped lint and prepared thousands of bandages, for bales of lint and stacks of bandages were needed after every battle and skirmish. In addition to mittens, they knitted socks, gloves, and caps. (In time, the Wisconsin Aid Society became part of a national organization called the United States Sanitary Commission; the Wisconsin society channeled its supplies through the Chicago branch of the commission.)

Early in the war, individual boxes were sent in a rather haphazard fashion to soldiers in various sectors and camps. The typical soldier notified his family when troops were to be stationed at one spot for several weeks, then carefully stipulated what he would like to have sent in a box at the earliest possible time. The local aid societies, on the other hand, prepared cooperative boxes and designated a certain military company as recipient. As a rule, this would be the military company recruited in their city or county. The company commander then distributed the goodies or the socks and mittens equitably among his men. In 1862, Governor Salomon called for contributions "for Wisconsin soldiers," rather than for individual soldiers or special military companies. The United States Sanitary Commission worked overtime trying to deliver and supervise the distribution of the hundreds of thousands of cartons which were collected and packed on the home front. The Milwaukee chapter of the Wisconsin Aid Society reported that it forwarded 2,142 boxes to Chicago during 1864—partial proof that Wisconsin women were solicitous about the welfare of their boys in blue.

Although Mrs. Colt gained statewide publicity because of her work in the Wisconsin Aid Society, it was Cordelia Harvey of Madison who became the best-known of all Wisconsin women in the war years. Her reputation as an angel of mercy became nationwide. Mrs. Harvey was the widow of Wisconsin's ill-fated seventy-three-day governor, Louis P. Harvey, who had drowned in the spring of 1862. Following his untimely death on a trip to visit wounded and sick Wisconsin troops, Mrs. Harvey dedicated her life to being the good Samaritan. She wanted to finish the work her husband had so nobly begun.

In September of 1862, Governor Salomon appointed Mrs. Harvey a "sanitary agent" and invited her to look after the needs and welfare of Wisconsin soldiers located in Missouri. Upon her arrival in St. Louis, Mrs. Harvey visited hospitals at Benton Barracks and at Fifth Street. These two hospitals were crowded with sick and wounded men from camps and battlefields. She noticed that the medical service was "poorly organized" and wholly inadequate. She noticed that many of the surgeons were "incompetent" and inept. The hospital at Cape Girardeau was understaffed and ill-managed, and contagious diseases cost many lives. She telegraphed the U.S. Sanitary Commission for hospital stores and medical supplies. Like a gadfly, she got attention and forced changes to be made. The sick and wounded soldiers applauded her efforts.

Mrs. Harvey returned to Madison to report to

Cordelia A. P. Harvey, c. 1865. (X3)32355.

the governor on her work and her observations. She told Salomon that Wisconsin soldiers in distant hospitals needed better care. Her enthusiasm permeated the ranks of the Wisconsin Aid Society. Auxiliaries of the organization boxed and shipped cartons of supplies.

After she returned to St. Louis, Gen. Samuel R. Curtis gave her permission to visit all the hospitals within his jurisdiction. He also ordered that stocks of sanitary stores be put at her command. Mrs. Harvey visited hospitals in Helena, Rolla, Ironton, and Memphis. She reached the conclusion that the system needed overhauling. She believed that men who were sick and dying because of inadequate care at faraway and understaffed hospitals could be saved if they were transferred to hospitals nearer home. They would get better care and would escape the suffocating atmosphere of death and corruption which pervaded the typical army hospital. On her own initiative she arranged for the transfer of many Wisconsin soldiers to hospitals in the North. She believed—probably correctly—that the "brisk Wisconsin air" and better care would put many sick men on the road to recovery.

Mrs. Harvey gained an interview with Gen. Ulysses S. Grant near Vicksburg in March of 1863. She explained her theories to the laconic general and he nodded in assent. Grant gave her permission to send patients who suffered from chronic dysentery to northern hospitals. He also agreed that medical inspectors should be named for every army corps and that medical inspectors should have full power to discharge disabled men or send convalescents to hospitals farther north.

Beyond this, however, Mrs. Harvey had in mind a grander scheme for convalescent care of the sick and wounded. She wanted to establish several military hospitals in Wisconsin, and she now took steps to achieve that end. She boldly

Sgt. Jefferson Coates of the Seventh Wisconsin, who won the Medal of Honor but lost his eyesight at Gettysburg. (X3)1800.

went to Washington, where she secured an interview with President Lincoln and presented her plan of hospitals in the soldiers' home states. Lincoln sent her on to the War Department to see Secretary of War Edwin M. Stanton. (On an envelope addressed to the crotchety Stanton, Lincoln wrote: "Admit Mrs. Harvey at once; listen to what she says; she is a lady of intelligence and talks sense.")

Stanton listened to the woman from Wisconsin, but he was in no mood to have a woman tell him how to revamp the hospital system. He saw a way out. He told Mrs. Harvey that he had just sent the U.S. Surgeon General to New Orleans on a hospital inspection tour. Before he took action on her suggestions, he would await the report of the Surgeon General. Mrs. Harvey was certain that Stanton was just finding an excuse to leave things as they were. The next day, therefore, she returned to President Lincoln's office, where she stubbornly and firmly restated her case. She would not leave until the president took action on her plea.

Her persistence paid dividends. Lincoln authorized her to establish three hospitals or convalescent camps in Wisconsin. The Harvey United States Army General Hospital (named for the deceased governor, not for Mrs. Harvey) was established in Madison in October, 1863. The second was established in Milwaukee the next year as an officer's hospital. A third, the Swift Hospital, was located in Prairie du Chien.

After the war, Mrs. Harvey returned to Madison. She heard reports that the War Department planned to close down and discontinue the Madison and Prairie du Chien hospitals. She talked of transforming the Harvey Hospital into a home for orphans of Wisconsin soldiers killed in the war, and she enlisted support for that proposal. She then organized a charitable association which acquired title to the vacant Harvey United States Army General Hospital buildings. By January 1, 1866, the orphanage was ready for occupancy. Several months later, the state assumed control of the institution's funding and governance. The Wisconsin Soldiers' Orphans' Home operated until 1875, a living monument to the energy and compassion of Cordelia Harvey.

Of course many thousands of Wisconsin women, in addition to Mrs. Harvey, made contributions to winning the war. In families where the breadwinners shouldered muskets and marched off to war, women took on added responsibilities. Some fields of activity previously closed to women were opened by the exigencies of the war—for example, higher education.

In a way, the doors of the University of Wisconsin were opened to women by the war. Before 1860, the university was strictly a men's institution. When many of the students volunteered for service in 1861, the student body dwindled appreciably, leaving the physical facilities largely empty and the faculty at loose ends. In 1863, therefore, the university's board of regents decided to create what they called a "normal department" to which young women would be admitted for training as public school teachers. Not surprisingly, some of the hidebound professors expressed apprehension, fearing that the "standards of culture" might be lowered.

Initially, ten women enrolled in the new department. By the end of the first term, they had proved that they deserved the opportunity open to them. One professor, sympathetic to the principle of educational opportunities for women, felt compelled to report that the "experiment" at the University of Wisconsin had been highly successful: "... I deem it my duty to communicate to the Board [of Regents] my experiences and views concerning the admittance of young ladies to the University classes. As far as my department is concerned, the experiment has proved a successful one. In earnestness, application, and quickness of perception they, in general, were certainly not inferior to the young men, while their presence evidently exerted a beneficial influence on the deportment of the latter."

If the war brought opportunities to some women, it also brought sacrifice and sadness to many others. The death of a son or husband meant much more than just an empty chair; it meant anguish and an aching heart. Of an estimated 80,000 Wisconsin men who enlisted in the war to save the Union, more than 11,000 were killed in action or died of wounds and disease. It is no exaggeration to say that in many thousands of homes across the state, the war turned wives into widows, children into orphans, and hope into despair. Ella Wheeler, a Dane County poet who achieved success in the postwar years, aptly described in "The Messenger" the scene that ensued when a Union soldier brought a woman terrible news about one of her sons:

A deathly pallor shot across
Her withered face. She did not weep.
She said, "It is a grievous loss;
But God gives his beloved sleep.
What of the living? —of the three?
And when can they come back to me?"
The soldier turned away his head—
"Lady, your husband, too, is dead."

ᵇ 28 ᵇ

Economic Growth During the War

WHILE SOLDIERS FOUGHT AND DIED on faraway battlefields and their women kept the home fires burning, major economic changes occurred in Wisconsin—changes that were sometimes swift, sometime gradual. They affected virtually every one of the state's diverse industries.

For one thing, agriculture gradually became mechanized. There was a scarcity of farm laborers. Farm prices climbed during the last half of the war. Those two factors encouraged farmers to turn to labor-saving machinery. Farmers bought a variety of agricultural machines: reapers and seed drills, mowers and harrows. By the end of the war, most farmers had invested heavily in machinery. One railroad reported that it shipped 2 million pounds of farm machinery out of Milwaukee in the war years.

Wisconsin farmers needed reapers to harvest their bumper crops of wheat. Each machine could do the work of four to six men. When farm laborers left for the army, machines took their place. Wisconsin wheat contributed to the winning of the war. It helped to feed the armies and it helped to ensure the neutrality of England and France, who relied upon American grain. "The farmers of the Northwest, in producing this surplus grain," claimed a writer for the Milwaukee *Daily Wisconsin*, "have fought a battle for the Union of greater significance than any possible achievement of the Grand Army of the Potomac."

The war brought several other changes to agriculture in Wisconsin. It introduced the factory system of cheesemaking to the state. The making of butter and cheese by individual farmers gave way to the cooperative factory where an expert utilized "the milkings" of an entire community. The first cheese factory was established during wartime at Ladoga in Fond du Lac County, and the system soon swept the state.

Diversified farming also developed in the state as wheat-cropping exhausted the soil. The dairy cow became a more important farm animal as quality cheese and butter helped to erase the evil reputation of midwestern butter in the markets of the East.

The war also helped to popularize some new commercial crops in Wisconsin. It prompted many farmers to turn to the production of sugar cane, sugar beets, and flax. When Louisiana, "the sugar-cane state," joined the Confederacy, there was a new interest in crops which could produce sugar. In his message of January, 1861, Governor Alexander Randall urged that bonuses be paid to farmers who tried their hand at raising sugar cane or sorghum. The Madison area developed into the center of sorghum culture. By the end of the war, Wisconsin was producing 800,000 gallons of sorghum syrup a year. The sorghum mill became a common sight in the countryside as the "sorghum craze" swept the state. Prophets predicted that sorghum would continue to become a more important Wisconsin crop with each passing year. The end of the war, however, witnessed the retreat of sorghum culture in Wisconsin. "King Sorghum" abdicated and Louisiana again became the land of sugar cane fields and sugar mills.

Flax, too, became a notable wartime crop. When the Southern states seceded, the mills of the North could no longer obtain cotton for clothing. Several flax companies took steps to introduce and extend flax culture in Wisconsin by distributing free flaxseed in some eastern and southern counties. The companies contracted for the flax crop which the farmers agreed to raise. These entrepreneurs also established several linen factories and linseed mills in the state. The new industry seemed well-established when the war ended; but, when Southern cotton reappeared on the market, the flax industry in Wisconsin went the way of the sorghum industry.

As might be expected, the demands of the war gave an impetus to sheep husbandry and wool production. Wool commanded top prices, rising from 25 cents per pound in 1860 to $1.50 in the fall of 1864. Manufacturers of woolen cloth for soldiers' uniforms outbid each other in the wool market; those engaged in sheep-raising noticed that wool possessed a golden glint. They increased the size of their flocks as they tried to take advantage of the high price of new wool. The number of sheep in Wisconsin grew from 332,954 in 1860 to 1,260,900 in 1865. Although wool prices tumbled after Appomattox, wool-producing remained an important Wisconsin industry in the postwar years.

The prices which Wisconsin farmers secured for their commercial and surplus crops put them in a firm financial position. Handsome wartime profits enabled farmers to pay off their mortgages, mechanize their farms, and purchase new acreage. In four or five years they evolved from frontier farmers into well-established businessmen. Not surprisingly, their success and security affected their political views. Most of them became Republicans in the postwar era, and rural Wisconsin became known as "solid Republican country."

While agriculture enjoyed prosperity in the war years, mining also experienced a boom. The lead-mining industry had reached its peak in Wisconsin about fifteen years before the war. Many mines had been abandoned as non-productive during the 1850's, and the panic of 1857 had seemingly dealt a coup de grace to that dying industry. The demands of war, however, put a premium upon lead. Miners hurried back to the lead districts as prices on pig lead skyrocketed. Eastern capital entered the picture; lead-mining methods changed and lead production steadily climbed upward. By 1862 Wisconsin was producing 17 million pounds of lead a year—enough to provide 100 bullets for every Union soldier in uniform.

Manufacturing in Wisconsin received less stimulus from the war than did such industries as mining, lumbering, and agriculture. A shortage of capital prevented Wisconsin from taking a giant stride forward in manufacturing. Many of the areas of manufacturing hardly held their own. The flour-milling industry made slow progress, and Wisconsin continued to market wheat rather than flour. Iron smelting also remained constant. Wisconsin could boast of only three iron smelters in operation in 1860. No new ones were put in operation during the war.

Four manufactured products, however, benefited. The war gave a tremendous boost to the manufacture of farm machinery. Milwaukee, Whitewater, Horicon, La Crosse, Beaver Dam, and Racine increased their production of farm machinery. The J. I. Case Company of Racine built 300 threshing machines in 1860; by the end of the war the company was making nearly twice that number. The Van Brunt Company of Horicon produced sixty seeders in 1860; it built 700 machines in 1863. "The several agriculture shops in this city," wrote a La Crosse editor in 1863, "are driven with work and hardly able to meet the demands on them for threshing machines, reapers, fanning mills, etc. A million more dollars could be profitably invested here in the manufacturing of farm tools and labor saving implements of all kinds. There is no end to the demand which increases each year in astonishing ratio."

Leather products, like farm machinery, also experienced an upsurge because the war gave a boost to the leather industry. Soldiers' shoes and belts and saddlery and harnesses for horses helped to create a demand for good leather. Milwaukee had nine tanneries in 1860; by the end of the war, fifteen. In addition to the increase in the number of plants, there was also an expansion of the existing plants. In the postwar years, Milwaukee boasted of being "the tanning capital of America."

The pork-packing industry expanded dynamically in the early 1860's. It was centered in Milwaukee. Railroads carried hogs from Iowa, Minnesota, and rural Wisconsin into Milwaukee. Packers transformed the hogs into bacon, ham, salt pork, and lard. Smoked hams and salt pork became staple foods for the armies of the Union.

Beer was another fourth manufactured product which improved its position during the war. Milwaukee produced 36,000 barrels of beer in 1860 and 55,000 in 1865. The discriminatory excise tax on distilled spirits helped make beer a "respectable drink." Milwaukee, with its large German population, consumed most of the beer produced in that city.

The lumbering industry, like agriculture and mining, enjoyed a Civil War boom. The lumbering industry was already well established by 1860, and by the end of the warm it was a major industry. Some of the finest stands of white pine anywhere were concentrated in the vast region drained by the Chippewa River and its tributaries.

Lumber prices spiraled upward in 1863, and a lumber boom soon followed. The editor of the Appleton *Crescent* compared the "lumber rush"

of 1863–1864 with the Pike's Peak gold rush of 1859–1860. Chicago was experiencing growing pains, and Chicagoans begged for lumber, shingles, lath, and pickets. The growing populations of relatively treeless states like Kansas and Iowa were also begging for lumber for homes, barns, and sheds. Wisconsin lumbermen hustled to meet the unprecedented demand for their products. The Wisconsin pineries produced lumber by the billions of feet and created profits in the millions of dollars. Several of the lumber barons of the postwar years got their start as lumbermen during the Civil War years.

Merchants as well as manufacturers claimed a portion of the wartime bonanza; indeed, Milwaukee was better known for its trade than its manufacturing in 1860. Her excellent harbor and expanding railroad network brought northern Iowa and all of Minnesota into her orbit. Many thousands of bushels of wheat were exported from Milwaukee's wharves. Like bees the stevedores collected the golden harvest, and the harbor was their hive. From 1861 through 1865, Milwaukee loaded and shipped 60 million bushels of wheat and claimed the title "greatest primary wheat market in the world." No other city successfully challenged that claim.

Milwaukee was known for her imports as well as her exports. By 1860 the city had gained a reputation as an outfitting center where emigrants bound for points north and west secured their supplies. Merchants dominated the city government. Most of the Milwaukeeans who boasted an income over $10,000 were merchants. John Plankinton, who reported an income of $104,000 in 1864, made most of his profits from investments in wool.

Prosperity in trade meant growth in population. Milwaukee's population in 1860 bordered on 45,000. It increased nearly 25 per cent during the war years, and in 1865 totaled 55,641.

During the Civil War years, railroad building in Wisconsin experienced a standstill. The wartime trend was not to build more lines, but to consolidate local lines already built. The process of concentration and consolidation brought into being two famous rail systems: the Chicago & North Western and the Chicago, Milwaukee & St. Paul. With the lower Mississippi Valley closed off by the war, these young giants began to monopolize traffic in the Upper Midwest and to reap profits which outraged farmers and critics of big business. In the postwar years, Wisconsin's railroads would embark upon a golden age of growth and expansion. Wisconsin was only a dozen years old when the Civil War began in 1861. By the end of the conflict, the state had matured. It had become the granary of the Midwest and had taken Herculean strides in manufacturing and industry. The war years were a catalyst for many sectors of the state's economy and prepared the way for postwar expansion.

☙ 29 ❧

Politics and the Elections of 1864

IN 1864, the political caldron began to bubble and boil earlier than usual. It was a presidential election year, and Lincoln's supporters wanted him renominated and reelected. Early in January—just eight days after the state legislature had convened—fervid Wisconsin Republicans introduced a series of resolutions to show that there existed a groundswell for the president. The resolutions endorsed the war policy of the Lincoln administration, praised the president as a constructive and effective leader, and endorsed him for renomination and reelection. The fourth resolution proclaimed the president "a statesman of liberal and enlarged views, great ability, and unswerving integrity, and if the wishes of the people of Wisconsin are complied with by the National Union Convention that assembles to nominate candidates for the presidency, Abraham Lincoln will again be nominated."

Not surprisingly, the Democratic members of the legislature criticized the resolutions and argued against their adoption. One Democrat offered an amendment to substitute the name of Gen. George B. McClellan for Abraham Lincoln in the fourth resolution. George B. Smith, onetime attorney general and floor leader of the minority party, harangued for three hours against the pro-Lincoln resolutions. Smith insisted that most Wisconsin citizens did not favor the resolutions or the renomination of Lincoln; that Lincoln had not hewed to the Constitution in fighting war; and that the president should be rebuked be-

cause of the many arbitrary arrests made and the many civil rights violated. Smith contended that Democrats were the true defenders of the Constitution—that they were determined to preserve "their liberties and the Constitution at all hazards." (Although Democrats would not say so publicly, many preferred Lincoln to either Salmon P. Chase or John C. Fremont, the pair upon whom the Radical Republicans showered their blessings.)

Smith spoke in vain, for the Republicans defeated his amendment in the assembly, 54 to 21, and steamrolled the pro-Lincoln resolutions through both houses of the legislature.

Alexander Randall, who had served as the state's first Civil War governor, dutifully tried to tie the knot which fastened Wisconsin Republicans to President Lincoln's coattails. Randall and Lincoln stood on good terms. After Randall had relinquished the governor's chair to Louis P. Harvey in January, 1861, Randall wanted to enter the military service and dreamed of a brigadier general's star. But the astute president, already embarrassed by an overabundance of such "political generals," sent Randall to Rome as envoy and minister extraordinary. There Randall served as U.S. representative to the Papal States and enjoyed the salubrious climate of sunny Italy. But he soon tired of the inactivity associated with his diplomatic post and returned to the United States to meet with Lincoln.

Again Randall requested an army assignment, but Lincoln prudently sidetracked him. Instead, he proffered Randall to accept a domestic post in which he could serve as liaison with Republicans in Wisconsin. The able ex-governor thereupon accepted the position of assistant postmaster-general and took a desk job in Washington. Randall spent considerable time mending Lincoln's political fences in Wisconsin. It was he who deserved most of the credit for the introduction and passage of the pro-Lincoln resolutions, which were intended to launch the Lincoln boom of 1864.

In February, Randall's long arm again reached to Madison. He appointed Elisha W. Keyes a "special commissioner" to canvass Wisconsin for the president and to solicit more riders for the Lincoln bandwagon. Boss Keyes, Madison postmaster and titular head of the "Madison Regency," performed his task well, effectively quashing what little support was developing for Chase and Fremont. He gave hope to long-time Lincoln supporters and found new supporters for the president's war policies.

In an effort to recruit independent or uncommitted voters, Republican party strategists decided to claim that their approach to the election was bipartisan. They tentatively laid aside the Republican cloak and designated their state conclave a "Union Party" convention. They met in Madison on March 30 to select sixteen state delegates to the National Union Convention and of course to sing the praises of the Lincoln administration. All sixteen delegates were pledged to Abraham Lincoln—testament that Alexander Randall and Elisha W. Keyes had done their spadework thoroughly. Then the delegates turned to the task of cementing their hold upon the machinery of state government.

The Democrats, somewhat disorganized, also gave attention to the political hustings. Some of the "Peace Democrats" liked Horatio Seymour of New York, who had served a term as Civil War governor of the Empire State and had criticized the Lincoln administration with both perception and decorum. Most Democrats, however, seemed to favor George B. McClellan, who remained a war hero despite his chronic failure to secure a Union victory in the field. Many Democrats believed that "Little Mac" was a good general who had suffered injustice at Lincoln's hand. He possessed color and his name was widely known. So at their Madison convention, state Democrats pinned their hopes on McClellan and sat back to await their party's national convention.

As the meeting date for the Republican-sponsored National Union convention approached, Alexander Randall expressed some fear that John C. Fremont and Salmon P. Chase were gaining in favor. Randall wrote to Boss Keyes, urging him to bring his friends and his influence to Baltimore early. It was a needless fear. When the convention opened on June 7, the revolt of the Radical Republicans failed to materialize. Lincoln easily won renomination; his lieutenants had the situation well in hand. The Democrats in turn tried to give shape to criticism of Lincoln and the convention which nominated him. Assuming a holier-than-thou attitude, they charged that the convention which nominated Lincoln was an assemblage of officeholders, crooked contractors, cotton speculators, and recipients of patronage.

The Democrats, hoping for a split in the Republican ranks, decided to postpone their national convention until late in August. They also hoped that time would favor them and their cause; after all, war weariness was extensive and new calls for troops might have political repercussions. When the delegates finally met in Chicago, they nominated Gen. McClellan as their candidate and placed a peace plank in their platform—a plank which McClellan quickly repudiated.

Because there was no state ticket before the people that autumn, Wisconsin politicos had trouble whipping up much enthusiasm during the campaign of 1864. There were a couple of spirited contests for seats in Congress, but the campaigners generally pled their case before a lethargic jury.

Two Democratic editors did their best to enliven the campaign. "Pump" Carpenter and "Brick" Pomeroy each made a distinctive contribution to the cause of political partisanship. Carpenter put together a weekly column entitled "The Logic of History," in the Madison *Patriot*. It consisted of a collection of miscellaneous items, mostly excerpts from speeches or statements made by Lincoln and the Radical Republicans, as well as words of wisdom uttered by Democrats from Thomas Jefferson to George McClellan. Carpenter sought to prove that the Radical Republicans were irresponsible and irrational and that Abraham Lincoln was unprincipled, inconsistent, and incompetent.

Carpenter's editorials were long on vehemence, short on discretion. The ghost of abolition seemed haunt the editor, even in late 1864. He never ceased to denounce Lincoln's emancipation measures and his suspension of the writ of habeas corpus. "The idea of suspension," Carpenter recorded for posterity, "is akin to the quack doctor who cut his patient's throat to cure a tumor on his neck." Shrill and partisan to the very bone, Carpenter voiced his disapproval of every measure of the Lincoln administration. He wrote that peace would be a blessing and that Lincoln's reelection would have the direst consequences; but like other Democrats, he had no formula to bring an end to hostilities.

"Brick" Pomeroy of the La Crosse *Democrat* exhibited even more malevolence toward the president. Indeed, it might be said that Pomeroy made the denunciation and vilification of Lincoln an art. Pomeroy's unhappy experience with the Union army, combined with his aversion to abolition, transformed him from a mild critic into a madman whose hatred of Abraham Lincoln became an obsession which he cultivated without pause or restraint. When Pomeroy first learned that Lincoln sought reelection and a second term, he wrote, "May God Almighty forbid that we are to have two terms of the rottenest, most-stinking, ruin-working small-pox ever conceived by fiends or mortals in the shape of two terms of Abe Lincoln." And on August 23, 1864, Pomeroy published a picture of Lincoln on the front page beneath the caption "The Widow Maker of the 19th Century and Republican Candidate for the Presidency."

That day's editorial shocked even Pomeroy's friends. In part it read: "The man who votes for Lincoln now is a traitor and murderer. He who pretending to war for, wars against the Constitution of our country is a traitor, and Lincoln is one of these men. . . . And if he is elected to misgovern for another four years, we trust some bold hand will pierce his heart with dagger point for the public good." The bloodthirsty editor even suggested Lincoln's epitaph:

Beneath this turf the Widow Maker lies,
Little in everything, except in size.

Brick Pomeroy gained national notoriety for his venomous criticism of President Lincoln. The national spotlight turned upon La Crosse, and Pomeroy reveled in the publicity he received. But his rantings embarrassed his more moderate Democratic colleagues, who recognized that Pomeroy's campaign of abuse and animosity hurt rather than helped the cause of the Wisconsin Democracy.

While Pomeroy and Carpenter carried on their private war against Lincoln, the tide of the war inexorably turned. Sherman moved on Atlanta, Grant savaged Lee's army in front of Richmond, and the naval blockade continued to squeeze the life out of the Confederacy. By late 1864, Republicans could jubilantly (and rightly) claim that the war was not the miserable failure which the carping Copperhead critics claimed it to be.

War prosperity also strengthened Lincoln's chances for reelection. The failure of the Ohio wheat crop in 1864 boosted prices on the abundant wheat yield in Wisconsin. Army purchases of

the farm surpluses also helped to bring better prices. Wisconsin farmers consequently enjoyed "a prosperity so enormous as almost to challenge disbelief." These flush times for farmers helped to heal some of the wounds of the war. One newspaperman viewed the good times as "the lance of Achilles, healing by its touch the wounds of war and desolation." And as Lincoln's stock rose, McClellan's declined.

Lincoln's ability to appeal to the masses and to transform his aims into the people's ideals also affected the election returns. Lincoln had an innate ability to gain the confidence of the people. He spoke their language, and his words carried the ring of sincerity and conviction. His apparent humility and his thorough honesty disarmed many critics. The people sensed that the charges of despotism and corruption which some Democrats circulated were distortions and exaggerations. They simply did not ring true. The proof was in the elections of November, 1864.

George B. McClellan actually ran better in Wisconsin than his supporters thought he would. He carried twenty-two of the state's fifty-eight counties, and he trailed Lincoln by only 6,000 votes. (The final tally among votes cast in Wisconsin was Lincoln, 68,887, to McClellan, 62,586.) Milwaukee County, bucking the trend, gave McClellan 6,875 votes to Lincoln's 3,175. But, as in previous wartime elections, votes cast by soldiers in the field told a different story. Ultimately, Lincoln's majority in Wisconsin rose to 15,000 votes.

In the congressional races, the Democrats fared badly. They lost two of the three seats they had won in 1862. Wisconsin, in the new Congress, would be represented by five Republicans and but one Democrat. The Republicans also retained control of both houses of the state legislature.

Governor James T. Lewis, Elisha W. Keyes, and Alexander Randall gave thanks for Lincoln's victory at the polls in Wisconsin. Republican editors expressed their jubilation in their editorials. Republican spokesmen contended that the election returns proved that their views were the true views. The Democrats, on the other hand, offered the usual stale and staid excuses and alibis. The Madison *Patriot*, for example, blamed the Democratic defeats upon fraud, forgeries, threats, intimidations, and patronage—upon what it termed "the power of the sword and the purse." Democrats hoped that Lincoln and his generals would end the war in a hurry and reunite the war-torn and war-weary nation.

⊰ 30 ⊱

The End of the War, and After

AFTER GEN. SHERMAN presented the city of Savannah, Georgia, as a "Christmas present" to President Lincoln in 1864, Northerners knew that the end of the war was not far off. During the spring of 1865, telegraphic reports told of Sherman's march through the Carolinas and of Grant's relentless hammering of Lee's depleted ranks south of Richmond in Virginia. Citizens of Wisconsin waited impatiently for the news that the war was over so they could release the emotions pent up through four long years of struggle and sacrifice. Early in April, word came at last over the telegraph wires. "On the receipt of the news of the fall of Richmond, April 2, 1865, and the capture of Jefferson Davis, April 9, 1865," recalled a Menasha resident, "the town was alive with crowds of people and with demonstrations of joy, the blowing of horns, the clanging of bells, the firing of anvils, and the shouting of the people." The observer added wonderingly, "I never expect to see such a demonstration again."

While Wisconsin communities planned victory celebrations for main street and services of thanksgiving in their churches, the shocking news of Abraham Lincoln's assassination a few days later cast a shadow of gloom over the North. That same Menasha resident recalled how the joy of victory was eclipsed by the tragic news from Washington: "In marked contrast with the joy of the hour was the deep sorrow into which the nation was plunged by the news of Lincoln's assassination, April 14. I remember where I stood when I heard the news that morning. I said, 'It cannot be.' There were faces blanched with grief and fear. Business was suspended. At such a time the Nation bereft of its great leader and chief, it seemed the greatest calamity of all that had befallen us. . . . We were all mourners."

Just as four bitter years of war had transformed a confederation of sovereign states into a nation, they had transformed a regional politician into a statesman. "Lincoln," wrote a historian long afterward, "grew with the war; he was a party politician when he was elected in 1860, but he was a statesman by the war's end." John Wilkes Booth's pistol turned the president into a martyr as well. Most of Lincoln's wartime critics admitted that his death represented a grievous loss to the country, both North and South. They liked the temper and the tone of his second inaugural address in which he had called for "malice toward none . . . charity toward all." Even Brick Pomeroy reversed the column rules of the *Democrat* and decked his newspaper in mourning garb. (Before a month had passed, however, Pomeroy's editorials again bordered on blasphemy. By June he was ranting that "God generously permitted an agent to make a martyr of the late president. . . .")

While most people thanked God that the fraternal war was over and mourned the loss of Abraham Lincoln, the federal government took steps to transform Union soldiers into civilians. During the summer of 1865, the War Department closed the provost marshals' offices in Wisconsin; recruiting had been discontinued on April 13. During the fall and winter, most of the state's regiments returned to Wisconsin to be mustered out, though a few Wisconsin troops received orders to go to the Southwest to keep Mexican raiders from crossing into the United States, and others headed for the Dakota frontier to fight Indians. These, however, were few in comparison to the many battle-tested veterans who came home to receive the thanks of Governor James T. Lewis and to return to farms, offices, and workshops. Citizen-soldiers became just plain citizens.

In his inaugural address of January 1, 1866, one-armed Lucius C. Fairchild, who was elected governor in November, 1865, noted the peaceful transformation: "A million of men have returned from the war, been disbanded in our midst, and resumed their former occupations. . . . The transition from the citizen to the soldier was not half so rapid, nor half so wonderful, as has been the transition from the soldier to the citizen."

Governor Fairchild stated what the war had cost the state of Wisconsin. He reported that 10,752 Wisconsin soldiers—"about one in every eight"—had died while in the service of their country. The state had paid out approximately $3,900,000 for "war purposes," which included the expense of recruiting, aid to families of sol-

diers, and the costs of operating the military offices of the state. Wisconsin's counties, cities, villages, and townships raised an additional
$7,752,000 for the war through taxes and other
levies. (Nor did this reckoning include the many
thousands of dollars raised at war rallies or by
soldiers' aid societies.)

Adjutant Gen. Augustus Gaylord, commis-
sioned January 7, 1862, and reappointed by governors Salomon and Lewis, took pride in Wisconsin's contribution to the war. He paid special
tribute to Quartermaster Gen. William T. Tredway and Surgeon Gen. Erastus B. Wolcott, both
of whom performed their work efficiently and
well. Gaylord also reported that twelve different
Wisconsin soldiers wore general's stars, and three
of these held the rank of major general: Charles S.
Hamilton, Carl Schurz, and Cadwallader C.
Washburn. Hamilton left for the front as colonel
and commander of the Third Wisconsin. A West

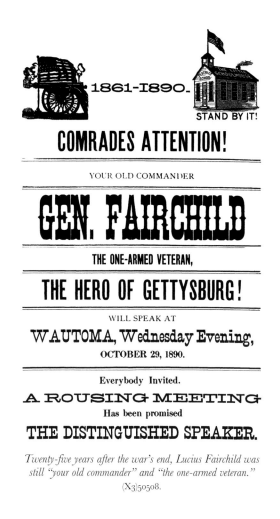

*Twenty-five years after the war's end, Lucius Fairchild was
still "your old commander" and "the one-armed veteran."*
(X3)50508.

Pointer, he led his troops to victory at Iuka and
Corinth and seemed marked for success; indeed,
he was promoted to major general in September,
1862. But he became embroiled in a dispute with
his higher-ups and resigned from the army in
1863.

Carl Schurz, after a stint as U.S. minister to
Spain, received a commission as brigadier general
of volunteers in 1862. For his services at Second
Bull Run, Chancellorsville, and Gettysburg, he at-
tained the rank of major general; after the war he
settled in Missouri, where he won election to the
U.S. Senate in 1869. Schurz was not a great soldier, but he made a reputation as a political reformer, newspaperman, and historian.

Cadwallader C. Washburn, Wisconsin's third
major general, had a career nearly as varied as
that of Schurz. Washburn was serving as a congressman at the start of the Civil War. Late in
1861, he received special permission from the federal government to raise a regiment of cavalry in
Wisconsin. In March of 1862, Col. Washburn and
his regiment departed for the front. Successful
campaigns and successive promotions earned him
a brigadier's and then a major general's stars.
During the final year of the war, he commanded
the District of West Tennessee. Washburn afterward served two terms in Congress and a single
term as governor of Wisconsin (1872–1874).

Nine Wisconsin soldiers wore the single star of
the brigadier general: Lysander Cutler, Thomas
H. Ruger, Frederick Salomon, Joseph Bailey, Edward S. Bragg, Lucius Fairchild, Rufus King, Halbert E. Paine, and John C. Starkweather. (The
first three were brevet major generals, denoting a
provisional wartime rank.) Cutler commanded the
reconstituted Iron Brigade on a temporary basis
for six weeks early in 1864. Then Edward S.
Bragg, one of the state's best-known soldiers, led
that brigade during the Petersburg campaign. Bailey, whose ingenuity had saved the federal fleet
entrapped on the Red River, received more honors
than any other Wisconsin soldier. Fairchild, who
lost his left arm at Gettysburg, later served three
terms as governor of Wisconsin. He also served as
national commander of the Grand Army of the
Republic (the national soldiers' organization), and
as both consul and minister abroad. Twenty-eight
other Wisconsin soldiers achieved the brevet rank
of brigadier general.

While the generals and the soldiers were be-than Wisconsin. Those soldiers consumed 17,456 meals—an average of forty-eight a day.

Mrs. Hewitt and her friends determined to sponsor a huge "soldiers' fair" to raise funds for the building of a soldiers' home. Governor Lewis encouraged the project and communities from every part of Wisconsin made contributions or sponsored exhibits. The Soldiers' Home Fair of June 18, 1865, was a greater success than even the most optimistic had anticipated; its profits exceeded $110,000.

A delegation of Milwaukeeans then went off to Washington to urge the building of a national soldiers' home in Milwaukee, offering to turn over the site and the funds of the Wisconsin Soldiers' Home Association to the federal government. The government consequently agreed to build one of its soldiers' homes in Milwaukee. In July of 1867, the Wisconsin Soldiers' Home Association turned over its funds and property to a board of commissioners of the National Asylum for Disabled Soldiers. The Wisconsin Soldiers' Home thus became the United States National Soldiers' Home, and the association itself was dissolved, its objectives achieved and its work completed.

Lysander Cutler (1808–1866), first commander of the Sixth Wisconsin. (X3)23123.

coming civilians in 1865 and 1866, the Wisconsin Soldiers' Home was gaining a reputation for giving hospitalization and care to those in need. The history of that institution dated back to March 5, 1864. On that day, several Wisconsin women were returning from a meeting in Chicago where they had discussed a proposal for the founding of a soldiers' home project for Chicago. Mrs. Lydia Hewitt of Milwaukee wondered why a soldiers' home could not just as well be established in Wisconsin—preferably in Milwaukee. She therefore suggested that Wisconsin women abandon the Chicago project and devote themselves to establishing a soldiers' home in Milwaukee. She took the lead in organizing the Wisconsin Soldiers' Home Association. The association rented several large rooms on Water Street and made arrangements to receive sick and wounded Wisconsin soldiers. Prominent Milwaukee businessmen contributed generously to the association, and the volunteer organization expanded its work accordingly. During the year ending April 15, 1865, the association's headquarters cared for and in their words "entertained" 4,842 soldiers, more than half of whom represented nineteen states other

Thomas H. Ruger (1833–1907), who commanded the Third Wisconsin early in the war and rose to brevet general's rank in 1864. (X3)50393.

Wisconsin not only originated the idea of a national home for needy ex-soldiers but also established the first state-sponsored home. The proponents of such a home argued that some veterans were unable to care for themselves and that the state should establish an institution where crippled or "helpless" veterans could take up residence with their wives. Veterans and legislators favored the proposal and voted funds for the Wisconsin Veterans' Home. The home was located on a site of sixty-eight tree-studded acres on the Chain o' Lakes in Waupaca County, at present-day King. The quarters were ready for occupancy on November 16, 1887, and within a month the Wisconsin Veterans' Home had acquired its first fifty residents. In time, a regular village grew up on the grounds as new residence halls, maintenance and amusement buildings, and cottages were added.

Similarly, in Madison, the Soldiers' Orphans' Home founded by Cordelia Harvey provided education and a nurturing environment for youthful victims of the war until its closure in 1875. Such institutions, always well managed, became models upon which other states planned their soldiers' home projects.

The war had touched the lives and the minds of all those who had taken part in it. But during the first few years afterward, most veterans were fully occupied with reconnecting with family and friends, and reestablishing jobs as farmers, mechanics, and clerks. Before many years, however, the veterans of Shiloh and Chickamauga, of Antietam and Atlanta began to crave an opportunity to talk with one another. Those regiments with the most esprit de corps were the quickest to arrange postwar reunions at which the old soldiers could reminisce, renew old acquaintances, and embellish their stories of life in camp and in the field. Among their own kind, they could recall not only the humorous aspects of the war, but also the tragic and terrible ones which were indelibly inscribed upon mind and memory. One Wisconsin soldier tried to put into words a scene which had haunted him in the years that followed. He told of a fellow soldier who was standing close to him in the regimental line of battle: "Just as I happened to glance at him he was struck in the neck by a musket ball. He let fall his gun and dropped, turning toward me as he fell. As he did so, by a convulsive movement of the muscles of his throat, his

tongue was forced out of his mouth to its utmost extent. A sickening shudder involuntarily passed over me at the fearful sight."

The old soldier went on to say how a feeling of great pity and sympathy welled up in him—how he wished to minister to his dying friend. But the regiment was advancing, and he advanced with it. War shows no pity for the fallen, he said, and it soon hardens the hearts of all participants. (A generation of armless and legless men, both North and South, knew of what he spoke.)

No reunion received the publicity or developed such intense loyalties as those held by veterans of the Iron Brigade. A brigade reunion association came into being in 1880, presided over by John Gibbon, the man who had molded inexperienced troops into a proud fighting unit. Gibbon remained president until his death in 1896, when he was succeeded by another fighting general, Edward S. Bragg.

In addition to reminiscing at reunions, veterans organized local posts or associations. In Illinois, a group of veterans created an association which they named the Grand Army of the Republic and which became popular (and powerful) as "the G.A.R." When Madison veterans established a post in 1866, Wisconsin could claim the honor of being the second state in the Union to have a branch of the G.A.R. The Wisconsin Department of the G.A.R. had a number of dedicated and able commanders, including Lucius C. Fairchild, who later became commander-in-chief of the national organization.

The G.A.R. preached patriotism and exerted pressure in behalf of veterans' legislation. It supported radical Reconstruction policies, anathematized Democrats and former rebels, and relentlessly "waved the bloody shirt." In so doing, it prevented the healing of the wounds of the Civil War and prolonged the bitterness of the postwar years. In 1887, as a gesture of good will toward the conquered South, President Grover Cleveland (a Democrat) sanctioned the return of some captured battle flags to the former Confederate states. Lucius Fairchild, national commander of the G.A.R., protested angrily against such sacrilege, declaiming before an assemblage of Union veterans: "May God palsy the hand that wrote that order! May God palsy the brain that conceived it! May God palsy the tongue that dictated it!"

In the face of such strident opposition, Presi-

Lucius Fairchild (seated, center), commander of the Grand Army of the Republic, and his staff, c. 1885. (X3)50510.

dent Cleveland judiciously rescinded his order. It was another thirteen years, when Fairchild was gone and the power of the G.A.R. had faded, that President Theodore Roosevelt returned most of the captured Confederate banners to their respective states.

Women whose husbands had fought in the Civil War felt the need to join together "to serve as the strong right arm" of the Grand Army of the Republic. Interested wives launched the Women's Relief Corps in Denver in 1883, and Wisconsin women organized a branch of the order in the same year. The purposes of the society were threefold: to perpetuate the memory of the Union soldiers of the Civil War, to promote patriotism, and to lend assistance to widows and orphans of the order. The Wisconsin branch of the Women's Relief Corps contributed considerably to the establishment and improvement of the Wisconsin Veterans' Home.

The sons of veterans also took steps to organize. Their intent was to pay tribute to the honored dead and "to assist at memorial exercises." Logically enough, they adopted the name of Sons of Veterans.

Pride in achievement brought forth many regimental histories. Twenty-five histories of Wisconsin regiments reached print. Some were sound as to scholarship and long on detail. Others were brief, discursive, and somewhat inaccurate. (As might be expected, few regimental histories dealt with cowardice, incompetence, or desertion in the ranks.) But Rufus R. Dawes's *Service with the Sixth Wisconsin Volunteers*, published in 1890, was a shining exception. It excelled all other regimental histories, gaining a reputation as a readable as well as an accurate firsthand account; no better book was written about any regiment of any state in the Union.

Each of the three most prominent Wisconsin Copperheads of the Civil War era enjoyed a measure of success and a modicum of fame in the postwar era. Stephen D. Carpenter found time to turn his talents from journalism to invention. In addition to increasing his influence in Democratic party councils, he devised a binding machine which was fitted to the Marsh harvester, and patented a half-dozen other inventions.

Marcus Mills Pomeroy was discredited as a prophet when the North won the war, but he enjoyed astonishing success in rebuilding both his reputation and his fortune. By 1868 he had increased subscriptions to the La Crosse *Democrat* to 100,000, with many subscribers in the South. He also gained a reputation as a humorist and a novelist. Then he sought new fields to conquer. At "Boss" Tweed's invitation, Pomeroy moved to New York to edit the New York *Democrat*. There, he soon quarreled with Tweed and ended up levying charges which helped to wreck the notorious Tweed Ring. He then returned to the Midwest, editing *Pomeroy's Democrat* in Chicago and becoming a top chieftain in the Greenback party wigwam. Next, "Brick" moved to Denver where he edited the *Great West*, invested in mines, and promoted a tunnel company. He spent his last years in New York as editor of *Advance Thought* and promoter extraordinaire. He frequently talked of La Crosse where he had gotten his start and won national notoriety as a critic of the Lincoln administration. His detractors, however, never forgave him for his wartime ravings. The editor of the La Crosse *Republican* bitterly recalled how Pomeroy had "out-jeffed Jeff Davis in treasonable utterances and out-deviled the Devil in deviltry."

Edward G. Ryan prospered after the war. Condemned by Lincoln's supporters in the war years, he was afterward praised by reform-minded farmers who sought relief from the railroad monopoly. In a famous address he delivered before University of Wisconsin graduates in 1873, Ryan eloquently described the coming of "a new and dark power" wielded by "vast corporate combinations of unexampled capital." He warned: "The question will arise . . . which shall rule—wealth or man; which shall lead—money or intellect; who shall fill public stations—educated and patrotic freemen, or the feudal serfs of corporate capital." (Robert M. La Follette, aged eighteen, heard the speech, understood its import, and later traced his political views back to it.)

In 1874 Ryan was named to the Wisconsin Supreme Court and went on to become the most celebrated and perhaps the greatest justice in all Wisconsin history. His decision in *Pike v. The Chicago, Milwaukee & St. Paul Railway Company* made him the idol of the Grangers. When the case went before the U.S. Supreme Court,

Ryan's argument and decision became the basis for the U.S. Court's verdict in the Granger cases of 1876–1877.

Wisconsin was a young state—just twelve years old—when the Civil War began. In a sense, the war tested the thirtieth state of the Union to see if it really belonged in the company of such old and famous members as New York, Pennsylvania, and Massachusetts. Wisconsin, like her sister states of the Old Northwest, met the challenge successfully—though not, to be sure, without much partisan bickering and occasional outbursts of disorder. Probably friction was inevitable in any newly minted state whose peoples represented a dozen European stocks and as many languages and folkways. By war's end, however, most of Wisconsin's 868,000 citizens agreed that the Union must prevail over secession, no matter what the cost. Most also agreed that chattel slavery was an evil system that deserved to be destroyed—though perhaps only a bare majority of people were prepared to grant equal rights to the freedman. Some politicians would prosper by "waving the bloody shirt" and nursing a grudge against their old adversaries, and Wisconsin was to remain a bastion of the Republican party for almost a century.

Yet the healing process had begun even before the guns fell silent. A few days after the Battle of Gettysburg, Capt. Frank Haskell walked reflectively along the littered crest of Cemetery Ridge, near the stone wall and the little clump of oaks where Pickett's men had died before the muzzles of Cushing's battery. Afterward, he wrote his brother Harrison in Portage: "Another Spring shall green these trampled slopes, and flowers, planted by unseen hands, shall bloom upon these graves; another Autumn and the yellow harvest shall ripen there—all not in less, but higher, perfection for this poured-out blood. In another decade of years, in another century, or age, we hope that the Union, by the same means, may repose in a securer peace, and bloom in a higher civilization."

Frank Haskell was not destined to see the Union triumphant; he died on a Virginia battlefield the following summer, aged thirty-six. But his vision of a more perfect Union arising from the blood and sacrifice of a terrible war was amply borne out in the years that followed.

⇥ *Select Bibliography* ⇤

WHAT FOLLOWS IS A HIGHLY SELECTIVE list of books, articles, and academic theses which bear upon Wisconsin's role in the Civil War. Most of these are available in larger public libraries, in the libraries of colleges and universities, or through the Wisconsin Interlibrary Loan Service (WILS). Probably these will satisfy the needs and interests of most readers.

The library and the manuscript collections of the State Historical Society of Wisconsin in Madison are rich in books, periodicals, and public records about the war. There, for example, the reader may consult regimental histories, census volumes, muster rolls, maps, monographs, and such daunting but invaluable documentary sources for military history as the 128 volumes of *The War of the Rebellion: A Compilation of the Official Records of the Union and Confederate Armies*— usually referred to as *The Official Records*.

Serious students of the topic will also want to explore manuscript collections, state documents, soldiers' letters and diaries, and newspapers from the period 1861–1865. To begin, they should consult Alice E. Smith, ed., *Guide to the Manuscripts of the State Historical Society* (Madison, 1944) and two supplements: Josephine L. Harper and Sharon C. Smith, eds., *Guide to the Manuscripts of the State Historical Society of Wisconsin: Supplement Number One* (Madison, 1957), and Josephine L. Harper, ed., *Guide to Manuscripts of the State Historical Society of Wisconsin: Supplement Number Two* (Madison, 1966). Examples of manuscript collections held by the State Historical Society of Wisconsin include, for example, the Wisconsin Civil War Governors' Papers, and the papers of Edward S. Bragg, Lucius Fairchild, Elisha W. Keyes, Lucius Fairchild, and George B. Smith.

An invaluable supplement to these other sources are the ten scrapbook volumes assembled by Edwin B. Quiner under the title "Correspondence of Wisconsin Volunteers, 1861–1865." These are arranged by regiments and indexed. (Quiner is the author of another vitally important book, *The Military History of Wisconsin*, published in 1866 and listed below.)

Although somewhat dated, William G. Paul's *Wisconsin Civil War Archives* (Madison, 1965) is still useful as a guide to state records held by the State Historical Society. The Wisconsin State Archives contain (among other items) the records of the Wisconsin Adjutant General, which are essential for information on Wisconsin regiments.

The State Historical Society's *Wisconsin Magazine of History*, published quarterly since 1917, contains not only many articles about the war (see below) but also lists of manuscript and archival accessions which are not in the *Guides* cited above. The *Magazine* is indexed both annually and decennially.

Newspapers are indispensable sources for Civil War history, especially for soldiers' letters, local news, and editorial opinion. Donald E. Oehlerts, comp., *Guide to Wisconsin Newspapers, 1833–1957* (Madison, 1958) describes hundreds of newspapers, most of which are available on microfilm at the State Historical Society in Madison. Among them, the Milwaukee *Sentinel*, the La Crosse *Republican*, the Oshkosh *Northwestern*, and the Madison *Wisconsin State Journal* typify Republican newspapers. The La Crosse *Democrat*, the Sheboygan *Journal*, the Milwaukee *News*, and the Madison *Wisconsin Patriot* are examples of Democratic newspapers. The Milwaukee *See-Bote*, a German-language paper, criticized the Lincoln administration on many counts. The Milwaukee County Historical Society has a good collection of Civil War newspapers as well as soldiers' letters and manuscript material. These are indexed by names of individuals as well as by subject. Finally, the Milwaukee Public Library has a card index for the Milwaukee *Sentinel* which is truly a researcher's delight.

Books

Ambrose, Stephen E., editor. *A Wisconsin Boy in Dixie: The Selected Letters of James K. Newton.* Madison, 1961.

Aubery, James M. *The Thirty-Sixth Wisconsin Volunteer Infantry, 1st Brigade, 2nd Division, 2nd Army Corps, Army of the Potomac.* Milwaukee, 1890.

Beaudot, William J. K., and Lance Herdegen. *An Irishman in the Iron Brigade: The Civil War Memoirs of James P. Sullivan, Sergt., Company K, 6th Wisconsin Volunteers.* New York, 1993.

Beitzinger, Alfons J. *Edward G. Ryan: Lion of the Law.* Madison, 1960.

Blegen, Theodore C., editor. *The Civil War Letters of Colonel Hans Christian Heg.* Northfield, Minnesota, 1936.

Bradley, George S. *The Star Corps; Or, Notes of an Army Chaplain, During Sherman's Famous "March to the Sea".* Milwaukee, 1865.

Brobst, John F. *Well, Mary: Civil War Letters of a Wisconsin Volunteer.* Edited by Margaret Brobst Roth. Madison, 1960.

Brown, Kent M. *Cushing of Gettysburg: The Story of a Union Artillery Commander.* Lexington, Kentucky, 1993.

Bryant, Edwin F. *History of the Third Regiment of Wisconsin Veteran Infantry, 1861–1865.* Madison, 1891.

Byrne, Frank L., editor. *The View From Headquarters: Civil War Letters of Harvey Reid.* Madison, 1965.

Byrne, Frank L., and Andrew T. Weaver, editors. *Haskell of Gettysburg: His Life and Civil War Papers.* Madison, 1970.

Cheek, Philip, and Mair Pointon. *History of the Sauk County Riflemen, Known as Company "A," Sixth Wisconsin Veteran Volunteer Infantry, 1861–1865.* Gaithersburg, Maryland, 1984.

Current, Richard N. *The History of Wisconsin. Volume II: The Civil War Era, 1848–1873.* Madison, 1976.

Dawes, Rufus R. *Service With the Sixth Wisconsin.* Marietta, Ohio, 1890 (reprinted, Madison, 1962).

Eden, Robert C. *The Sword and the Gun: A History of the 37th Wis. Volunteer Infantry, From Its First Organization to Its Final Muster Out.* Madison, 1865.

Fitch, Michael H. *The Chattanooga Campaign, With Especial Reference to Wisconsin's Participation Therein.* Madison, 1911.

Hagdeburg, F. H. *Wisconsin at Shiloh.* Madison, 1909.

Haskell, Frank A. *The Battle of Gettysburg.* Madison, 1908.

Herdegen, Lance J., and William J.K. Beaudot. *In the Bloody Railroad Cut at Gettysburg.* Dayton, Ohio, 1990.

Hincks, Elizabeth Eaton. *Undismayed: The Story of a Yankee Family in the Civil War.* Chicago, 1952.

Hurn, Ethel Alice. *Wisconsin Women in the War Between the States.* Madison, 1911.

Jones, Evan T. *Four Years in the Army of the Potomac: A Soldier's Recollections.* London, 1882.

Jones, Jenkin L. *An Artilleryman's Diary.* Madison, 1914.

Kellogg, John A. *Capture and Escape: A Narrative of Army and Prison Life.* Madison, 1908.

Klement, Frank L. *Wisconsin and the Civil War.* Madison, 1963.

Livermore, Mary A. *My Story of the War: A Woman's Narrative of Four Years Personal Experience as Nurse in the Union Army, and in Relief Work at Home, in Hospitals, Camps, and at the Front. . . .* Hartford, Connecticut, 1889.

Love, William DeLoss. *Wisconsin in the War of Rebellion.* Chicago, 1866.

Lyons, Adelia C., compiler. *Reminiscences of the Civil War.* San Jose, California, 1907.

McLain, David. *The Story of Old Abe, the Eighth Wisconsin War Eagle: A Full Account of His Capture and Enlistment, Exploits in War and Honorable as well as Useful Career in Peace.* Madison, 1885.

Mattern, Carolyn J. *Soldiers When They Go: The Story of Camp Randall, 1861–1865.* Madison, 1981.

Merck, Frederick. *Economic History of Wisconsin During the Civil War.* Madison, 1916 (reprinted, Madison, 1971).

Nolan, Alan. *The Iron Brigade: A Military History.* New York, 1961 (reprinted, Madison, 1975).

Otis, George H. *The Second Wisconsin Infantry.* Dayton, Ohio, 1894.

Quiner, Edwin B. *The Military History of Wisconsin.* Chicago, 1866.

Rood, Hosea W. *Story of the Service of Company E, and of the Twelfth Wisconsin Regiment, Veteran Volunteer Infantry, in the War of the Rebellion.* Milwaukee, 1893.

Rood, Hosea W. *Wisconsin at Vicksburg.* Madison, 1914.

Ross, Sam. *The Empty Sleeve: A Biography of Lucius Fairchild.* Madison, 1964.

Thwaites, Reuben G., editor. *Civil War Messages and Proclamations of Wisconsin War Governors.* Madison, 1912.

Wells, Robert W. *Wisconsin in the Civil War.* Milwaukee, 1962.

Whipple, Henry E. *The Diary of a Private Soldier.* Waterloo, Wisconsin, 1906.

Zeitlin, Richard H. *Old Abe the War Eagle: A True Story of the Civil War and Reconstruction.* Madison, 1986.

Williams, John R. *"The Eagle Regiment," 8th Wis. Inf'ty Vols., A Sketch of Its Marches, Battles and Campaigns, From 1861 to 1865. . . .* Belleville, Wisconsin, 1890.

Wisconsin Commission on Civil War Records. *Records and Sketches of Military Organizations, Population, Legislation, Election and Other Statistics, Relating to Wisconsin in the Period of the Civil War.* Madison, 1914.

Wisconsin Commission on Civil War Records. *Wisconsin Losses in the Civil War: A List of the Names of Wisconsin Soldiers Killed in Action, Mortally Wounded or Dying From Other Causes in the Civil War, Arranged According to Organization, and Also in a Separate Alphabetical List.* Madison, 1915.

Pamphlets

Alexander, Edward P. *Lincoln Comes To Wisconsin.* Historical bulletin no. 2, Lincoln Fellowship of Wisconsin. Madison, 1961.

Hambrecht, George P. *Abraham Lincoln in Wisconsin.* Historical bulletin no. 4, Lincoln Fellowship of Wisconsin. Madison, 1953.

Hesseltine, William B. *Lincoln's Problems in Wisconsin.* Historical bulletin no. 10, Lincoln Fellowship of Wisconsin. Madison, 1961.

Hunter, John P. *Wisconsin Responds to President Lincoln: Treasures from the State Archives.* Historical Bulletin no. 22, Lincoln Fellowship of Wisconsin. Madison, 1974.

Klement, Frank L. *Lincoln's Critics in Wisconsin.* Historical bulletin no. 14, Lincoln Fellowship of Wisconsin. Madison, 1966.

[Lincoln, Abraham.] *Lincoln on Agriculture.* Historical bulletin no. 1, Lincoln Fellowship of Wisconsin. Madison, 1950.

List of Persons, Residents of the State of Wisconsin, Reported as Deserters from the Military and Naval Service of the United States. Madison, 1868. [Bound in Wisconsin Miscellaneous Pamphlets, vol. 17, in the State Historical Society of Wisconsin.]

Noyes, Edward. *Wisconsin's Reaction to Abraham Lincoln's Emancipation Proclamation, with Especial Reference to Editorial Opinion.* Historical bulletin no. 41, Lincoln Fellowship of Wisconsin. Oshkosh, 1966.

Noyes, Edward. *Wisconsin's Reactions to the Assassination of Abraham Lincoln.* Historical bulletin no. 25, Lincoln Fellowship of Wisconsin. Oshkosh, 1969.

Articles

Balasubramanian, D. "Wisconsin's Foreign Trade in the Civil War Era." *Wisconsin Magazine of History,* 46 (Summer, 1963), 257–262.

Beitzinger, Alfons J. "The Father of Copperheadism in Wisconsin." *Wisconsin Magazine of History,* 39 (Autumn, 1995), 17–25.

Blegen, Theodore C. "Colonel Hans Christian Heg." *Wisconsin Magazine of History,* 4 (December, 1920), 140–165.

Current, Richard N. "Wisconsin's Civil War Historians." *Wisconsin Magazine of History,* 70 (Autumn, 1986), 21–31.

Fish, Carl R. "The Raising of the Wisconsin Volunteers, 1861." *Military Historian and Economist,* 1 (1916), 258–273.

Fishel, Leslie H. "Wisconsin and Negro Suffrage." *Wisconsin Magazine of History,* 46 (Spring, 1963), 180–196.

Grant, Marilyn. "One More Civil War Memoir." *Wisconsin Magazine of History,* 65 (Winter, 1981–1982), 122–129.

Harrsch, Patricia. "'This Noble Monument': The Story of the Soldiers' Orphans' Home." *Wis-*

consin Magazine of History, 76 (Winter, 1992–1993), 83–121.

Harstad, Peter T., editor. "A Civil War Medical Examiner: The Report of Dr. Horace O. Crane." *Wisconsin Magazine of History*, 48 (Spring, 1965), 222–231.

Hesseltine, William B. "Lincoln's Problems in Wisconsin." *Wisconsin Magazine of History*, 48 (Spring, 1965), 187–195.

Holzhueter, John O., editor. "William Wallace's Civil War Letters: The Virginia Campaign." *Wisconsin Magazine of History*, 57 (Autumn, 1973), 28–59.

Holzhueter, John O., editor, "William Wallace's Civil War Letters: The Atlanta Campaign." *Wisconsin Magazine of History*, 57 (Winter, 1973–1974), 91–116.

Hoogenboom, Ari. "What Really Caused the Civil War?" *Wisconsin Magazine of History*, 44 (Autumn, 1960), 3–5.

Johnson, Peter Leo. "Port Washington Draft Riot of 1862." *Mid-America*, new series, 1 (January, 1930), 212–222.

Kaiser, Leo M., editor. "Civil War letters of Charles W. Carr of the 21st Wisconsin Volunteers." *Wisconsin Magazine of History*, 43 (Summer, 960), 264–272.

Klement, Frank L. "'Brick' Pomeroy: Copperhead and Curmudgeon." *Wisconsin Magazine of History*, 35 (Winter, 1961), 106–113, 156–157.

Klement, Frank L. "Copperheads and Copperheadism in Wisconsin: Democratic Opposition to the Lincoln Administration." *Wisconsin Magazine of History*, 42 (Spring, 1959), 182–188.

Klement, Frank L. "Milwaukee Critics of Lincoln." *Historical Messenger of the Milwaukee County Historical Society*, 16 (September, 1960), 2–7.

Klement, Frank L. "Milwaukee Women and the Civil War." *Historical Messenger of the Milwaukee County Historical Society*, 21 (March, 1965), 9–14.

Klement, Frank L. "A Milwaukeean Witnesses Lincoln's Gettysburg Address." *Milwaukee History*, 9 (Summer, 1986), 34–49.

Klement, Frank L. "Peter V. Deuster, the *See-Bote*, and the Civil War." *Historical Messenger of the Milwaukee County Historical Society*, 16 (December, 1960), 2–6.

Klement, Frank L. "The Soldier Vote in Wisconsin During the Civil War." *Wisconsin Magazine of History*, 28 (September, 1944), 37–47.

Klement, Frank L. "Wisconsin and the Re-election of Lincoln in 1864." *Historical Messenger of the Milwaukee County Historical Society*, 22 (March, 1966), 20–42.

Krynski, Elizabeth, and Kimberly Little, editors. "Hannah's Letters: The Story of a Wisconsin Pioneer Family, 1856–1864." *Wisconsin Magazine of History*, 74 (Spring, 1991), 163–195; (Summer, 1991), 272–296.

Kuhns, Luther M., editor. "An Army Surgeon's Letters to His Wife." *Proceedings of the Mississippi Valley Historical Association, 1913–1914*, pp. 306–320.

Larsen, Lawrence H. "Draft Riot in Wisconsin, 1862." *Civil War History*, 7 (December, 1961), 421–427.

Lathrop, Stanley E. "Vital Statistics of the First Wisconsin Cavalry in the Civil War." *Wisconsin Magazine of History*, 5 (March, 1922), 296–300.

Madaus, Howard M. "Into the Fray: The Flags of the Iron Brigade, 1861–1865." *Wisconsin Magazine of History*, 69 (Autumn, 1985), 3–35.

Mott, Margaret Ann. "Lydia Ely Hewitt and the Civil War Monument." *Historical Messenger of the Milwaukee County Historical Society*, 23 (December, 1966), 10–15.

Mott, Margaret Ann. "Lydia Ely Hewitt and the Soldiers' Home." *Historical Messenger of the Milwaukee County Historical Society*, 22 (September, 1966), 101–111.

Noyes, Edward. "A Negro in Mid-Nineteenth Wisconsin Life and Politics." *Wisconsin Academy Review*, 15 (Fall, 1968), 2–6, 21.

Noyes, Edward. "The Negro in Wisconsin's War Effort." *The Lincoln Herald*, 69 (Summer, 1967), 70–82.

Noyes, Edward. "White Opposition to Black Migration into Civil War Wisconsin." *The Lincoln Herald*, 73 (Fall, 1971), 181–193.

Plumb, R. G., editor. "Letters of a Fifth Wisconsin Volunteer." *Wisconsin Magazine of History*, 3 (September, 1919), 52–83.

Porter, Daniel R. "The Colonel and the Private Go to War." *Wisconsin Magazine of History*, 42 (Winter, 1958–1959), 124–127.

Quaife, Milo M. "The Panic of 1862 in Wisconsin." *Wisconsin Magazine of History*, 4 (December, 1920), 166–195.

[Schafer, Joseph, editor.] "A Badger Boy in Blue: The Letters of Chauncey H. Cooke." *Wiscon-*

sin Magazine of History, 4 (September, December, March, June, 1920), 75–100, 208–217, 322–344, 431–456; 5 (September, 1921), 63–98.

Starr, Stephen Z. "The Grand Old Regiment." *Wisconsin Magazine of History*, 48 (Autumn, 1964), 21–31.

Swint, Henry L., editor. "With the First Wisconsin Cavalry, 1862–1865: The Letters of Peter J. Williamson." *Wisconsin Magazine of History*, 26 (March–June, 1943), 333–345, 433–448.

Thomas, Benjamin P. "A Wisconsin Newsman with Grant." *Wisconsin Magazine of History*, 39 (Summer, 1956), 238–244.

Thompson, William Fletcher, Jr. "Illustrating the Civil War." *Wisconsin Magazine of History*, 45 (Autumn, 1961), 10–20.

Thompson, William Fletcher, Jr. "Pictorial Propaganda and the Civil War." *Wisconsin Magazine of History*, 46 (Autumn, 1962), 21–31.

Walsh, John Evangelist. "A Statue for Billy." *Wisconsin Magazine of History*, 76 (Summer, 1993), 235–247.

Williams, T. Harry. "Badger Colonels and the Civil War Officer." *Wisconsin Magazine of History*, 47 (Autumn, 1963), 35–46.

Wintherbotham, William W. "Memoirs of a Civil War Sleuth." *Wisconsin Magazine of History*, 19 (December, 1935; March, 1936), 131–160, 276–293.

Zeitlin, Richard H. "Beyond the Battle: The Flags of the Iron Brigade, 1863–1918." *Wisconsin Magazine of History*, 69 (Autumn, 1985), 36–66.

Masters' Theses

Bascom, Elizabeth A. "Why They Fought: A Comparative Account of the Impact of the Civil War on Five Wisconsin Soldiers, with Selections from Their Civil War Records." University of Wisconsin, 1941.

Glazer, Walter S. "Wisconsin Goes to War: April 1861." University of Wisconsin, 1963.

Horton, Jackson R. "The Demobilization of Wisconsin Troops after the Civil War." University of Wisconsin, 1952.

Jacobi, Robert H. "Wisconsin Civil War Governors." University of Wisconsin, 1948.

Kroncke, Robert N. "Race and Politics in Wisconsin, 1854–1865." University of Wisconsin, 1968.

Meyer, Mary D. "The Germans in Wisconsin and the Civil War: Their Attitude Toward the Union, the Republicans, Slavery, and Lincoln." Catholic University of America, 1937.

Schoonover, Lynn I. "A History of the Civil War Draft in Wisconsin." University of Wisconsin, 1915.

Schwab, Robert L. "Wisconsin and Compromise Efforts on the Eve of the Civil War." Marquette University, 1957.

Scott, Spencer C. "The Financial Effects of the Civil War on the State of Wisconsin." University of Wisconsin, 1939.

Shannon, James W. "State Aid to Wisconsin Soldiers and Their Families: Financial and Humanitarian." University of Wisconsin, 1915.

Vollmer, William J. "The Negro in a Midwest Frontier City, 1835–1870." Marquette University, 1968.

⊰ *Index* ⊱